PENGUIN HANDBOOKS

GETTING YOURS

Matthew Lesko is the founder of Washington Researchers, an information service based in Washington, D.C., which through consulting, seminars, and publications helps business clients draw on the vast informational resources of the federal government for their own needs. He lectures widely to business groups, does a regular feature on National Public Radio on finding free help from the government in many different areas, and writes a monthly column for *Good Housekeeping* on money and personal finance. His articles have appeared in *Inc.*, *Boardroom Reports*, *Industry Week*, and other publications.

GETTING YOURS

THE COMPLETE GUIDE TO GOVERNMENT MONEY

BY MATTHEW LESKO

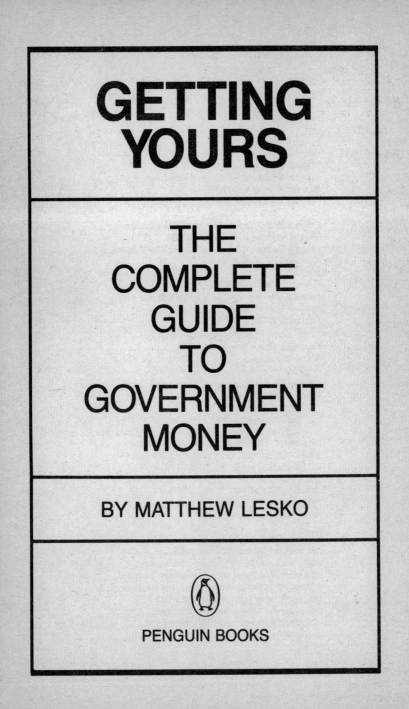

PENGUIN BOOKS

Penguin Books Ltd, Harmondsworth,
Middlesex, England
Penguin Books, 625 Madison Avenue,
New York, New York 10022, U.S.A.
Penguin Books Australia Ltd, Ringwood,
Victoria, Australia
Penguin Books Canada Limited, 2801 John Street,
Markham, Ontario, Canada L3R 1B4
Penguin Books (N.Z.) Ltd, 182–190 Wairau Road,
Auckland 10, New Zealand

First published in simultaneous hardcover and
paperback editions by The Viking Press and
Penguin Books 1982
Reprinted 1982

LIBRARY OF CONGRESS CATALOGING IN PUBLICATION DATA
Lesko, Matthew.
    Getting yours.
    Includes index.
    1. Economic assistance, Domestic—United States—
Directories.   2. Administrative agencies—United
States—Directories.   I. Title.
HC110.P63L37   658.1′522   81-11979
ISBN 0 14 146.510 3   AACR2

Printed in the United States of America
Set in Linotron Times Roman

CONTENTS

ACKNOWLEDGMENTS

I would like to thank the Office of Management and Budget of the federal government for publishing the *Catalog of Federal Domestic Assistance*. The *Catalog* provided the main source of information for the programs described in this book.

I also thank Michael Glennon for compiling the success stories and for his writing and editing assistance; Eudice Daly for her enthusiasm and editorial help; the program and information officers at the federal agencies kind enough to supply success stories; and my partner, Leila Kight, and Washington Researchers for their encouragement and patience.

M.L.

INTRODUCTION

If you want to build a house or chicken coop, get a job, start a business, get a college degree, improve your neighborhood, or even build a tennis court or a golf course, it is likely you can do it with funds from the federal government. Many people already have done so. If you are not one of them, this book is for you.

For generations the federal government has provided money to its citizens in order to accomplish a number of social and economic objectives, such as alleviating human miseries, improving the environment of a community, bolstering business and creating jobs, smoothing over dislocations in the economy, funding the ambitious and scholarly as well as scientific research, and improving the quality of life through support for the arts and humanities. Thousands of programs have come and gone as the needs of the country have changed, and as administrations have won and lost elections. There are currently some 1,000 programs that annually give over $190 billion in loans and loan guarantees and $287 billion in grants and direct payments. Individuals are eligible for 519 programs, nonprofit organizations for 496 programs, and state and local governments for 796 programs.

Each year this money has to go to someone. The government is not always able to make the best of investments because the best of situations and needs are not presented to them. For some funding programs, the same handful of individuals apply for and receive their money year in and year out because although thousands are eligible, no one knows that the funding is available. More efficient use can be made of these programs if more people are aware of their availability.

You may think that getting government money requires something magical like taking a congressman to dinner or knowing the right people with influence. Perhaps you are convinced that it is not you but others who are always eligible. The fact is, with so many programs covering so many different areas, it is hard to be ineligible for all of them, and the only magic involved is finding the right program and persevering until you get the funds.

Getting Yours will attempt to help you identify those federal funds which you are eligible for and have already paid for with your taxes. It will also attempt to provide you with a few easy steps to follow to help you get through the federal government maze.

The programs listed in this book represent over 95 percent of the available money programs. Because of space and timeliness, it is close to impossible to include every program that is currently available. This book also does not include other types of available government assistance such as training services, advisory and counseling services, dissemination of technical information, investigation of complaints, use of property, and other specialized services. To keep current on the latest of all federal programs see the section titled Further Sources of Information.

PART 1
HOW TO USE THE BOOK

DEFINITIONS

The following are terms used frequently throughout the book:

Loans: money lent by a federal agency for a specific period of time and with a reasonable expectation of repayment. Loans may or may not require payment of interest.

Guaranteed/insured loans: programs in which federal agencies agree to pay back part or all of a loan to a private lender if the borrower defaults.

Grants: money given by federal agencies for a fixed period of time. Grants include money dispersed to states according to a prescribed formula (formula grants), fellowships, scholarships, research grants, evaluation grants, planning grants, technical assistance grants, survey grants, construction grants, and unsolicited contracts.

Direct payments: funds provided by federal agencies to individuals, private firms, and institutions. The use of direct payments may be "specified" to perform a particular service or "unrestricted," e.g., retirement and pension payments.

Insurance: coverage under specific programs to assure reimbursement for losses sustained. Insurance may be provided directly by federal agencies or through insurance companies and may or may not require the payment of premiums.

THE NUMBERING SYSTEM

Each of the government programs described in this book is identified by a unique five-digit federal program number. The programs are listed in numerical order and referred to by these numbers throughout the book and the index.

FINDING A PROGRAM

The following steps will help identify the program for you.

Step 1   Read the examples: These stories will stir your curiosity, expand your mind, and give you insights into using government funds in ways you never dreamed of. They will also lead you to sources of money for similar aims. An agency that supports one endeavor is likely to help another in a related area.

Step 2   Refer to the subject index: Start with a broad subject area such as crime or health, and then look for the specific program within that category. If you cannot find it at first, don't despair. It does not mean that there is no such program. In fact, most likely there *is* one. It only means that you and the government use different terms to describe the same program.

Step 3   Find the relevant agency: If you are unsuccessful with the index, use the Contents to find the agency or office interested in your subject. For example, if you are interested in trade, look under the U.S. Department of Commerce; for starting a small business, see Small Business Administration. Then review all the programs included with it, since the arrangement of the book groups them together.

Step 4   Contact a program in a related area: If you still cannot find the program that meets your particular requirements, find one that covers a related subject. For example, look under the U.S. Department of Education for libraries or the U.S. Department of Commerce for fishing. Then contact that department or agency for further guidance.

GETTING THE MONEY

Once you have identified the program or programs that can help you, your work has just begun. Now you have to get the money. Volumes and volumes have been written and consultants have been paid thousands of dollars to counsel individuals and organizations on the ways and means of obtaining government financing. There is no mystery in the method. You do not need a Ph.D. or a Washington office. All you need is patience, determination, and hard work, if you are eligible.

ELEVEN LESSONS FOR APPLICANTS

The following tips are meant to offer advice and encouragement to both the novice and the "old pro" government money seeker.

1. When You Find One Program, Assume That There Are More. When you identify a program that comes close to meeting your needs, ask the program director about similar programs in other departments. Find out whether new programs are in the offing. The alternatives may present opportunities more suited to your needs, or they may be combined with the existing program for a package funding.

2. The Money May Not Be Where You Think It Is. As the examples in the following sections will show, much of the money comes from unexpected sources. For example, the Department of Agriculture supports teenage entrepreneurs, and the Department of Labor will finance doctoral dissertations.

3. Don't Be Discouraged If You Think You Are Not Eligible. You may discover a program that meets your needs only to find that the funding is not available to individuals. Don't be discouraged. Examples in the following sections describe how people have formed nonprofit organizations or worked with local governments in order to receive the available money. Moreover, many of the programs for state and local governments make individuals their ultimate beneficiaries. Contact the program director to identify for you the local office administering the funds.

4. Examine a Successful Application. You have the right, in most cases, to see copies of successful applications. If you encounter any difficulty, write the federal office in charge of the program, and request a copy under the Freedom of Information Act.

5. Talk to Those Who Give the Money. Before you actually fill out any applications, it is well worth your time to review your forms with the program officials, either in person if at all possible, or over the telephone. Many of the funding agencies have offices throughout the country to assist you. Such contact should help tailor your answers to the government's expectations. It will give them what they want to see.

6. Obtain Copies of Appropriation Committee Hearings. Each government agency has to justify to the Congress, annually, its request for money. Public hearings are held by both the House and the Senate for government officials to present their cases. Often the program of your interest may be discussed in these hearings and these transcripts are available to add insight into their objectives and future. If you need extra background information on your subject, contact your congressman's office for information on how to obtain copies of these published hearings.

7. Personalize Your Approach. Remember that the program officers are there to help you if you give them half a chance. Be friendly, open, and courteous. Establish yourself as an individual so that you are more to them than just a faceless number. Even getting money from the federal government can be a people business, and it is up to you to encourage it.

8. Give Them What They Want. When you prepare your applications, give the government exactly what it asks for, even though it may not make much sense to you. Don't fight it. You will need all your energy to get your money. It is unlikely that you will have any to spare for changing the government's ways, even if you are right.

9. Start Small. Even if you need a large amount of money, start small. It may be wiser and easier. Initially, ask for enough money to complete a small portion of your project. The next year, ask for the rest. In this way the program officer can get to know you before he gives you a large amount of money.

10. Try Again. If your proposal is rejected, learn what you did wrong and try again next year, or try with a different program. Many proposals are rejected because of bad timing or a relatively minor hitch. Don't worry. Your failure will not be held against you.

11. When the Bureaucracy Is Stuck, Use Your Congressman.
Try to use your congressman's office only for those times when the
bureaucracy comes to a halt on your paperwork. Sometimes this is
the only way to get it moving again.

FURTHER SOURCES OF INFORMATION

If you are looking for further information on government programs, you may find one or more of the following sources helpful.

1. Catalog of Federal Domestic Assistance. This 1,000-page document is the most complete source of information on government programs. It is published by the Office of Management and Budget once a year with updates. Subscriptions are available for $20.00 from:

> Superintendent of Documents
> U.S. Government Printing Office
> Washington, DC 20402
> 202-783-3238

2. Federal Assistance Programs Retrieval System (FAPRS). This is a computerized information system containing much of the same information in the *Catalog of Federal Domestic Assistance*. It is designed to identify quickly specific federal assistance programs for which applicants are eligible. It can be accessed through computer terminals in many government regional offices and in university libraries. The price of a search varies with the request. For an access point near you contact:

> Federal Program Information Branch
> Budget Review Division
> Office of Management and Budget
> 17th and Pennsylvania Avenues, N.W.
> Washington, DC 20503

3. Federal Information Centers. There are thirty-eight such centers throughout the country and their job is to personally assist the public in finding information in the federal government. For a center near you, check the white pages of your telephone book under "U.S. Government" or contact:

Coordinator
Federal Information Center
7th and D Streets, S.W.
Washington, DC 20024
202-755-8660

4. Your Congressman's Office. This is a good place to turn to when all else fails. Remember, your congressman works for you in Washington. He can be reached by contacting his local district office or:

c/o U.S. Capitol
Washington, DC 20515
202-224-3121

EXAMPLES

The examples that follow are grouped into eight topical categories. Each shows how specific individuals and organizations have used a government program to improve themselves or their environment.

PURSUING THE ARTS

Artists and scholars can obtain government funds to help them through their struggling periods as well as their prosperous ones. The following stories show how some of the famous and not-so-famous have used government funds to help their careers.

Students Take a Walk for the Humanities. Nine students at Oberlin College walked 412 miles in January 1980, financed by a $10,000 youth grant from the National Endowment for the Humanities (program #45.115). The students were following the exact route taken by hundreds of escaping slaves on the Underground Railway during the mid-nineteenth century. At stops along the way, the students gave a slide presentation on the Underground Railway, generating great interest in the historical significance of the region.

Texas Choreographer Receives $7,500. Deborah Hay, a choreographer in Austin, Texas, received $7,500 worth of grants (program #45.002), which enabled her to rent rehearsal space, pay dancers, and choreograph.

Young Filmmaker Preserves Harlem's Cotton Club. The historical and musical importance of the Cotton Club, Harlem's most famous nightclub and the showcase of some of the best-known black performers, including Duke Ellington and Billie Holiday, is being preserved on film thanks to a youth grant (program #45.115) from the National Endowment for the Humanities. A twenty-five-year-old filmmaker (youth grants are made to individuals under the age of thirty) received a $10,000 grant in 1979 to make his film on the Cotton Club. The money was used to offset the cost of collecting old film clips and still photos and to film interviews with people associated with the club in its heyday.

Gloria Steinem Among Distinguished Fellows.
The Smithsonian Institution's Woodrow Wilson International Center for Scholars offers year-long fellowships (program #60.020) for scholars and other distinguished individuals from nonacademic professions. Here are a few examples from recent years:

- Robert Donovan, author and journalist, did research for a book on "National Security Policy in President Harry S Truman's Second Term in Office."
- Polish scholar Bronislaw Geremek, director of medieval studies at the Academy of Sciences in Warsaw, worked on "Social Marginality in the Pre-Industrial Age."
- Journalist Gloria Steinem investigated "Feminism and Its Impact on the Premises and Goals of Current Political Theory."

All Kinds of Music.
The National Endowment for the Arts funds a variety of musicians and composers under its music program (#45.005). Here is a sampling:

- The Amarillo Symphony in Amarillo, Texas, received an $8,000 grant in 1980 to support the continuation of concerts in the schools in the region and to help pay traveling expenses of guest artists.
- Joseph Schwantner wrote "Aftertones of Infinity" while he was receiving a $7,500 Arts Endowment music grant in 1979. His orchestral composition went on to win the 1979 Pulitzer Prize for music.
- Jazz saxophonist Jimmy Giuffre of West Stockbridge, Massachusetts was the recipient of a $10,000 grant which helped support him while he composed and performed.
- Music lovers in West Virginia will continue to hear performances by the Charleston Symphony Orchestra in their hometowns as a result of a $15,000 grant given to defray the costs of the orchestra's extensive touring program throughout the state.

Support for Rural Theater in Iowa.
The Old Creamery Theater in Garrison, Iowa, provides live theater to folks who normally wouldn't see it: farmers in the rural areas of Iowa. Because it plays on tour and gives workshops in acting and other phases of the theater, the Old Creamery has received over $50,000 from the National Endowment for the Arts (program #45.010). In addition, it has received $1,500

in 1980 and $5,000 in 1981 (program #45.008) to subsidize its resident theater program.

Grants Help Filmmakers Win Academy Awards. In 1975 a filmmaker named Barbara Kopple received a grant (program #45.006) of $27,980 to make a movie about coal miners. The film, *Harlan County U.S.A.* went on to win an Academy Award for feature documentaries in 1976. The same program gave Ira Wohl $25,000 in 1978 to help him with the costs of a movie he was making about a retarded member of his family. The film, *Best Boy,* won the feature documentary Academy Award in 1979.

Getting Seen in the Visual Arts. Two examples of artists who received money from the Arts Endowment's Visual Arts Program (#45.009) follow:

- Ed Ruscha, a Los Angeles painter and printmaker, received $5,000 in 1967 to work on his art. Since then, he has become well known and widely admired in art circles.
- In 1972, Robert Arneson obtained a $7,500 grant to work on ceramics. Arneson's pieces are now featured in major exhibitions and are in the collections of many major American museums.

Researchers Can Work with Smithsonian Specialists. Each year scholars performing pre- and postdoctoral research are selected to receive an average stipend of $14,000 to work for one year with Smithsonian specialists (program #60.001). Recent projects included "The 1940s in New York—Radical Politics and Avant Garde Art"; "A History of Music in the White House"; "Research in Experimental Radio Astronomy"; and "Socioecology of Venezuelan Red Howler Monkeys."

Funding for Writers. The following are writers who received grants ranging from $5,000 to $6,000 from the National Endowment for the Arts Literature Program (#45.004) in the early to mid-1970s: Alice Adams, author of *Families and Survivors* and *Listening to Billie*; Erica Jong, author of *Fear of Flying* and *Fanny*; William Gaddis, author of *JR*, which won a National Book Award, and John Milton, author of *Notes to a Bald Buffalo*. Poets who have benefited from the program include Lucille Clifton, Daniel Mark Epstein, Linda Pastan, and Charles Wright.

BUSINESS

There are close to two hundred programs available to entrepreneurs and corporations. These programs range from providing a few thousand dollars of seed money for a part-time venture to the well publicized $500,000,000 loan guarantee for the Chrysler Corporation. For complete coverage of financial assistance available to the business community, review the programs available within the following organizations:

> U.S. Department of Agriculture
> U.S. Department of Commerce
> U.S. Department of Defense
> U.S. Department of Health and Human Services
> U.S. Department of Housing and Urban Development
> U.S. Department of the Interior
> U.S. Department of Labor
> U.S. Department of State
> U.S. Department of Transportation
> U.S. Department of the Treasury
> Equal Employment Opportunity Commission
> Federal Trade Commission
> General Services Administration
> National Credit Union Administration
> Community Services Administration
> Small Business Administration
> Overseas Private Investment Corporation
> Department of Energy
> Federal Emergency Management Agency

The stories presented below show how various individuals and corporations have used government programs to start or help their businesses. In each case a federal program was used to help fulfill the dreams of a small businessman or woman, as well as to provide employment and economic opportunity to members of the local community.

Posh Health Spa Saved. The Golden Door, one of the country's most glamorous health spas, was once threatened with a major setback when it was notified that its facility stood in the path of a proposed freeway. Undaunted, owner Deborah Magganti applied for and received $1.75 million worth of technical and financial assistance from the Small Business Administration (program #59.001) to build a new fitness farm that now counts famous Hollywood personalities among its regular customers.

Loans for Lucille's Auto Shop. A $25,000 Small Business Administration loan (program #59.012) provided the working capital for the first woman-owned automobile transmission repair shop in the United States. "Transmissions by Lucille" in Pittsburgh opened its doors in 1975 and has grown into a half-million-dollar business, employing eighteen people, most of whom are men.

Insurance for U.S. Plants Abroad. In order to protect its investment in the troubled Middle East, Baldwin Piano Company received $162,000 worth of Foreign Investment Insurance (program #70.003) for its plant in Israel. This insurance, offered by the Overseas Private Investment Corporation, protects Baldwin against the threat of war, revolution, and expropriation.

Jimmy Carter and Miss Lillian. In 1962 Jimmy Carter and his mother, Miss Lillian, received a $175,000 Small Business Administration loan (program #59.012) to construct a cotton gin building, a cotton warehouse, and an office building. They also used the money to buy and install machinery and equipment. The loan was fully paid off on schedule.

From Family Business to Fortune 500. When Rose and Jim Totino decided to expand the market for the pizzas that were so popular at their restaurant in Minneapolis, a $50,000 Small Business Administration loan (program #59.012) enabled them to open a pizza manufacturing plant. Totino's Finer Foods grew from 25 pies a week to 200,000 daily. The business was then purchased by the Pillsbury Company and Mrs. Totino was named a corporate vice president, the first woman to hold the position in the firm's history.

Dairy Man Parlays Excess Cream into Ice Cream Parlor. The owner of a dairy in Wilkes-Barre, Pennsylvania, decided that the best way to dispose of his dairy's excess cream was to start his own ice cream parlor and restaurant. After local banks refused to lend him the $550,000 needed to open the restaurant, the Department of Agriculture agreed to guarantee the loan through their Business and Industry Loan Program (#10.423). The restaurant now provides an outlet for the dairy's excess cream as well as jobs for some eighty-five area residents.

Cure for Nursing Home. A small nursing home failed to meet state requirements and was faced with a shutdown. The facilities required a costly new fire sprinkler system along with a number of new beds. Because the owner was a woman and lived in a rural section of Ohio, the Department of Agriculture provided her with a $90,000 insured loan (program #10.422) to purchase the needed equipment.

Money to Meet OSHA Standards. The Maywood Packing Company, an olive-packing business in Corning, California, was about to go out of business because its aging plant failed to meet many of the requirements of the Occupational Safety and Health Act (OSHA). Maywood was the community's largest employer, and if it closed, 250 people would be left jobless. A $696,700 Occupational Safety and Health loan from the Small Business Administration (program #59.018) saved the day. Most of the money was used to reconstruct the facility in order to meet OSHA standards. The remaining $50,000 was earmarked for working capital in order to carry the business during the eight-month construction period.

Millions for Small Business. A $24 million loan guarantee from the Department of Commerce (program #11.502) enabled a small Philadelphia-based shipping concern to purchase a $30 million oil tanker. In another case, the Department of Commerce guaranteed a $5 million loan (program #11.502) that enabled a Chicago-area shipper to purchase three new barges for the transportation of petroleum products on the Great Lakes.

Big Catch for Small Fisherman. A shrimp boat operator in Louisiana made his living on an old but reliable boat. When the boat finally broke down, the fisherman faced paying $400,000 for a new boat or going out of business. Luckily he was able to qualify for a Department of Commerce fishing vessel loan (program #11.415) which provided him with the needed money at a lower interest rate and longer payment schedule than standard commercial financing.

Condemned Sausage Company Salvaged. In 1972 Discovery Foods, a successful sausage and meat processing factory in Los Angeles, was facing a forced shutdown because it had failed to meet consumer health standards. A $1,250,000 Consumer Protection Loan from the Small Business Administration (program #59.017) provided the money to construct a new processing plant. The facility contained costly cooking and refrigeration machinery that enabled it to comply with health standards.

Baseball Star Hits Home Run with SBA. Lou Brock, a former major league baseball star who holds the all-time record for stolen bases, received a $100,000 loan guarantee from the Small Business Administration (program #59.012) to buy a Dodge dealership in East St. Louis, Illinois.

Franchising Made Easy. Three businessmen in a suburb of Detroit decided to pool their resources and buy a Dunkin' Donuts franchise. Because none of them had any experience running a restaurant, the local banks refused to provide them with additional financing. So they applied to the Small Business Administration and received a 90 percent guarantee on a $265,000 loan (program #59.012). In 1980, when they started their Dunkin' Donuts, they expected sales to reach $5,000 a week eventually. To their surprise, they earned more than that the first week they were open.

For additional business examples see the section on Rural Living. A handy compilation of the various money and nonmoney programs available to business is presented in *Handbook for Small Business: A Survey of Small Business Programs of the Federal Government* ($5.50). Copies are available from:

> Superintendent of Documents
> U.S. Government Printing Office
> Washington, DC 20402
> 202-783-3238

EDUCATION

Individuals can advance their education with federal funds through a wide range of programs that either offer money directly or indirectly through financial institutions, schools, social service organizations, and nonprofit groups. Although most of the money is from the Department of Education, there are a number of educational opportunities scattered throughout the government. The stories below describe many of the major programs.

Upward Bound Pulls Up Neglected Iowan. A young cerebral palsy victim in Iowa was neglected by his parents. He was forced to sleep alone in an unheated bedroom and sent to public schools while his brothers and sisters attended private schools. No one seemed to care about him until he joined Upward Bound (program #84.047). The program provided him with extensive counseling and tutoring in reading, writing, and speech. His grades improved, and he was accepted at a local college. He is now a counselor at a school in Minnesota working with mentally and physically impaired students and adults.

Bilingual Program Trains Machine Operator. In 1975 a Spanish-speaking machine operator in New York City lost his job of fifteen years when a local textile factory closed down. Through the Department of Education's Bilingual Vocational Training Program (#84.077), he took courses in basic maintenance and was hired as a maintenance man at a large New York housing project. He continued to take advanced courses through the program and today he supervises a crew of fifteen maintenance men.

Work-Study Helps Pay for Student's Studies. The Department of Education's College Work-Study Program (#84.033) provides money to colleges and universities for up to 80 percent of the salaries of part-time jobs held by students in financial need. For example, a student in Massachusetts was able to support his day-to-day expenses and pay part of his tuition by working about fifteen hours a week clearing tables and serving meals in the school dining hall. Other typical positions funded under the program include work in libraries, athletic facilities, and departmental offices.

From Maine Marines to Nuclear Navy. State marine schools, which receive support from the federal government (program #11.506), offer a low-cost education for future engineers and ship-builders. For example, a student from Maine entered the Maine Maritime Academy in 1964. Upon graduation he fulfilled a three-year commitment to the school by working as an engineer on an oil tanker in the U.S. Merchant Marine. After completing his stint at sea, he took a job at a steam turbine manufacturing company and a year and a half later joined a shipbuilding firm, where he helped design a power plant for a nuclear-powered submarine.

German Studies Lead to Book, Articles, Course, and Award. Wayne Thompson, a professor at Lynchburg College, a school of 2,200 students in Lynchburg, Virginia, received a $15,000 stipend in 1977 from the National Endowment for the Humanities (program #45.144). Thompson used the fellowship to attend the University of California at Santa Barbara where he researched the topic "German Social Democracy in the 20th Century." Out of his fellowship work came a book, *In the Eye of the Storm: Kurt Riezler and the Crisis of Modern Germany*, and five articles published in scholarly journals. In addition, Thompson initiated a new course at Lynchburg College, "German Political Thought," and was given a faculty award for distinguished scholarship by his colleagues.

Supplemental Funds Make Ends Meet. A Department of Education Supplemental Educational Opportunity Grants program (#84.007) gives money to colleges that use it to subsidize the tuition of poverty-stricken students. For example, Tri-County Technical College in Pendleton, South Carolina, received $43,000 worth of supplemental grant money in 1980. This money in turn was parceled out to extremely needy students, allowing them to complete their college education.

Counselor Cuts College Costs. A young woman hoped to attend a college that charges $3,600 a year, but her parents were afraid that the cost would be too much for them to bear. After consulting her high school counselor, she discovered that she was eligible for a $1,300 a year educational opportunity grant from the Department of Education (program #84.063).

Famous Fulbrights. Fulbright Scholarships (program #82.001) enable talented students to spend a year studying abroad. Here are some of the more well known Fulbright scholars: Harrison Schmitt, the Republican senator from New Mexico and a former astronaut, received a Fulbright in 1957 to study geology at the University of Oslo. One of his Senate colleagues, Senator Daniel Patrick Moynihan, Democrat from New York, studied at the London School of Economics under a Fulbright Scholarship in 1950. Opera star Anna Moffo went to Italy in 1954. Dancer Yuriko Kimura received a scholarship in 1966 to study modern dance with Martha Graham.

Doctoral Student Finances Dissertation. The Department of Labor provides grants averaging around $11,500 for graduate students working on doctoral dissertations on topics related to training and employment. For example, the Rev. William Byron, S.J., received a grant (program #17.218) while he researched his dissertation on "The Applicability of the Job Bank Concept to the Washington, D.C., Market for Domestic Day Workers." He received his Ph.D. from the University of Maryland in 1969 and is now president of the University of Scranton.

RNs Score Scholarships. Prospective nurses can receive government money to help pay for nursing school. Under the Department of Health and Human Services Nursing Scholarships program (#13.363), Arizona State University in Tempe, Arizona, received $33,000 in nursing scholarship funds to help defray tuition costs for full- or part-time students in the nursing baccalaureate program.

Cure for Medical School Bill. Dr. David B. Flannery made it through his last two years of medical school with the help of a National Health Service Corps Scholarship (program #13.288). After he completed his three years of residency in 1979, Dr. Flannery, a pediatrician, repaid his scholarship by serving two years as head of the Louisa Health Center for Young People in Louisa, Virginia (population 2,000).

Loan Helps Student to Attend College of His Choice. The college education of a New Jersey student was made possible by a Department of Education guaranteed student loan (program #84.032). The student's mother, a widow, could afford to send her son to a local school, but he wanted to attend a more costly out-of-state college. A guaranteed loan made by a local bank—$5,500 at seven percent interest paid out over four years—helped cover the additional expense. The student is now paying off the loan in monthly installments spread over ten years.

For a free booklet describing six federal financial aid programs for college students, *Student Consumer's Guide*, contact:

> U.S. Department of Education
> P.O. Box 84
> Washington, DC 20033
> 800-638-6700
> (in Maryland, 800-492-6602)

ENERGY

Although the actual number of energy-related programs is small, their growth is something to watch. It appears that a new program is created every week. In no time at all, the number of energy programs may outnumber those for agriculture. The following stories identify the major programs available.

Conservation Grants to Schools. Chadron State College in Nebraska received an $18,000 grant from the Department of Energy (program #81.052) to insulate a classroom building and install thermostats that automatically lower classroom temperatures at night. Energy savings amounted to more than $6,000 a year.

Energy Audits Reduce Consumption. Money from the Department of Energy's State Energy Conservation program (#81.041) is being put to use in Rhode Island to cut heating bills. Since 1978 the Rhode Island state energy office has channeled $75,000 to a nonprofit corporation named RISE (Rhode Island Is Saving Energy), which provides free energy audits and also suggests ways to reduce energy consumption. In one particularly successful example of RISE's work, the consumption of heating oil at a large older home in Providence dropped from twenty-three gallons per day to twelve gallons after the owners received their free energy audit and decided to insulate their home.

Thermal Window Blinds. Alan Ross of Brattleboro, Vermont, received an $8,000 grant from the Energy Department's Appropriate Technology program (#81.050) to design and produce thermal insulating window blinds made from paper boxboard, jute, pine, and reflective foil.

Photoelectric Cells Get Boost. Two loans from the Small Business Energy Loan Program (#59.030) worth $350,000 provided working capital to SOLEC International, Inc., and enabled the Los Angeles firm to buy sophisticated machinery to manufacture photoelectric cells that transform the sun's rays into electric energy. SOLEC's products have had many successful applications and have been used in devices to activate attic fans and to recharge batteries of boats at sea.

Weatherization Lowers Fuel Bills. From 1976 through 1979 low-income residents of Pennsylvania saved more than $5 million on their fuel bills. They participated in a Department of Energy grant program (#81.042) that gives money to low-income citizens to insulate and otherwise weatherize their homes. The money is sent to states and distributed to individuals through local nonprofit community action agencies. During the first four years of the program over 50,000 homes received weatherization treatment, including storm windows, insulation, and weather stripping.

Dallas Goes Big for Conservation. The Texas state energy office is using the Department of Energy's Energy Extension Service program (#81.050) to help individuals and small businesses resolve energy problems. The $800,000 received in 1980 was distributed throughout the state to perform energy audits on homes and small businesses and to give workshops for businessmen on how to save energy in their offices and stores. In Dallas alone, over two hundred energy audits were performed in the first half of 1980.

Stove Business Gets Hot. A nonprofit community action group in Vermont began making wood-burning stoves with the help of a $45,000 grant from the New England Regional Commission. The plant, which began in 1975, was manned by local residents whose wages were paid by funds from the CETA program (#17.232). The stoves were originally given away or sold at reduced prices to low-income people in the area, but as word of the new stove spread, demand increased and the operation started to show a profit. Its success almost stopped federal funding until new regulations were promulgated that allowed the community action agency to own 51 percent of the stove-making company as long as all profits were earmarked for economic development projects. To set the new, profit-making firm on its feet, the Community Services Administration awarded it an Emergency Energy Conservation Services Program grant (#49.014) for $172,500.

First Grant for Electric Vehicle Manufacturers. Electric Vehicle Associates, Inc., in Cleveland, Ohio, is the first firm in the nation to receive a loan guarantee under the Energy Department's Electric and Hybrid Vehicle Loan program (#81.060). The company received $2.5 million in 1980 to produce electric-powered cars. The money was used for working capital, equipment, expenses, and other costs associated with transforming Ford Fairmonts into electric cars.

Success in Hot Water. An inventor in New Orleans, Harry E. Wood, received a $72,000 grant from the Department of Energy (program #81.036) to perfect his design of a high-efficiency water heater. The grant enabled Wood to construct and install a large water heater in an apartment building. The experimental unit worked so well that Wood subsequently received orders for eight more of the heaters.

Resort No Longer Suffers from Gas Shortage. Business at La Cortina, a year-round recreational facility in Killington, Vermont, suffered badly during the gasoline shortage in the summer of 1974. The future of the lodge seemed uncertain until the Small Business Administration granted it a $40,000 Emergency Energy Economic Injury Loan (program #59.022). The loan saved the day, allowing La Cortina's owners to gear up for the winter season.

BUYING AND IMPROVING A HOME

The examples in this section will only refer to single family dwellings. There are a large number of programs covering multifamily dwellings, and most of these can be found within the Departments of Agriculture and Housing and Urban Development.

Hill House Gets HUD Help. Terry Savage of Lolo, Montana, built his home into the side of a hill in order to retain the earth's heat. As an experimental home, it qualified for the Department of Housing and Urban Development's mortgage insurance for unusual domiciles (program #14.152). Tapping another source of money, Savage obtained a grant from the state of Montana to build a small-scale hydroelectric dam in a nearby stream to generate his own electricity.

Condos and Co-ops. The Department of Housing and Urban Development provides mortgage insurance to help individuals buy condominiums (program #14.133) and cooperative apartments (program #14.163). In Washington, D.C., for example, long-time residents of areas undergoing rehabilitation were being forced out of their apartments as their buildings were converted into condominiums. With the help of HUD mortgage insurance, they were able to buy their own apartments and remain in their neighborhoods.

Advantages to Older Areas. Rundown areas of St. Petersburg, Florida, are being revitalized as a result of a mortgage insurance program administered by the Department of Housing and Urban Development (program #14.123). Young people settling in St. Petersburg can use the money not only to buy their homes but also to repair and reconstruct them.

Solar Outhouse. A man in Jamestown, Missouri, received a $1,200 grant from the Department of Energy (program #81.051) in 1979 to design and build a solar-heated outhouse. The "Above Ground Aerobic and Solar-Assisted Composting Toilet" uses solar heat to warm the structure and to aid the decomposition of waste material.

Solar Fence Keeps in Pigs. The Department of Energy awarded a $1,120 grant (program #81.051) to Dr. David A. Sleep, Department of Agriculture, American Samoa Government in Pago Pago, to build a solar-powered electric fence. The fence was built to enclose wild pigs that had been overrunning a part of the island not served by electrical power.

Couple's First House. A young married couple living outside Cleveland were eager to buy a house before their first child was born. But because they were young and had yet to establish a credit rating, private banks refused to give them a mortgage. Luckily they qualified for mortgage insurance issued by the Department of Housing and Urban Development (program #14.117). They got their house, and thanks to the HUD insurance, their down payment and their interest rates were lower than on conventional mortgages.

Rehabilitation Loan Reduces Monthly Payments. In the late 1970s a young couple in Bradford, Pennsylvania, bought a large old home that was in dire need of repair. Almost immediately they began to have trouble meeting their monthly mortgage payments. They discovered, however, they were eligible for a Section 312 Rehabilitation Loan from the Department of Housing and Urban Development (program #14.220), which enabled them to refinance their mortgage and reduce their monthly payments drastically.

Veteran Keeps Moving Up. The Veterans Administration's Direct Loans and Advances program (#64.113) enabled a young Vietnam veteran to buy a house even though his financial resources were scarce. In 1975 the veteran and his wife were living in a small apartment in Pennsylvania. They wanted to buy a house but had never been able to save enough money. The veteran sought advice from his local Veterans Administration office and discovered that he was eligible to receive a $30,000 direct loan (program #64.113) to finance the house they wanted. A few years later their fortunes improved and they decided to move to a bigger house. This time they took advantage of the VA's guaranteed loan program (#64.114) and were able to buy the new house without spending a fortune on the down payment.

First Home Is on Wheels. A young man in Oklahoma was able to buy his first house—a mobile home—with some help from the Department of Housing and Urban Development. Too young to have established a credit rating, the potential homeowner was turned down by local lenders when he applied for a mortgage. With HUD mortgage insurance (program #14.110), however, he secured a loan with a lower down payment than nonguaranteed financing and a reduced rate of interest.

House for $1.00. A divorced mother of two bought a rundown house in 1979 in Columbus, Ohio, for $1.00 through a program funded by the Department of Housing and Urban Development (program #14.222). Before the purchase, the woman, a machinist at a factory, was paying $250 a month to rent an apartment. Working with officials of the state housing agency, she developed a rehabilitation plan for her $1.00 house. After the plan was approved, she received a long-term $10,500 loan to finance the improvements, 20 percent of which she completed herself. Now this urban homesteader owns her home and pays only $140 a month on her improvement loan.

Country Living. Lloyd P. Klabunde, a wheat farmer in Emmet, North Dakota, began his farm career in 1946 on 320 acres of land he rented from a neighbor. As he prospered, he added to his leased land and in 1964 he took out a $48,000 farm ownership loan (program #10.407) from the Department of Agriculture to buy 800 acres of farmland, including the original parcel of 320 acres that constituted his first farm. Mr. Klabunde now operates an 1,800-acre farm (he rents the additional 1,000 acres) and is one of the most successful farmers in the region.

For additional examples see the section on Rural Living.

GETTING A JOB

In addition to direct employment, the government offers a wide range of programs with employment opportunities. Here are a few examples.

Unemployed Take Four Months to Be Entrepreneurs. A group of five young men, all previously unemployed, joined the Young Adult Conservation Corps (program #10.663) to receive training in the lumber business. They worked near Oakridge, Oregon, learning how to operate chain saws and how to safely burn debris after trees were felled. Within four months they developed enough expertise to be hired by the Weyerhauser lumber company as independent contractors to clean up after the firm's tree-cutting crews. As a result, their wages rose from the minimum wage paid by the Young Adult Conservation Corps to over $5.00 per hour.

Job Corps Student Gets Top Job. James Daniels was out of school and out of work when he joined the Job Corps (program #17.211) in 1966. He was hired as a security officer at a Job Corps Center in Kentucky and resumed school part-time. In 1977 Daniels received his bachelor's degree in sociology from Indiana State University and was named manager of residential living at the Job Corps Center in Crystal Springs, Mississippi. The following year he was made director of the Crystal Springs Center. He is the first person helped by the Job Corps to head a Job Corps Center.

New Money for Older Americans. Money from the Older Americans Opportunities and Services program of the Community Services Administration (program #49.010) is being utilized by the Hill County Community Action Association in Sana Saba, Texas, to give part-time jobs to older Americans. The center employs thirteen local senior citizens as drivers and clerical assistants. The center also operates an employment service that matches the skills of older area residents to the needs of local businesses.

Help for Those Hurt by Imports. It looked as if a laid-off assembly line worker near Jackson, Mississippi, would have to put his house on the market to make ends meet. He lost his job when the electronics company he worked for cut back production due to competition from low-cost imports. His savings were almost gone when he took advantage of the Department of Labor's weekly trade readjustment allowance (program #17.400) to supplement his unemployment income. The extra money meant that the family home was saved.

Welfare Mother Wins Job. A mother of five in Lowell, Massachusetts, had been collecting welfare for five years when she joined the Department of Labor's Work Incentive program (#13.646). A high school graduate, she received counseling and training at the local Work Incentive (WIN) program office and was accepted into a technical institute, where she received training in computer sciences;

WIN paid her tuition. Upon graduation, she took a job as a computer technician earning over $5 per hour. She was so pleased with the program, she urged her sister to enroll in WIN. She is now a wage earner as well.

IMPROVING YOUR NEIGHBORHOOD

There are hundreds of federal programs available that can assist communities in improving their neighborhoods. Although most of the money is earmarked for local governments and nonprofit organizations, individuals can play an instrumental role in obtaining federal funds by identifying a relevant program and helping local government officials prepare the necessary paperwork. Once funds are received, local residents are often hired to become paid directors of the project. Citizens can also band together and form a nonprofit organization to receive federal funds. Here are a few success stories.

Eyesore Transformed into Gym and Playground. Due to efforts of the local Boys' Club, an abandoned coal bunker in Jersey City, New Jersey, is now the centerpiece of a new park and recreational facility. With a $227,500 grant from the Department of the Interior's Urban Park and Recreation Recovery Program (#15.417), and with additional money from foundations, the local United Way, a local bank, community groups, and the Colgate-Palmolive Company, the Boys' Club built a solar-heated swimming pool, a 12,000-square-foot rooftop playground, community and craft rooms, and a gymnasium.

Government Subsidizes Home Improvement. Dismayed by the unsightly appearance of homes in a low-income area in Indianapolis, a community group worked through the city government to receive a Community Development Block Grant (program #14.203) in order to subsidize expensive home improvements. The poor residents received grant money directly to spruce up their homes; higher-income homeowners in the area received partial rebates for their repairs.

Rats on the Run. With the help of a $1.2 million grant from the Department of Health and Human Services (program #13.267), the

District of Columbia mounted one of the most successful rat eradication programs in the country. In sections of the city where rats infested as many as 70 percent of the households, the rate was reduced to less than 4 percent.

New Lease on Life for Nursery School. When two women who ran a successful nursery school were informed that they were going to lose their lease, they applied for a $45,000 Department of Agriculture insured loan (program #10.422). The money was used to buy property and put up a new building, thus insuring the school's survival.

Ski Town Transformed to Resort Area. The famous ski town of Steamboat Springs, Colorado, the home and training ground of more Olympic skiers than any other American ski area, began to develop in the late 1960s thanks to over $5 million worth of loans provided by the Small Business Administration (program #59.013) in cooperation with a local bank. The money was channeled through a local development company to aid hotels, motels, restaurants, lodges, ranches, campgrounds, an auto dealership, a gas station, a supermarket, and ski facilities. As a result, the number of full-time jobs available in Steamboat Springs has more than doubled.

Greenhouse Grows into Victory Garden. To help relieve chronic food shortages among poor residents of Cheyenne, Wyoming, a non-profit community action agency applied for and received a $42,000 grant from the Community Services Administration (program #49.005) to build a community solar greenhouse. The greenhouse produces about $75,000 worth of fresh vegetables annually, most of which is given to area groups to supplement the diets of the poor, elderly, and handicapped. Surplus crops are sold to the public and profits are used to pay the greenhouse operating expenses. The greenhouse is staffed chiefly by volunteers, including several senior citizens. It offers courses in gardening to the handicapped and it employs juvenile offenders ordered to work off court fines.

Local Food Bank Flourishes. Two men who ran a dining room in Arizona for the needy in the mid-1960s discovered they could get discarded but edible food free from markets and food processing plants. They soon found that they could obtain so much food that they organized a food bank and began distributing it to other charitable organizations. The Department of Labor (program #17.232) provided them with funds to hire nine staff members and the Community Services Administration (program #49.005) provided them with $160,000 to hold workshops and seminars in communities around the country to spread information about establishing food banks.

Day Care Centers Fortified with Breakfast Program. In 1977 MANNA, a local anti-hunger group in Nashville, Tennessee, generated enough support among teachers, parents, and students to force the local school board to adopt a Department of Agriculture free breakfast program (#10.553) in one Nashville school. As the program grew to include other schools so did MANNA. The group now has a staff of forty and has also received money from the Community Food and Nutrition Program (#49.005) as well as the Child Care Food Program (#10.558). The funds are used to feed lower-income preschoolers in local day care centers.

Neighborhood Arts Center Off and Running. The Neighborhood Arts Center in Atlanta, Georgia, got its start in 1975 when a group of community activists blocked the demolition of an old school building and persuaded city officials to rent it for $100 a year. The arts center, which emphasizes black culture, is financed in part by three federal agencies. The National Endowment for the Arts gave it a $22,000 grant (program #45.010) to continue providing cultural outlets to the predominantly black population in the neighborhood. The Department of Agriculture provides funds to serve free lunches to children attending classes during the summer (program #10.559). And salaries of the center's twenty-six-member staff are paid from funds provided by the Department of Labor's Comprehensive Employment and Training Programs (#17.232).

Marine Museum Remains Afloat. The Penobscot Marine Museum continues to serve the community around Searsport, Maine, thanks in part to help from the Department of Education's Institute of Museum Services (program #84.115). The museum's collection features paintings and ship models and is housed in several buildings, including the old town hall and three former homes of sea captains. The $10,000 grant it received in 1980 went to pay for heating, electricity, and staff salaries.

Historic Mill Reopens. The historic Valley Falls Mill complex in Central Falls, Rhode Island, is once again operating thanks to help from the Department of the Interior. Built in 1849, the mill was operated until the 1930s when it fell into disrepair. In 1977 the state historic preservation commission performed a survey of the mill, aided by a $14,000 grant from the Department of the Interior (program #15.411), and placed it on the National Register of Historic Places. A corporation was then founded to rehabilitate the mill, the largest building in the town, to make housing units for senior citizens. In addition to being eligible for the Small Business Adminstration's section 8(a) funds to finance the rehabilitation, the officers of the for-profit corporation also received a special challenge grant of $240,000 from the Department of the Interior to reactivate the electrical generating capacity of the mill. Now the mill provides the electricity and heat for the entire housing project. The special grant that enabled the corporation to reactivate the mill is similar to another Department of the Interior program (#15.411); this one, however, offered the corporation more money.

Money Channeled for Youngsters. In 1973 the Department of Health and Human Services gave a three-year seed-money grant (program #13.275) worth $300,000 to Al Duca, a painter and sculptor in Gloucester, Massachusetts, to refine further his program that kept teenagers drug-free and out of trouble. Seventy percent of the money was used to pay stipends to youngsters involved in useful community projects. The rest financed administrative costs and the development of training programs and materials to spread word of the project. Out of that experiment grew Channel One, an organization primarily supported by local businesses and community agencies, as well as the state and federal governments. In Gloucester, youngsters from all walks of life worked on several projects, including construction of an education center and the restoration of an historic graveyard. Other Channel One programs have sprung up in hundreds of communities across the country, all based on the Gloucester model. And now, in addition to his painting and sculpture, Al Duca works as the Channel One program director for the Gloucester Community Development Corporation.

For additional examples see sections on Rural Living, and on Buying or Improving a House. The 400-page publication, *People Power: What Communities Are Doing to Counter Inflation* provides countless stories showing how individuals have improved their communities by using federal programs. Copies are free from Consumer Information Center, Department 682-H, Pueblo, CO 81009.

SURPLUS PROPERTY

Not all government programs simply provide money. A number of programs offer surplus property as well as goods and services at no cost, or at prices that would be substantially higher elsewhere. The following list identifies the more popular nonmoney programs:

- Nonprofit organizations can receive free surplus food (program #10.550).
- More than 140 varieties of grasses, legumes, shrubs, and trees are free for conservation purposes (program #10.905).
- Tools, machinery, and other surplus equipment are free to educational institutions through the Tools for Schools Program of the Department of Defense (program #12.001).
- The Department of Defense offers free ships, cannons, works of art, manuscripts, books, and other military property (program #12.700).
- Free pigs, goats, and other wild animals are available to nonprofit organizations (program #15.900).
- Federal surplus land can be purchased at substantial savings, if used for low- and moderate-income housing (program #14.211).
- Individuals can receive houses for next to nothing in urban areas (program #15.603).
- Surplus automobiles, airplanes, office supplies, and other items are free to some and for sale to others (programs #39.002, #39.003, and #39.007).

RURAL LIVING

Most of us are aware that the Department of Agriculture offers hundreds of programs to help farmers produce, store, and market their products. However, what is not so well known is that you can also qualify for Department of Agriculture money if:

- you are not in the agriculture business but are simply living in a small town;
- you are in the winery, beekeeping, or aquaculture business;
- you wish to build a tennis court or golf course;
- you are twelve years old and want to start a business.

For a majority of the programs available to farmers and those people living in small towns, review the list described under the Department of Agriculture. Keep in mind also that small communities can benefit from programs in some of the other government departments, such as the Department of Housing and Urban Development and the Department of Commerce.

The following stories demonstrate how individuals have used Department of Agriculture money and other agencies to resolve other-than-typical farming problems.

Mortgage Money for Young Teachers. A young couple fresh out of college moved to a small Oklahoma town to take teaching jobs. They found a house they wanted to buy for $50,000 but could not meet the local bank's demand for a 20 percent down payment ($10,000). They solved their problem by applying for and receiving an Above-Moderate-Income Housing Loan (program #10.429) which required only a $2,000 down payment.

Barn and Farm Transformed into Golf Course and Clubhouse. A farmer in Alabama received a $22,000 Recreation Facility Loan (program #10.413) to convert part of his land into a nine-hole golf course with a clubhouse. Another Alabama farmer used a $13,000 loan (program #10.413) to help build a 20-acre sport fishing lake complete with cottages and concession stands.

Nearly Half a Million for Catfish. A $400,000 loan (program #10.407) enabled an Arkansas man to start a catfish farm in the southeastern section of the state, where the confluence of several rivers and the ready availability of moisture-holding clay make conditions ideal for aquaculture. The loan was used to construct dams to form breeding and storage pools, build an irrigation and drainage system between the pools, and to buy the land and fish food. The fish are sold cleaned and ready to cook to fishmongers in Arkansas, Tennessee, Kentucky, Illinois, and Indiana, and alive to farmers in Indiana and Illinois to stock their sport fishing ponds.

Loan for Tot Lot and Tennis Courts. The people living in Kinnen, Alabama, lacked local recreational facilities until the town received a $50,000 insured loan from the Department of Agriculture (program #10.423) to build a park, complete with tennis courts, a baseball diamond, a picnic area, and a playground for toddlers called a "Tot Lot."

Money for Loss of Honey. In 1971 beekeeper Ken Moore of southwestern Ohio received $6,000 from the Department of Agriculture (program #10.060) when the honey produced from his field bee colony dropped from forty to eighty pounds per hive to ten or twelve pounds. Because Mr. Moore's bees were being affected by the insecticide used by local farmers to kill alfalfa weevil he was eligible for Beekeeper Indemnity Payments.

Employee Turns Employer. A man in Oil City, Louisiana, was making a good living as a heavy equipment operator for a company that prepared and cleaned up oil well sites, when his employer suddenly died. Because he is a member of a minority group, he was able to obtain a $225,000 insured loan (program #10.422) from the Department of Agriculture to buy the business from the employer's heirs. It is now a true family business. The owner manages the firm's field operations, his son is employed as a heavy equipment operator, and his wife and daughter run the office.

Bouquet from USDA for Winery. After heavy rain wiped out most of the year's crop of raisins, a vineyard owner near Fresno, California, turned to the Department of Agriculture for help. He received a

$16,000 operating expenses loan (program #10.406) to hire workers, repair machinery and buildings, and buy fertilizer and insurance. In addition, he received a $22,400 equipment loan to buy posts and wire to stake his grape vines properly.

Seed Money for Teenage Entrepreneurs. A group of youngsters in Erie County, Pennsylvania, received a $500 loan from the Department of Agriculture (program #10.406) to buy a young steer. They raised the steer, fattened it up, and sold it at the county fair for a profit. A young teenager in Pennsylvania received a $500 loan (program #10.406) to start a summer landscaping business on a small scale. The money was used to purchase a lawnmower, grass clippers, saws, pruning shears, and other equipment. The initial loan money enabled him to operate his small business for three consecutive summers.

Aid for Small-Town Airlines. Big Sky Transportation Company was started in 1978 to provide commuter air service to small cities and towns in Montana, Idaho, and Wyoming. Almost immediately the airline began to run into trouble due to the harsh Montana winters that played havoc with the airplanes. Faced with mounting financial woes, the officers of the company looked to federal agencies for help and received a Federal Aviation Administration loan guarantee (program #20.105) worth $500,000 to buy two Cessna airplanes better suited to winter flying conditions. Moreover, another airline, Frontier Airways, decided in 1979 to cancel service to eight small cities in Montana and North Dakota. The Civil Aeronautics Board determined that flights to and from these cities constituted "essential" air service and awarded Big Sky Transportation Company a $15 million one-year subsidy (program #26.003) to take over the route in July 1980. Both sources of federal assistance helped Big Sky turn the corner and develop into a financially healthy enterprise.

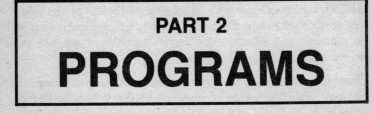

PART 2
PROGRAMS

The following federal government assistance programs are arranged numerically according to a unique five-digit federal program numbering system. This numbering system is used within the federal government when referring to these programs, and the index to this book is also based on these numbers.

U.S. DEPARTMENT OF AGRICULTURE

ANIMAL AND PLANT HEALTH INSPECTION SERVICE

10.051 COMMODITY LOANS AND PURCHASES (PRICE SUPPORTS)

Type of Assistance: Direct payments and loans ranging from $50 to $2,000,000.
Applicant Eligibility: Individuals.
Objective: To improve and stabilize farm income, to assist in bringing about a better balance between supply and demand of the commodities, and to assist farmers in the orderly marketing of their crops. Funds provide farmers a ready means of promoting more orderly marketing. Producers are not obligated to make good any decline in the market price of the commodity they have put up as collateral.
Contact: Price Support and Loan Division, Agricultural Stabilization and Conservation Service, Department of Agriculture, P. O. Box 2415, Washington, DC 20013, 202-447-8837.

10.052 COTTON PRODUCTION STABILIZATION (COTTON DIRECT PAYMENTS)

Type of Assistance: Direct payments ranging from $3 to $50,000.
Applicant Eligibility: Individuals.
Objective: To attract the cotton production that is needed to meet domestic and foreign demand for fiber, to protect income for farmers, and to assure adequate supplies at fair and reasonable prices. Payments are used to provide producers with a guaranteed price whenever average prices drop below the established or "target" price.
Contact: Production Adjustment Division, Agricultural Stabilization and Conservation Service, Department of Agriculture, P. O. Box 2415, Washington, DC 20013, 202-447-7641.

10.053 DAIRY INDEMNITY PAYMENTS (MILK AND DAIRY COW INDEMNITY PAYMENTS)

Type of Assistance: Direct payments ranging from $940 to $22,430.
Applicant Eligibility: Individuals.
Objective: To indemnify dairy farmers and manufacturers of dairy products who are directed to remove their milk, milk cows, or dairy products from commercial markets because of contamination with residues of pesticides re-

sulting from no misaction on the part of the dairy farmer or the manufacturer of the dairy product. Fair market value for the milk is paid.

Contact: Emergency and Indemnity Programs Division, Agricultural Stabilization and Conservation Service, Department of Agriculture, P. O. Box 2415, Washington, DC 20013, 202-447-7997.

10.054   EMERGENCY CONSERVATION PROGRAM

Type of Assistance: Direct payments ranging from $400 to $10,000.

Applicant Eligibility: Individuals.

Objective: To enable farmers to perform emergency conservation measures to control wind erosion on farmlands, or to rehabilitate farmlands damaged by wind erosion, floods, hurricanes, or other natural disasters; and to carry out emergency water conservation or water enhancing measures during periods of severe drought.

Contact: Conservation and Environmental Protection Division, Agricultural Stabilization and Conservation Service, Department of Agriculture, P. O. Box 2415, Washington, DC 20013, 202-447-6221.

10.055   FEED GRAIN PRODUCTION STABILIZATION (FEED GRAIN DIRECT PAYMENTS)

Type of Assistance: Direct payments ranging from $3 to $50,000.

Applicant Eligibility: Individuals.

Objective: To attract the production needed to meet domestic and foreign demand, to protect income for farmers, and to assure adequate supplies at fair and reasonable prices. Payments are used to provide producers with a guaranteed price on their planted acreage in the event average prices drop below the established or "target" price.

Contact: Production Adjustment Division, Agricultural Stabilization and Conservation Service, Department of Agriculture, P. O. Box 2415, Washington, DC 20013, 202-447-7633.

10.056   STORAGE FACILITIES AND EQUIPMENT LOANS (FARM FACILITY LOANS)

Type of Assistance: Direct loans ranging from $200 to $50,000.

Applicant Eligibility: Individuals.

Objective: To complement the commodity loan and grain reserve programs by providing adequate financing for needed on-farm storage facilities, drying equipment, and operating equipment, thereby affording farmers the opportunity for orderly marketing of their crops. Loans are used to finance the purchase of storage structures, drying equipment, and operating equipment, and to remodel existing facilities.

Contact: Price Support and Loan Division, Agricultural Stabilization and Conservation Service, Department of Agriculture, P. O. Box 2415, Washington, DC 20013, 202-447-4634.

10.058 WHEAT PRODUCTION STABILIZATION (WHEAT DIRECT PAYMENTS)

Type of Assistance: Direct payments ranging from $3 to $50,000.
Applicant Eligibility: Individuals.
Objective: To attract the production that is needed to meet domestic and foreign demand for food, to protect income for farmers, and to assure adequate supplies at fair and reasonable prices. Payments are used to provide producers with a guaranteed price on their planted acreage in the event average prices drop below the established or "target" price.
Contact: Production Adjustment Division, Agricultural Stabilization and Conservation Service, Department of Agriculture, P. O. Box 2415, Washington, DC 20013, 202-447-7633.

10.060 BEEKEEPER INDEMNITY PAYMENTS

Type of Assistance: Direct payments ranging from $7.50 to $125,000.
Applicant Eligibility: Individuals.
Objective: To indemnify beekeepers who through no fault of their own have suffered losses of honey bees as a result of utilization of poisons near or adjacent to the property on which the bee hives were located. The beekeeper is paid for his loss resulting from the damage done to his bees as a result of the use of pesticides.
Contact: Emergency and Indemnity Programs Division, Agricultural Stabilization and Conservation Service, Department of Agriculture, P. O. Box 2415, Washington, DC 20013, 202-447-7997.

10.062 WATER BANK PROGRAM

Type of Assistance: Direct payments ranging from $4 to $55 per acre.
Applicant Eligibility: Individuals.
Objective: To conserve surface waters; preserve and improve migratory waterfowl habitat and wildlife resources; and secure other environmental benefits. Agreements are for 10 years with eligible landowners to help preserve important breeding and nesting areas of migratory waterfowl. During the agreement, the participants agree in return for annual payments not to drain, burn, fill, or otherwise destroy the wetland character of such areas and not to use areas for agricultural purposes.
Contact: Conservation and Environmental Protection Division, Agricultural Stabilization and Conservation Service, Department of Agriculture, P. O. Box 2415, Washington, DC 20013, 202-447-6221.

10.063 AGRICULTURAL CONSERVATION PROGRAM

Type of Assistance: Direct payments ranging from $3 to $10,000.
Applicant Eligibility: Individuals.
Objective: Control of erosion and sedimentation, voluntary compliance with federal and state requirements to solve point and nonpoint source pollution, priorities in the National Environmental Policy Act, improvement of water

quality, and assurance of a continued supply of necessary food and fiber. The program is directed toward the solution of critical soil, water, woodland, and pollution abatement problems on farms and ranches. The conservation practices are to be used on agricultural land and must be performed satisfactorily and in accordance with applicable specifications.
Contact: Conservation and Environmental Protection Division, Agricultural Stabilization and Conservation Service, Department of Agriculture, P. O. Box 2415, Washington, DC 20013, 202-447-7333.

10.065   RICE PRODUCTION STABILIZATION (RICE DIRECT PAYMENTS)

Type of Assistance: Direct payments ranging from $3 to $50,000.
Applicant Eligibility: Individuals.
Objective: To provide the production needed to meet domestic and foreign demand, to protect income for farmers, and to assure adequate supplies at fair and reasonable prices. Payments are used to provide producers with a guaranteed price on the portion of the crop produced on the allotment in the event average prices drop below the established or "target" price.
Contact: Production Adjustment Division, Agricultural Stabilization and Conservation Service, Department of Agriculture, P. O. Box 2415, Washington, DC 20013, 202-447-8480.

10.066   EMERGENCY FEED PROGRAM

Type of Assistance: Direct payments ranging from $3 to $100,000.
Applicant Eligibility: Individuals.
Objective: To assist in the preservation and maintenance of livestock in any area of the United States where because of flood, drought, fire, hurricane, earthquake, storm, or other natural disaster, it is determined that an emergency exists.
Contact: Emergency and Indemnity Programs Division, Agricultural Stabilization and Conservation Service, Department of Agriculture, P. O. Box 2415, Washington, DC 20013, 202-447-7997.

10.067   GRAIN RESERVE PROGRAM (FARMER-HELD AND OWNED GRAIN RESERVE)

Type of Assistance: Direct payments ranging from $25 to $50,000.
Applicant Eligibility: Individuals.
Objective: To insulate sufficient quantities of grain from the market to increase price to farmers. To improve and stabilize farm income and to assist farmers in the orderly marketing of their crops.
Contact: Price Support and Loan Division, Agricultural Stabilization and Conservation Service, Department of Agriculture, P. O. Box 2415, Washington, DC 20013, 202-447-3215.

10.068 RURAL CLEAN WATER PROGRAM

Type of Assistance: Direct payments up to $50,000.

Applicant Eligibility: Individuals.

Objective: To improve water quality in approved project areas in the most cost effective manner; to assist agricultural landowners to reduce agricultural nonpoint source water pollutants; and to develop and test programs, policies, and procedures for controlling agricultural nonpoint source pollution.

Contact: Conservation and Environmental Protection Division, Agricultural Stabilization and Conservation Service, Department of Agriculture, P. O. Box 2415, Washington, DC 20013, 202-447-7333.

AGRICULTURE MARKETING SERVICE

10.156 FEDERAL-STATE MARKETING IMPROVEMENT PROGRAM

Type of Assistance: Grants ranging from $6,000 to $500,000.

Applicant Eligibility: State governments.

Objective: To solve marketing problems at the state and local level through pilot marketing service projects conducted by the states. Projects may deal in such areas as providing marketing services for improving the marketability of agricultural products, expanding export markets, improving economic and physical efficiency of marketing, and assembling and disseminating marketing information.

Contact: Director, Federal-State Marketing Improvement Program, Agricultural Marketing Service, Department of Agriculture, Washington, DC 20250, 202-447-2704.

FARMERS HOME ADMINISTRATION

10.404 EMERGENCY LOANS

Type of Assistance: Guaranteed/insured loans ranging from $500 to $6,400,000.

Applicant Eligibility: Individuals.

Objective: To assist farmers, ranchers, and aquaculture operators with loans to cover losses resulting from a major and/or natural disaster, for annual farm operating expenses, and for other essential needs necessary to return the disaster victims' farming operation(s) to a financially sound basis in order that they will be able to return to local sources of credit as soon as possible. Loans may be used to repair, restore, or replace damaged or destroyed farm property and supplies which were lost or damaged as a direct result of a natural disaster; provide annual operating expenses for up to six full crop-years following the disaster; under certain conditions, refinance debts made necessary by the disaster; and finance adjustments in the farming, ranching, or aquaculture operation(s) determined necessary to restore or maintain applicants on a sound financial basis.

Contact: Administrator, Farmers Home Administration, Department of Agriculture, Washington, DC 20250, 202-447-4671.

10.405 FARM LABOR HOUSING LOANS AND GRANTS (LABOR HOUSING)

Type of Assistance: Grants and guaranteed/insured loans ranging from $3,000 to $1,978,000.

Applicant Eligibility: Individuals, nonprofit organizations, state and local governments.

Objective: To provide decent, safe, and sanitary low-rent housing and related facilities for domestic farm laborers. Funds may be used for construction, repair, or purchase of housing; acquiring the necessary land and making improvements on the land for the housing; and developing related facilities including recreation areas, central cooking and dining facilities, small infirmaries, laundry facilities, and other essential equipment and facilities.

Contact: Administrator, Farmers Home Administration, Department of Agriculture, Washington, DC 20250, 202-382-1621.

10.406 FARM OPERATING LOANS

Type of Assistance: Guaranteed/insured loans up to $200,000.

Applicant Eligibility: Individuals.

Objective: To enable operators of not larger than family farms (primarily limited resource operators, new operators, and low-income operators) to make efficient use of their land, labor, and other resources. Youth loans enable rural youths to establish and operate modest income-producing farm or nonfarm projects that are educational and practical and provide an opportunity to learn basic economic and credit principles. Funds may be used for a wide range of necessary agricultural expenses.

Contact: Director, Production Loan Division, Farmers Home Administration, Department of Agriculture, Washington, DC 20250, 202-447-2288.

10.407 FARM OWNERSHIP LOANS

Type of Assistance: Guaranteed/insured loans ranging from $16,000 to $200,000.

Applicant Eligibility: Individuals.

Objective: To assist eligible farmers and ranchers, including farming cooperatives, partnerships, and corporations to become owner-operators of not larger than family farms; to make efficient use of the land, labor, and other resources; to carry on sound and successful operations on the farm, and afford the family, cooperative, partnership, or corporation an opportunity to have a reasonable standard of living. Farm ownership loans are also available to eligible applicants with limited incomes and resources who are unable to pay the regular interest rate and have special problems such as undeveloped managerial skills. Loans may be used for a wide range of necessary agricultural expenses.

Contact: Administrator, Farmers Home Administration, Department of Agriculture, Washington, DC 20250, 202-447-5044.

10.408 GRAZING ASSOCIATION LOANS

Type of Assistance: Guaranteed/insured loans ranging from $44,300 to $1,029,900.

Applicant Eligibility: Nonprofit organizations.

Objective: To increase the income of farm families and those who reside in rural areas and to readjust the use of land so that each acre is used for a purpose which will better serve the community. Loans may be made to associations of family farmers and ranchers to acquire and develop grazing land to provide seasonal grazing for livestock belonging to association members.

Contact: Administrator, Farmers Home Administration, Department of Agriculture, Washington, DC 20250, 202-447-4572.

10.409 IRRIGATION, DRAINAGE, AND OTHER SOIL AND WATER CONSERVATION LOANS

Type of Assistance: Guaranteed/insured loans ranging from $32,000 to $612,000.

Applicant Eligibility: Nonprofit organizations.

Objective: To increase the income of farm families and other rural residents and to readjust the use of land so that each acre is used for a purpose which will better serve the community. Loans may be made to eligible applicants for irrigation, drainage, or other soil conservation measures.

Contact: Farm Real Estate Loan Division, Farmers Home Administration, Department of Agriculture, Washington, DC 20250, 202-447-4572.

10.410 LOW- TO MODERATE-INCOME HOUSING LOANS

Type of Assistance: Guaranteed/insured loans ranging from $1,000 to $60,000.

Applicant Eligibility: Individuals.

Objective: To assist rural families to obtain decent, safe, and sanitary dwellings and related facilities. Loans may be used for construction, repair, or purchase of housing; to provide necessary and adequate sewage disposal facilities; for water supply for the applicant and his family; for weatherization; to purchase or install essential equipment which upon installation becomes part of the real estate; and to buy a site on which to place a dwelling for applicant's own use.

Contact: Single Family Housing, Farmers Home Administration, Department of Agriculture, Washington, DC 20250, 202-382-1470.

10.411 RURAL HOUSING SITE LOANS

Type of Assistance: Direct and guaranteed/insured loans ranging from $45,200 to $571,000.

Applicant Eligibility: Nonprofit organizations.

Objective: To assist public or private nonprofit organizations interested in providing sites for housing to acquire and develop land in rural areas to be subdivided as adequate building sites and sold on a nonprofit basis to families eligible for low- and moderate-income loans; to also aid cooperatives and broadly based nonprofit rural rental housing applicants. Funds may be used for the purchase and development of adequate sites, including necessary equipment which becomes a permanent part of the development; water and sewer facilities if not available; payment of necessary engineering, legal fees, and closing costs; and needed landscaping and other necessary building-related facilities.

Contact: Single Family Housing, Farmers Home Administration, Department of Agriculture, Washington, DC 20250, 202-382-1470.

10.413 RECREATION FACILITY LOANS

Type of Assistance: Guaranteed/insured loans ranging from $20,000 to $100,000.

Applicant Eligibility: Individuals.

Objective: To assist eligible farm and ranch owners or tenants, including cooperatives, corporations, or partnerships, to convert all or a portion of the farms they own or operate to income-producing outdoor recreational enterprises which will supplement or supplant farm or ranch income and permit carrying on sound and successful operations. Recreation enterprises that may be financed include: campgrounds, horseback riding stables, swimming facilities, tennis courts, shooting preserves, vacation cottages, lodges and rooms for visitors, lakes and ponds for boating and fishing, docks, nature trails, hunting facilities, and winter sports areas.

Contact: Community Programs, Farmers Home Administration, Department of Agriculture, Washington, DC 20250, 202-447-7287.

10.414 RESOURCE CONSERVATION AND DEVELOPMENT LOANS

Type of Assistance: Guaranteed/insured loans ranging from $2,400 to $250,000.

Applicant Eligibility: Nonprofit organizations and local governments.

Objective: To provide loan assistance to local sponsoring agencies in authorized areas where acceleration of program of resource conservation, development, and utilization will increase economic opportunities for local people. Loan funds may be used for rural community public outdoor-oriented water-based recreational facilities; soil and water development, conservation, control, and use facilities; shift-in-land use facilities; community water

storage facilities; and special purpose equipment to carry out the above purposes.
Contact: Director, Community Facilities Division, Farmers Home Administration, Department of Agriculture, Washington, DC 20250, 202-447-7287.

10.415 RURAL RENTAL HOUSING LOANS
Type of Assistance: Guaranteed/insured loans ranging from $27,000 to $2,000,000.
Applicant Eligibility: Individuals, nonprofit organizations, state and local governments.
Objective: To provide economically designed and constructed rental and co-operative housing and related facilities suited for independent living for rural residents. Loans can be used to construct, purchase, improve, or repair rental or cooperative housing.
Contact: Administrator, Farmers Home Administration, Department of Agriculture, Washington, DC 20250, 202-447-5177.

10.416 SOIL AND WATER LOANS
Type of Assistance: Guaranteed/insured loans ranging from $3,300 to $100,000.
Applicant Eligibility: Individuals.
Objective: To facilitate improvement, protection, and proper use of farmland by providing adequate financing and supervisory assistance for soil conservation; water development, conservation, and use; forestation; drainage of farmland; the establishment and improvement of permanent pasture; the development of pollution abatement and control facilities on farms; and related measures. Loans may be used for a wide range of soil and water conservation methods.
Contact: Administrator, Farmers Home Administration, Department of Agriculture, Washington, DC 20250, 202-447-3646.

10.417 VERY LOW-INCOME HOUSING REPAIR LOANS AND GRANTS
Type of Assistance: Direct loans and grants ranging from $200 to $5,000.
Applicant Eligibility: Individuals.
Objective: To give very low-income rural homeowners an opportunity to make essential repairs to their homes to make them safe and to remove health hazards to the family or the community. This includes repairs to the foundation, roof, or basic structure as well as water and waste disposal systems, and weatherization.
Contact: Administrator, Farmers Home Administration, Department of Agriculture, Washington, DC 20250, 202-382-1474.

10.418 WATER AND WASTE DISPOSAL SYSTEMS FOR RURAL COMMUNITIES

Type of Assistance: Grants and guaranteed/insured loans ranging from $1,000 to $20,917,000.

Applicant Eligibility: Nonprofit organizations and local governments.

Objective: To provide human amenities, alleviate health hazards, and promote the orderly growth of the rural areas of the nation by meeting the need for new and improved rural water and waste disposal facilities. Funds may be used for the installation, repair, improvement, or expansion of a rural water facility including distribution lines, well-pumping facilities and costs related thereto, and the installation, repair, improvement, or expansion of a rural waste disposal facility including the collection and treatment of sanitary, storm, and solid wastes.

Contact: Administrator, Farmers Home Administration, Department of Agriculture, Washington, DC 20250, 202-447-5717.

10.419 WATERSHED PROTECTION AND FLOOD PREVENTION LOANS

Type of Assistance: Guaranteed/insured loans ranging from $4,000 to $5,450,000.

Applicant Eligibility: Nonprofit organizations, state and local governments.

Objective: To provide loan assistance to sponsoring local organizations in authorized watershed areas for share of cost for works of improvement. Loan funds may be used to help local sponsors provide the local share of the cost of watershed works of improvement for flood prevention, irrigation, drainage, water quality management, sedimentation control, fish and wildlife development, public water-based recreation, and water storage and related costs.

Contact: Director, Community Facilities Division, Farmers Home Administration, Department of Agriculture, Washington, DC 20250, 202-382-1490.

10.420 RURAL SELF-HELP HOUSING TECHNICAL ASSISTANCE

Type of Assistance: Grants ranging from $45,000 to $801,400.

Applicant Eligibility: Nonprofit organizations, state and local governments.

Objective: To provide financial support for the promotion of a program of technical and supervisory assistance which will aid needy individuals and their families in carrying out mutual self-help efforts in rural areas. Organizations may use funds to hire the personnel to carry out a program of technical assistance for self-help housing in rural areas; to pay necessary and reasonable office and administrative expenses; to make essential equipment such as power tools available to families participating in self-help housing construction; and to pay fees for training self-help group members in construction techniques or for other professional services needed.

Contact: Administrator, Farmers Home Administration, Department of Agriculture, Washington, DC 20250, 202-382-1470.

10.421 LAND ACQUISITION PROGRAM

Type of Assistance: Guaranteed/insured loans ranging from $260,000 to $7,000,000.
Applicant Eligibility: Native Americans only.
Objective: To enable tribes and tribal corporations to mortgage lands as security for loans from the Farmers Home Administration to buy additional land within the reservation. Loan funds may be used to acquire land for lease to tribal members, to lease to cooperative grazing units, or for use for recreational and commercial purposes, rounding out grazing units, or elimination of fractional heirships.
Contact: Office of Indian Affairs, Farmers Home Administration, Department of Agriculture, Washington, DC 20250, 202-447-7597.

10.422 BUSINESS AND INDUSTRIAL LOANS

Type of Assistance: Guaranteed/insured loans ranging from $11,000 to $50,000,000.
Applicant Eligibility: Individuals, nonprofit organizations, and local governments.
Objective: To assist public, private, or cooperative organizations (profit or nonprofit), Indian tribes, or individuals in rural areas to obtain quality loans for the purpose of improving, developing, or financing business, industry, and employment; improving the economic and environmental climate in rural communities including pollution abatement and control; and for conservation, development, and utilization of water for aquaculture purposes.
Contact: Administrator, Farmers Home Administration, Department of Agriculture, Washington, DC 20250, 202-447-2925.

10.423 COMMUNITY FACILITIES LOAN

Type of Assistance: Guaranteed/insured loans ranging from $1,600 to $5,500,000.
Applicant Eligibility: Nonprofit organizations, state and local governments.
Objective: To construct, enlarge, extend, or otherwise improve community facilities providing essential services to rural residents. Funds may be for projects supporting overall community development such as fire and rescue services, transportation, traffic control, community, social, cultural, health and recreational benefits, industrial park sites, access ways, and utility extensions.
Contact: Director, Community Facilities Division, Farmers Home Administration, Department of Agriculture, Washington, DC 20250, 202-382-1490.

10.424 INDUSTRIAL DEVELOPMENT GRANTS

Type of Assistance: Grants ranging from $5,000 to $195,000.

Applicant Eligibility: State and local governments.

Objective: To facilitate the development of business, industry and related employment for improving the economy in rural communities. Grant funds may be used to finance industrial sites in rural areas, including the acquisition and development of land and the construction, conversion, enlargement, repair, or modernization of buildings, plants, machinery, equipment, access streets and roads, parking areas, transportation serving the site, utility extensions, necessary water supply and waste disposal facilities, pollution control and abatement incidental to site development, fees, and refinancing.

Contact: Director, Community Facilities Loan Division, Farmers Home Administration, Department of Agriculture, Washington, DC 20250, 202-382-1490.

10.426 AREA DEVELOPMENT ASSISTANCE PLANNING GRANTS

Type of Assistance: Grants ranging from $3,750 to $50,000.

Applicant Eligibility: Nonprofit organizations, state and local governments.

Objective: To contribute to the development of comprehensive planning for rural development, especially as such planning affects the unemployed, the underemployed, those with low family incomes, and minorities. Funds may be used for the development of comprehensive processes for rural areas, to enable rural areas which already have plans to revise them, and to support the development of any aspect of a comprehensive planning process.

Contact: Office of Area Development Assistance, Farmers Home Administration, Room 5449, South Building, Department of Agriculture, Washington, DC 20250, 202-447-6557.

10.427 RURAL RENTAL ASSISTANCE PAYMENTS

Type of Assistance: Direct payments (dollar amount not available).

Applicant Eligibility: Individuals, nonprofit organizations, state and local governments.

Objective: To reduce the rents paid by low-income families occupying eligible Rural Rental Housing (RRH), Rural Cooperative Housing (RCH), and Farm Labor Housing (FLH) projects financed by the Farmers Home Administration. Rental assistance may be used to reduce the rents paid by low-income senior citizens or families and domestic farm laborers and families whose rents exceed 25 percent of an adjusted annual income which does not exceed the limit established for the state.

Contact: Administrator, Farmers Home Administration, Department of Agriculture, Washington, DC 20250, 202-382-1612.

10.428 ECONOMIC EMERGENCY LOANS

Type of Assistance: Guaranteed/insured loans up to $400,000.
Applicant Eligibility: Individuals.
Objective: To make adequate financial assistance available in the form of loans insured or guaranteed for bona fide farmers, ranchers, and aquaculture operators. This is done so that they may continue their normal farming or ranching operations during the economic emergency which has caused a lack of agricultural credit due to national or areawide economic stress. Funds may be used for purposes that are essential to carrying on farming operations.
Contact: Emergency Loan Division, Farmers Home Administration, Department of Agriculture, Washington, DC 20250, 202-382-1632.

10.429 ABOVE-MODERATE-INCOME HOUSING LOANS

Type of Assistance: Guaranteed/insured loans ranging from $1,000 to $59,000.
Applicant Eligibility: Individuals.
Objective: To assist above-moderate-income families in obtaining adequate but modest, decent, safe, and sanitary dwellings and related facilities for their own use in rural areas by guaranteeing sound rural housing loans when loans would not be made available without a guarantee. Loans may be made for construction, repair, or purchase of housing; installation of necessary and adequate sewage disposal and water supply facilities; weatherization; purchase and installation of essential equipment; and purchase of a site on which to place the dwelling if the applicant does not already own such a site.
Contact: Single Family Housing, Farmers Home Administration, Department of Agriculture, Washington, DC 20250, 202-382-1470.

10.430 ENERGY-IMPACTED AREA DEVELOPMENT ASSISTANCE PROGRAM

Type of Assistance: Grants ranging from $1,870 to $825,000.
Applicant Eligibility: State and local governments.
Objective: To help areas impacted by coal or uranium development activities by providing assistance for the development of growth management and housing plans and in developing and acquiring sites for housing and public facilities and services. Funds may be used for the preparation of growth management and/or housing plans and up to 75 percent of the actual cost of developing or acquiring sites for public facilities, housing, or services for which other resources are otherwise not available in an approved designated area.
Contact: Office of Area Development Assistance, Farmers Home Administration, Rm. 5449, South Building, Department of Agriculture, Washington, DC 20250, 202-447-2573.

10.431 TECHNICAL AND SUPERVISORY ASSISTANCE GRANTS

Type of Assistance: Grants up to $100,000.

Applicant Eligibility: Nonprofit organizations and state governments.

Objective: To assist low-income rural families in obtaining adequate housing to meet their needs and/or to promote their continued occupancy of already adequate housing. These objectives will be accomplished through the establishment or support of housing delivery and counseling projects run by eligible applicants. Funds may be used to hire personnel to carry out a program of housing counseling and delivery to meet the needs of low-income families in rural areas; to pay necessary and reasonable office and administrative expenses; and to pay reasonable fees for training of organization personnel.

Contact: Multiple Family Special Authorities Division, Farmers Home Administration, Department of Agriculture, Washington, DC 20250, 202-447-7207.

FEDERAL CROP INSURANCE CORPORATION

10.450 CROP INSURANCE

Type of Assistance: Insurance ranging from $1 to $250,000.

Applicant Eligibility: Individuals.

Objective: To improve agricultural stability through a sound system of crop insurance by providing all-risk insurance for individual farmers to assure a basic income against droughts, freezes, insects, and other natural causes of disastrous crop losses. Insurance is available on crops in over 1,500 agricultural counties in 29 states.

Contact: Manager, Federal Crop Insurance Corporation, Department of Agriculture, Washington, DC 20250, 202-447-3287.

FOOD AND NUTRITION SERVICE

10.550 FOOD DISTRIBUTION (FOOD DONATION PROGRAM)

Type of Assistance: Donation of goods and grants (dollar amount not available).

Applicant Eligibility: State governments.

Objective: To improve the diets of school children; needy persons in households, on Indian reservations, and in charitable institutions; the elderly; and other individuals in need of food assistance, and to increase the market for domestically produced foods acquired under surplus removal or price support operations.

Contact: Food Distribution Division, Food and Nutrition Service, Department of Agriculture, Washington, DC 20250, 202-447-8371.

10.551 FOOD STAMPS
Type of Assistance: Direct payments averaging approximately $37.41 per month per person.
Applicant Eligibility: State governments.
Objective: To improve diets of low-income households by supplementing their food purchasing ability by providing households with a free coupon allotment which varies according to household size. The coupons may be used in participating retail stores to buy food for human consumption and garden seeds and plants to produce food for personal consumption by eligible households.
Contact: Deputy Administrator, Family Nutrition Programs, Food and Nutrition Service, Department of Agriculture, Washington, DC 20250, 202-447-8982.

10.553 SCHOOL BREAKFAST PROGRAM
Type of Assistance: Donation of goods and grants of approximately $.46 per meal.
Applicant Eligibility: Nonprofit organizations and state governments.
Objective: To assist states in providing nutritious breakfasts for school children through cash grants and food donations. Funds are available to reimburse participating public and nonprofit private schools of high school grade or under for breakfasts meeting the nutritional requirements prescribed by the Secretary of Agriculture and served to eligible children.
Contact: Director, School Programs Division, Food and Nutrition Service, Department of Agriculture, Washington, DC 20250, 202-447-9065.

10.554 EQUIPMENT ASSISTANCE FOR SCHOOL FOOD SERVICE PROGRAMS
Type of Assistance: Grants averaging $32,109.
Applicant Eligibility: Nonprofit organizations and state governments.
Objective: To provide states with cash grants to supply schools in low-income areas with equipment for storing, preparing, transporting, and serving food to children. Cash assistance is available to schools for purchase of equipment for storing, preparing, transporting, and serving food to children.
Contact: Director, School Programs Division, Food and Nutrition Service, Department of Agriculture, Washington, DC 20250, 202-447-8130.

10.555 NATIONAL SCHOOL LUNCH PROGRAM
Type of Assistance: Donation of goods and grants up to $.77 per meal.
Applicant Eligibility: Nonprofit organizations and state governments.
Objective: To assist states, through cash grants and food donations, in making the school lunch program available to all school children, thereby promoting their health and well-being. Funds are available to reimburse participating public and nonprofit private schools of high school grade or under, including residential child care institutions, for lunches meeting the nu-

tritional requirements prescribed by the Secretary of Agriculture and served
to eligible children.
Contact: Director, School Programs Division, Food and Nutrition Service,
Department of Agriculture, Washington, DC 20250, 202-447-8130.

10.556 SPECIAL MILK PROGRAM FOR CHILDREN

Type of Assistance: Grants averaging 8.7¢ per ½ pint of milk.
Applicant Eligibility: Nonprofit organizations and state governments.
Objective: To encourage the consumption of fluid milk by children of high
school grade and under through reimbursement to eligible schools and insti-
tutions which inaugurate or expand milk distribution service.
Contact: Director, School Programs Division, Food and Nutrition Service,
Department of Agriculture, Washington, DC 20250, 202-447-8130.

10.557 SPECIAL SUPPLEMENTAL FOOD PROGRAM FOR WOMEN, INFANTS, AND CHILDREN

Type of Assistance: Grants (dollar amount not available).
Applicant Eligibility: State governments.
Objective: To supply supplemental nutritious foods and nutrition education
to participants identified to be at nutritional risk with respect to their physical
and mental health. This includes making foods available to pregnant, post-
partum, and breastfeeding women, and infants and children up to five years
of age, through local public or nonprofit private health or welfare agencies.
Contact: Special Supplemental Food Programs Division, Food and Nutrition Service, Department of Agriculture, Washington, DC 20250, 202-447-
8206.

10.558 CHILD CARE FOOD PROGRAM

Type of Assistance: Grants averaging $.50 per meal.
Applicant Eligibility: Nonprofit organizations and state governments.
Objective: To assist states, through grants-in-aid and other means, to initiate, maintain, or expand food service programs for children in public and
private nonprofit, nonresidential child care institutions. Funds are made
available to, but not limited to, day care centers, settlement houses, recreation centers, family and group day care programs, Head Start Centers, and
institutions providing day care services for handicapped children.
Contact: Director, Child Care and Summer Programs Division, Food and
Nutrition Service, Department of Agriculture, Washington, DC 20250, 202-
447-8211.

10.559 SUMMER FOOD SERVICE PROGRAM FOR CHILDREN

Type of Assistance: Grants averaging $.94 per meal.
Applicant Eligibility: Nonprofit organizations and state governments.
Objective: To assist states, through grants-in-aid and other means, to initi-

ate, maintain and expand food service programs for children in public and nonprofit service institutions and summer camps when school is not in session. Funds are made available to eligible service institutions which conduct a regularly scheduled program for children from areas in which poor economic conditions exist, for any period during the months of May through September.
Contact: Director, Child Care and Summer Programs Division, Food and Nutrition Service, Department of Agriculture, Washington, DC 20250, 202-447-8211.

10.560 STATE ADMINISTRATIVE EXPENSES FOR CHILD NUTRITION
Type of Assistance: Grants ranging from $38,000 to $2,779,000.
Applicant Eligibility: State governments.
Objective: To provide each state educational agency with funds for use for its administrative expenses in supervising and giving technical assistance to the local school districts and institutions in their conduct of child nutrition programs.
Contact: Director, School Programs Division, Food and Nutrition Service, Department of Agriculture, Washington, DC 20250, 202-447-7351.

10.561 STATE ADMINISTRATIVE MATCHING GRANTS FOR FOOD STAMP PROGRAM
Type of Assistance: Grants ranging from $319,000 to $31,702,000.
Applicant Eligibility: State governments.
Objective: To provide federal financial aid to state and local governmental agencies for administrative costs incurred to operate the Food Stamp program.
Contact: Deputy Administrator, Family Nutrition Programs, Food and Nutrition Service, Department of Agriculture, Washington, DC 20250, 202-447-8982.

10.564 NUTRITION EDUCATION AND TRAINING PROGRAM
Type of Assistance: Grants ranging from $75,000 to $2,456,221.
Applicant Eligibility: State governments.
Objective: Grants are made to state education agencies to provide for the nutritional training of educational and food service personnel, the food service management training of school food service personnel, and the conduct of nutrition education activities in schools and child care institutions.
Contact: Nutrition and Technical Services Division, Food and Nutrition Service, Department of Agriculture, Washington, DC 20250, 202-447-8286.

FOREST SERVICE

10.652 FORESTRY RESEARCH
Type of Assistance: Grants ranging from $2,000 to $100,000.
Applicant Eligibility: Nonprofit organizations, state and local governments.
Objective: To provide funds for research in the fields of timber management, watershed management, forest range management, wildlife habitat management, forest recreation, forest fire protection, forest insect and disease protection and control, forest products utilization, forest engineering, forest production economics, forest products marketing, and forest survey.
Contact: Deputy Chief for Research, Forest Service, Department of Agriculture, P. O. Box 2417, Washington, DC 20013, 202-447-7075.

10.661 YOUTH CONSERVATION CORPS GRANTS TO STATES
Type of Assistance: Grants ranging from $70,000 to $1,500,000.
Applicant Eligibility: State governments.
Objective: To accomplish needed conservation on public lands, provide gainful employment for 15- through 18-year-olds, and develop an understanding and appreciation in participating youths of the nation's natural environment and heritage. Funds are provided to assist states in meeting the cost of projects for the employment of young men and women to develop, preserve, and maintain nonfederal public lands and waters within the states.
Contact: Staff Director, Human Resource Programs, Forest Service, Department of Agriculture, P. O. Box 2417, Washington, DC 20013, 202-447-7783.

10.663 YOUNG ADULT CONSERVATION CORPS GRANTS TO STATES
Type of Assistance: Grants ranging from $6,000 to $6,000,000.
Applicant Eligibility: State governments.
Objective: To provide employment and other benefits to youth, who would otherwise not be productively employed, through service in useful conservation work and other projects of a public nature on federal and nonfederal public lands and waters.
Contact: Administrator, Staff Director, Human Resources Programs, Forest Service, Department of Agriculture, P. O. Box 2417, Washington, DC 20013, 202-447-7783.

10.664 COOPERATIVE FORESTRY ASSISTANCE
Type of Assistance: Grants ranging from $40,000 to $5,000,000.
Applicant Eligibility: State governments.
Objective: To assist in the advancement of forest resources management; the encouragement of the production of timber; the prevention and control of insects and diseases affecting trees and forests; the prevention and control of

rural fires; the efficient utilization of wood and wood residues, including the recycling of wood fiber; the improvement and maintenance of fish and wildlife habitat; and the planning and conduct of urban forestry programs. Funds are made available to assist the State Forester or equivalent agencies in programs on private, state, local and other nonfederal forest lands.

Contact: Deputy Chief, State and Private Forestry, Forest Service, Department of Agriculture, P. O. Box 2417, Washington, DC 20013, 202-447-8921.

10.665   SCHOOLS AND ROADS—GRANTS TO STATES

Type of Assistance: Grants ranging from $63 to $121,081,427.
Applicant Eligibility: State governments.
Objective: To share receipts from the National Forests with the states in which the National Forests are situated.
Contact: Director of Fiscal and Accounting Management, Forest Service, Department of Agriculture, Rm. 701 RPE, P. O. Box 2417, Washington, DC 20013, 703-235-8159.

10.666   SCHOOLS AND ROADS—GRANTS TO COUNTIES

Type of Assistance: Grants ranging from $10 to $751,651.
Applicant Eligibility: Counties.
Objective: To share receipts from National Grasslands and Land Utilization Projects with the counties in which these are situated.
Contact: Director of Fiscal and Accounting Management, Forest Service, Department of Agriculture, Rm. 701 RPE, P. O. Box 2417, Washington, DC 20013, 703-235-8159.

10.667   SCHOOL FUNDS—GRANTS TO ARIZONA
AND NEW MEXICO

Type of Assistance: Grants ranging from $1,825 to $211,736.
Applicant Eligibility: States of Arizona and New Mexico.
Objective: To pay to the states of Arizona and New Mexico a portion of the gross proceeds of all the National Forests in each state.
Contact: Director of Fiscal and Accounting Management, Forest Service, Department of Agriculture, Rm. 701 RPE, P. O. Box 2417, Washington, DC 20013, 703-235-8159.

10.668   ADDITIONAL LANDS—GRANTS TO MINNESOTA

Type of Assistance: Grants up to $675,000.
Applicant Eligibility: State of Minnesota
Objective: To share National Forest receipts with the state of Minnesota in connection with lands situated in the counties of Cook, Lake, and St. Louis which are withdrawn from entry and appropriation under the public laws of the United States.

Contact: Director of Fiscal and Accounting Management, Forest Service, Department of Agriculture, Rm. 701 RPE, P. O. Box 2417, Washington, DC 20013, 703-235-8159.

RURAL ELECTRIFICATION ADMINISTRATION

10.850   RURAL ELECTRIFICATION LOANS AND LOAN GUARANTEES

Type of Assistance: Guaranteed/insured loans ranging from $250,000 to $1,500,000,000.
Applicant Eligibility: Nonprofit organizations, state and local governments.
Objective: To assure that people in eligible rural areas have access to electric services comparable in reliability and quality to the rest of the nation. Funds are used to supply central station electric services on a continuing basis in rural areas.
Contact: Administrator, Rural Electrification Administration, Department of Agriculture, Washington, DC 20250, 202-447-4413.

10.851   RURAL TELEPHONE LOANS AND LOAN GUARANTEES

Type of Assistance: Guaranteed/insured loans ranging from $200,000 to $20,000,000.
Applicant Eligibility: Nonprofit organizations, state and local governments.
Objective: To assure that people in eligible rural areas have access to telephone service comparable in reliability and quality to the rest of the nation.
Contact: Administrator, Rural Electrification Administration, Department of Agriculture, Washington, DC 20250, 202-447-5123.

10.852   RURAL TELEPHONE BANK LOANS

Type of Assistance: Direct loans ranging from $250,000 to $20,000,000.
Applicant Eligibility: Nonprofit organizations, state and local governments.
Objective: To provide supplemental financing to extend and improve telephone service in rural areas.
Contact: Governor, Rural Telephone Bank, Department of Agriculture, Washington, DC 20250, 202-447-4305.

10.853   COMMUNITY ANTENNA TELEVISION LOANS AND LOAN GUARANTEES

Type of Assistance: Guaranteed/insured loans (dollar amount not available).
Applicant Eligibility: Nonprofit organizations.
Objective: To overcome isolation in rural areas through modern communi-

cations systems in bringing health, education, information, and entertainment services to small towns and rural areas. Funds are used for the purpose of providing community antenna television services.

Contact: Administrator, Rural Electrification Administration, Department of Agriculture, Washington, DC 20250, 202-447-2960.

SCIENCE AND EDUCATION ADMINISTRATION

10.875 AGRICULTURAL RESEARCH— BASIC AND APPLIED RESEARCH

Type of Assistance: Dissemination of technical information and grants from $15,000 to $113,500.

Applicant Eligibility: Individuals, nonprofit organizations, state and local governments.

Objective: To make agricultural research discoveries, evaluate alternative ways of attaining goals, and provide scientific and technical information.

Contact: Deputy Director for Agricultural Research, Science and Education Administration, Department of Agriculture, Washington, DC 20250, 202-447-3656.

10.876 GRANTS FOR AGRICULTURAL RESEARCH, SPECIAL RESEARCH GRANTS

Type of Assistance: Grants ranging from $5,646 to $296,000.

Applicant Eligibility: Nonprofit organizations and state governments.

Objective: To carry out research to facilitate or expand promising breakthroughs in areas of the food and agricultural sciences of importance to the nation and to facilitate or expand ongoing state-federal food and agricultural research programs. Areas of research are generally limited to high priority problems of a regional or national scope.

Contact: Administrator, Cooperative Research, Science and Education Administration, Department of Agriculture, Washington, DC 20250, 703-235-2680.

10.877 COOPERATIVE FORESTRY RESEARCH

Type of Assistance: Grants ranging from $26,973 to $349,553.

Applicant Eligibility: State governments.

Objective: To encourage and assist the states in carrying on a program of forestry research at forestry schools, and to develop a trained pool of forest scientists capable of conducting needed forestry research.

Contact: Administrator, Cooperative Research, Science and Education Administration, Department of Agriculture, Washington, DC 20250, 202-447-7075.

10.878 PAYMENTS TO AGRICULTURAL EXPERIMENT STATIONS UNDER HATCH ACT

Type of Assistance: Grants ranging from $437,006 to $4,340,434.

Applicant Eligibility: State governments.

Objective: To support agricultural research at state agricultural experiment stations. Its purpose is to promote efficient production, marketing, distribution, and utilization of products of the farm as essential to the health and welfare of people and to promote a sound prosperous agriculture and rural life. Funds may be used for meeting expenses for research and investigations for printing and disseminating the results of such research, retirement of employees, administrative planning and direction, and for the purchase and rental of land and the construction, acquisition, alteration, or repair of buildings necessary for conducting research.

Contact: Administrator, Cooperative Research, Science and Education Administration, Department of Agriculture, Washington, DC 20250, 202-447-7075.

10.879 RURAL DEVELOPMENT RESEARCH

Type of Assistance: Grants ranging from $7,119 to $52,593.

Applicant Eligibility: State governments.

Objective: To support rural development research at administratively responsible land-grant institutions and at other private and publicly supported colleges and universities including the Land-Grant Colleges of 1890. Its purpose is to encourage and foster a balanced national development. Funds may be used to pay salaries and other expenses of personnel to carry out the functions authorized, to obtain necessary supplies, equipment, services, and rent, repair, and maintenance of other facilities needed, but may not be used to purchase or construct buildings.

Contact: Administrator, Cooperative Research, Science and Education Administration, Department of Agriculture, Washington, DC 20250, 202-447-4423.

10.880 PAYMENTS TO 1890 LAND-GRANT COLLEGES AND TUSKEGEE INSTITUTE

Type of Assistance: Grants ranging from $377,006 to $1,593,001.

Applicant Eligibility: Nonprofit organizations and state governments.

Objective: To support continuing agricultural research at eligible colleges, including Tuskegee Institute. Its purpose is to promote efficient production, marketing, distribution, and utilization of products of the farm as essential to the health and welfare of people and to promote a sound, prosperous agriculture and rural life. Funds can be used for expenses of conducting agricultural research, contributing to the retirement of employees, administrative planning and direction, the purchase and rental of land, and the construction, acquisition, alteration, or repair of buildings necessary for conducting agricultural research.

Contact: Administrator, Cooperative Research, Science and Education Administration, Department of Agriculture, Washington, DC 20250, 202-447-4423.

10.881   COOPERATIVE EXTENSION SERVICE
Type of Assistance: Grants ranging from $503,074 to $12,548,561.
Applicant Eligibility: State governments.
Objective: To provide educational programs based upon local needs in the broad fields of agricultural production, and marketing, rural development, home economics, and youth development. Funds are available to land-grant institutions which, through state and county extension service personnel, provide educational and technical assistance to farmers, producers, and marketing firms on how to apply new technical developments in agricultural research; community organizations to develop natural, economic, and human resources; homemakers and youth in the areas of food and nutrition, home management, family economics, child development, and parent education; and 4-H youth in the area of leadership development and career guidance through work projects, demonstration projects, camping, and achievement programs.
Contact: Science and Education Administration Extension, Department of Agriculture, Washington, DC 20250, 202-447-3377.

10.882   HIGHER EDUCATION—
LAND-GRANT COLLEGES AND UNIVERSITIES
Type of Assistance: Grants ranging from $151,031 to $479,252.
Applicant Eligibility: State governments.
Objective: Grants to land-grant colleges and universities to support instruction in agriculture, mechanical arts, English, mathematics, science, and economics.
Contact: Assistant Director for Higher Education, Science and Education Administration, Department of Agriculture, Washington, DC 20250, 202-447-5121.

10.884   GRANTS FOR AGRICULTURAL RESEARCH—
COMPETITIVE RESEARCH GRANTS
Type of Assistance: Grants ranging from $3,000 to $240,000.
Applicant Eligibility: Individuals, nonprofit organizations, and state governments.
Objective: To promote research in food, agriculture, and related areas to further the programs of USDA through the award of research grants on a competitive basis. The initially selected areas for research are biological nitrogen fixation, biological stress on plants, photosynthesis, genetic mechanisms of crop improvement, and human nutritional requirements. Funds may be used for costs necessary to conduct the research.
Contact: Director, Competitive Grants Office, Science and Education Ad-

ministration, Department of Agriculture, 1300 Wilson Boulevard, Suite 103, Arlington, VA 22209, 703-235-2628.

SOIL CONSERVATION SERVICE

10.900 GREAT PLAINS CONSERVATION
Type of Assistance: Direct payments up to $25,000.
Applicant Eligibility: Individuals.
Objective: To conserve and develop the Great Plains soil and water resources by providing technical and financial assistance to farmers, ranchers, and others in planning and implementing conservation practices. Funds are available only for soil and water conservation measures determined to be needed to protect and stabilize a farm or ranch unit against climatic and erosion hazards.
Contact: Administrator, Soil Conservation Service, Department of Agriculture, P.O. Box 2890, Washington, DC 20013, 202-382-1870.

10.901 RESOURCE CONSERVATION AND DEVELOPMENT
Type of Assistance: Grants ranging from $2,000 to $250,000.
Applicant Eligibility: Nonprofit organizations and local governments.
Objective: To assist local people in initiating and carrying out long-range programs of resource conservation and development for the purposes of achieving a dynamic rural community with a satisfactory level of income and a pleasing environment, and creating a favorable investment climate attractive to private capital.
Contact: Director, Resource Development Division, Soil Conservation Service, Department of Agriculture, P. O. Box 2890, Washington, DC 20013, 202-447-4554.

10.904 WATERSHED PROTECTION AND FLOOD PREVENTION
Type of Assistance: Advisory services, and grants ranging from $20,000 to $13,000,000.
Applicant Eligibility: Nonprofit organizations, state and local governments.
Objective: To provide technical and financial assistance in planning and carrying out works of improvement to protect, develop, and utilize the land and water resources in small watersheds. Assistance is provided in planning, designing, and installing watershed works of improvement; sharing costs of flood prevention, irrigation, drainage, sedimentation control, and public water-based fish and wildlife and recreation; and extending long-term credit to help local interests with their share of the costs.
Contact: Administrator, Soil Conservation Service, Department of Agriculture, P. O. Box 2890, Washington, DC 20013, 202-447-3527.

10.905 PLANT MATERIALS FOR CONSERVATION

Type of Assistance: Donation of property and goods.
Applicant Eligibility: Individuals, nonprofit organizations, state and local governments.
Objective: To assemble, evaluate, select, release, and introduce into commerce new and improved plant materials for soil, water, wildlife conservation, and environmental improvement.
Contact: Administrator, Soil Conservation Service, Department of Agriculture, P. O. Box 2890, Washington, DC 20013, 202-447-5667.

10.909 RESOURCE APPRAISAL
AND PROGRAM DEVELOPMENT

Type of Assistance: Grants ranging from $13,000 to $122,000.
Applicant Eligibility: State and local governments.
Objective: To insure that USDA soil and water conservation programs administered by the Secretary of Agriculture are responsive to the long-term needs of the nation and will further the conservation, protection, and enhancement of the nation's soil, water, and related sources. Funds may be used to cover costs incurred that directly relate to the implementation of the program, including appraisal of natural resources; development or updating conservation programs that utilize Resources Conservation Act-generated information; and for carrying out state and national level Resources Conservation Act activities.
Contact: Assistant Administrator for Planning and Evaluation, Soil Conservation Service, Department of Agriculture, P. O. Box 2890, Washington, DC 20013, 202-447-8388.

10.910 RURAL ABANDONED MINE PROGRAM

Type of Assistance: Grants ranging from $5,000 to $196,000.
Applicant Eligibility: Individuals, nonprofit organizations, state and local governments.
Objective: To protect people and the environment from the adverse effects of past coal mining practices and to promote the development of soil and water resources of unreclaimed mined lands. Funds are available only for conservation practices determined to be needed for the reclamation, conservation, and development of up to 320 acres per owner of rural abandoned coal mine land or lands and waters affected by coal mining activities.
Contact: Director, Conservation Operations Division, Soil Conservation Service, Department of Agriculture, P. O. Box 2890, Washington, DC 20013, 202-382-1870.

U.S. DEPARTMENT OF COMMERCE

ECONOMIC DEVELOPMENT ADMINISTRATION

11.300 ECONOMIC DEVELOPMENT—GRANTS AND LOANS FOR PUBLIC WORKS AND DEVELOPMENT FACILITIES

Type of Assistance: Grants and direct loans ranging from $5,000 to $7,138,000.

Applicant Eligibility: Nonprofit organizations, state and local governments.

Objective: To assist in the construction of public facilities needed to initiate and encourage long-term economic growth in designated geographic areas where economic growth is lagging behind the rest of the nation. Funds may be used for such public facilities as water and sewer systems, access roads to industrial parks or areas, port facilities, railroad sidings and spurs, public tourism facilities, vocational schools, and site improvements for industrial parks.

Contact: Director, Office of Public Investments, Economic Development Administration, Department of Commerce, Washington, DC 20230, 202-377-5265.

11.303 ECONOMIC DEVELOPMENT—TECHNICAL ASSISTANCE

Type of Assistance: Grants ranging from $1,000 to $476,000.

Applicant Eligibility: Nonprofit organizations, state and local governments.

Objective: To solve problems of economic growth in Economic Development Administration-designated geographic areas and other areas of substantial need through administrative and demonstration project grants, feasibility studies, management and operational assistance, and other studies.

Contact: Office of Technical Assistance, Economic Development Administration, Department of Commerce, Washington, DC 20230, 202-377-5111.

11.305 ECONOMIC DEVELOPMENT—STATE AND LOCAL ECONOMIC DEVELOPMENT PLANNING

Type of Assistance: Grants ranging from $50,000 to $300,000.

Applicant Eligibility: State and local governments.

Objective: To develop the capability of state and local governments to undertake an economic development planning process that is comprehensive in scope, coordinated with that of other levels of governmental planning activities, and leading to the formulation of development goals and specific strate-

gies to achieve them, with particular emphasis on reducing unemployment and increasing incomes.
Contact: Chief, State and Urban Program Management Division, Office of Development Organizations and Planning, Economic Development Administration, Department of Commerce, Washington, DC 20230, 202-377-4578.

11.309 TRADE ADJUSTMENT ASSISTANCE
Type of Assistance: Direct loans and guaranteed/insured loans up to $3,000,000.
Applicant Eligibility: Individuals and nonprofit organizations.
Objective: To provide trade adjustments assistance to firms, businesses, and industry associations and communities adversely affected by increased imports.
Contact: Deputy Director, Office of Private Investment, Economic Development Administration, Department of Commerce, 14th Street and Constitution Avenue, N.W., Washington, DC 20230, 202-377-5067.

NATIONAL OCEANIC AND ATMOSPHERIC ADMINISTRATION

11.405 ANADROMOUS AND GREAT LAKES FISHERIES CONSERVATION
Type of Assistance: Grants ranging from $2,950 to $127,609.
Applicant Eligibility: Individuals.
Objective: To cooperate with the states and other nonfederal interests in the conservation, development, and enhancement of the nation's anadromous fish (fish that go upriver to spawn) and the fish in the Great Lakes and Lake Champlain that ascend streams to spawn, and for the control of sea lamprey. Funds may be used for spawning area improvement, installment of fishways, construction of fish protection devices and hatcheries, and research to improve management and increase anadromous fish resources.
Contact: Chief, State/Federal Division, National Marine Fisheries Service, Page Bldg. 2, 3300 Whitehaven St., N.W., Washington, DC 20235, 202-634-7454.

11.406 COMMERCIAL FISHERIES DISASTER ASSISTANCE
Type of Assistance: Grants ranging from $160,000 to $505,000.
Applicant Eligibility: State governments.
Objective: Provides financial assistance to restore commercial fisheries that have failed due to a resource disaster arising from natural or undetermined causes and to prevent a similar failure in the future.
Contact: Chief, State/Federal Division, National Marine Fisheries Service,

Page Bldg. 2, 3300 Whitehaven Street, N.W., Washington, DC 20235, 202-634-7454.

11.407   COMMERCIAL FISHERIES RESEARCH AND DEVELOPMENT

Type of Assistance: Grants ranging from $2,500 to $210,000.
Applicant Eligibility: State governments.
Objective: To promote state commercial fishery research and development in the 50 states, Puerto Rico, the Virgin Islands, Guam, American Samoa, and trust territory of the Pacific Islands. Funds may be used for research and development of commercial fishery resources, including construction of facilities.
Contact: Chief, State/Federal Division, National Marine Fisheries Service, 3300 Whitehaven Street, N.W., Washington, DC 20235, 202-634-7454.

11.408   FISHERMEN'S CONTINGENCY FUND

Type of Assistance: Direct payments averaging $3,500.
Applicant Eligibility: Individuals.
Objective: To compensate U.S. commercial fishermen for damage to or loss of fishing gear and resulting economic loss due to oil and gas related activities in any area of the Outer Continental Shelf.
Contact: Chief, Financial Services Division, National Marine Fisheries Service, 3300 Whitehaven Street, N.W., Washington, DC 20235, 202-634-7496.

11.409   FISHING VESSEL AND GEAR DAMAGE COMPENSATION FUND

Type of Assistance: Direct payments averaging $7,000.
Applicant Eligibility: Individuals.
Objective: To compensate U.S. fishermen for the loss, damage, or destruction of their vessels by foreign fishing vessels and their gear by any vessel or "act of God."
Contact: Chief, Financial Services Division, National Marine Fisheries Service, Department of Commerce, 3300 Whitehaven Street, N.W., Washington, DC 20235, 202-634-7496.

11.415   FISHING VESSEL OBLIGATION GUARANTEES

Type of Assistance: Guaranteed/insured loans ranging from $15,000 to $1,500,000.
Applicant Eligibility: Individuals.
Objective: To provide government guarantees of private loans to upgrade the U.S. fishing fleet. Guarantees are made on mortgages for up to 87.5 percent of actual vessel costs, for lenders providing funds for construction, reconstruction, or reconditioning of fishing vessels.
Contact: Chief, Financial Services Division, National Marine Fisheries Ser-

vice, Department of Commerce, 3300 Whitehaven Street, N.W., Washington, DC 20235, 202-634-7496.

11.417   SEA GRANT SUPPORT
Type of Assistance: Grants ranging from $32,000 to $2,840,000.
Applicant Eligibility: Individuals and state governments.
Objective: To support establishment of major university centers for marine research, education, training, and advisory services, and also individual efforts in these same areas. Limited funds are available for organized national projects and for international cooperative assistance relative to ocean and coastal resources. Funds may be used for research and development, education and training, and advisory services.
Contact: Director, National Sea Grant College Program, National Oceanic and Atmospheric Administration, 6010 Executive Boulevard, Rockville, MD 20852, 301-443-8926.

11.419   COASTAL ZONE MANAGEMENT
PROGRAM ADMINISTRATION
Type of Assistance: Grants ranging from $470,000 to $4,500,000.
Applicant Eligibility: State governments.
Objective: To assist states in implementing and administering coastal zone management programs that have been approved by the Secretary of Commerce.
Contact: Director, Coastal Zone Management Programs Office, Office of Coastal Zone Management, National Oceanic and Atmospheric Administration, Department of Commerce, 3300 Whitehaven Street, N.W., Washington, DC 20235, 202-634-1672.

11.420   COASTAL ZONE MANAGEMENT
OF ESTUARINE SANCTUARIES
Type of Assistance: Grants ranging from $50,000 to $1,800,000.
Applicant Eligibility: State governments.
Objective: To assist states in the acquisition, development, and operation of estuarine sanctuaries for the purpose of creating natural field laboratories to gather data and make studies of the natural and human processes occurring within the estuaries of the coastal zone.
Contact: Director, Sanctuary Programs Office, Office of Coastal Zone Management, National Oceanic and Atmospheric Administration, Department of Commerce, 3300 Whitehaven Street, N.W., Washington, DC 20235, 202-634-4236.

11.421   COASTAL ENERGY IMPACT PROGRAM—
FORMULA GRANTS
Type of Assistance: Grants ranging from $555,000 to $10,406,000.
Applicant Eligibility: State governments.

Objective: To provide financial assistance to coastal states to plan and construct public facilities and services and for the amelioration of environmental and recreational loss attributable to Outer Continental Shelf (OCS) energy development activities. Funds are available only to those states which have or have had adjacent OCS oil and gas leasing and development activities.

Contact: Director, Coastal Energy Impact Program Office, Office of Coastal Zone Management, National Oceanic and Atmospheric Administration, Department of Commerce, 3300 Whitehaven Street, N.W., Washington, DC 20235, 202-254-8000.

11.422 COASTAL ENERGY IMPACT PROGRAM—PLANNING GRANTS

Type of Assistance: Grants ranging from $16,000 to $340,000.

Applicant Eligibility: State governments.

Objective: To assist the states and units of local government to study and plan for the social, economic, and environmental consequences on the coastal zone of new or expanded energy facilities, and to encourage rational and timely planning and management of energy facility siting and energy resource development.

Contact: Director, Coastal Energy Impact Program Office, Office of Coastal Zone Management, National Oceanic and Atmospheric Administration, Department of Commerce, 3300 Whitehaven Street, N.W., Washington, DC 20235, 202-254-8000.

11.423 COASTAL ENERGY IMPACT PROGRAM—LOANS AND GUARANTEES

Type of Assistance: Direct loans ranging from $200,000 to $38,000,000.

Applicant Eligibility: State governments.

Objective: To provide financial assistance for public facilities necessary to support increased populations stemming from new or expanded coastal energy activity. The public facilities eligible include, but are not limited to, highways and secondary roads, parking, mass transit, docks, navigation aids, fire and police protection, water supply, waste collection and treatment (including drainage), schools and education, and hospitals and health care.

Contact: Director, Coastal Energy Impact Program Office, Office of Coastal Zone Management, National Oceanic and Atmospheric Administration, Department of Commerce, 3300 Whitehaven Street, N.W., Washington, DC 20235, 202-254-8000.

11.424 COASTAL ENERGY IMPACT PROGRAM—ENVIRONMENTAL GRANTS

Type of Assistance: Grants ranging from $3,000 to $515,000.

Applicant Eligibility: State governments.

Objective: To help states and units of local governments prevent, reduce, or

ameliorate unavoidable loss of valuable environmental or recreational resources resulting from coastal energy activity, while ensuring that the person responsible for these environmental or recreational losses pays for their full cost.
Contact: Director, Coastal Energy Impact Program Office, Office of Coastal Zone Management, National Oceanic and Atmospheric Administration, Department of Commerce, 3300 Whitehaven Street, N.W., Washington, DC 20235, 202-254-8000.

11.425 COASTAL ENERGY IMPACT PROGRAM— OUTER CONTINENTAL SHELF STATE PARTICIPATION GRANTS
Type of Assistance: Grants ranging from $75,000 to $317,000.
Applicant Eligibility: State governments.
Objective: To allow states and units of general purpose local governments to participate effectively in policy, planning, and managerial decisions relating to management of Outer Continental Shelf oil and gas resources.
Contact: Director, Coastal Energy Impact Program Office, Office of Coastal Zone Management, National Oceanic and Atmospheric Administration, Department of Commerce, 3300 Whitehaven Street, N.W., Washington, DC 20235, 202-254-8000.

11.426 OCEAN DUMPING AND MONITORING PROGRAM
Type of Assistance: Grants ranging from $20,000 to $80,000.
Applicant Eligibility: Individuals, nonprofit organizations, state and local governments.
Objective: To determine the consequences of dumping industrial, municipal, and dredged waste materials into the ocean.
Contact: National Oceanic and Atmospheric Administration, Ocean Dumping and Monitoring Division, National Ocean Survey, 6001 Executive Blvd., Rockville, MD 20852, 301-443-8241.

11.427 FISHERIES DEVELOPMENT AND UTILIZATION RESEARCH AND DEVELOPMENT GRANTS AND COOPERATIVE AGREEMENTS PROGRAM
Type of Assistance: Grants ranging from $5,000 to $2,500,000.
Applicant Eligibility: Individuals, nonprofit organizations, state and local governments.
Objective: To foster the development and strengthening of the fishing industry of the United States and increase the supply of wholesome, nutritious fish and fish products available to consumers.
Contact: Office of Utilization and Development, National Marine Fisheries Service, National Oceanic and Atmospheric Administration, Department of Commerce, Washington, DC 20235, 202-634-7252.

11.428   INTERGOVERNMENTAL CLIMATE-DEMONSTRATION PROJECT

Type of Assistance: Grants (dollar amount not available).

Applicant Eligibility: State and local governments, profit and nonprofit organizations, and individuals.

Objective: To conduct climate-related studies, to improve information to users regarding climate and climatic effects, and to provide advice to regional, state, and local government agencies on climate-related issues.

Contact: National Climate Program Office, National Oceanic and Atmospheric Administration, Department of Commerce, 6010 Executive Blvd., Rockville, MD 20852, 301-443-8981.

MARITIME ADMINISTRATION

11.500   CONSTRUCTION-DIFFERENTIAL SUBSIDIES

Type of Assistance: Direct payments ranging from $19,629,000 to $45,100,000.

Applicant Eligibility: Individuals.

Objective: To promote the development and maintenance of the U.S. Merchant Marine by granting financial aid to equalize cost of construction of a new ship in a U.S. shipyard with the cost of constructing the same ship in a foreign shipyard.

Contact: Assistant Administrator for Maritime Aids, Maritime Administration, Department of Commerce, Washington, DC 20230, 202-377-3797.

11.502   FEDERAL SHIP-FINANCING GUARANTEES

Type of Assistance: Guaranteed/insured loans ranging from $106,000 to $126,300,000.

Applicant Eligibility: Individuals.

Objective: To promote construction and reconstruction of ships in the foreign and domestic commerce of the United States by providing government guarantees of obligations so as to make commercial credit more readily available.

Contact: Assistant Administrator for Maritime Aids, Maritime Administration, Department of Commerce, Washington, DC 20230, 202-377-3797.

11.503   MARITIME WAR RISK INSURANCE

Type of Assistance: Insurance (dollar amount not available).

Applicant Eligibility: Individuals.

Objective: To provide war risk insurance whenever it appears to the Secretary of Commerce that adequate insurance for waterborne commerce cannot be obtained on reasonable terms and conditions from authorized insurance companies in the United States.

Contact: Director, Office of Marine Insurance, Maritime Administration, Department of Commerce, Washington, DC 20230, 202-377-4091.

11.504   OPERATING-DIFFERENTIAL SUBSIDIES
Type of Assistance: Direct payments ranging from $2,400 to $6,390 per day.
Applicant Eligibility: Individuals.
Objective: To promote development and maintenance of U.S. Merchant Marine by granting financial aid to equalize cost of operating a U.S. flagship with cost of operating a competitive foreign flagship.
Contact: Assistant Administrator for Maritime Aids, Maritime Administration, Department of Commerce, Washington, DC 20230, 202-377-3797.

11.506   STATE MARINE SCHOOLS
Type of Assistance: Grants of $1,200 per year to each student, plus $100,000 per year per school.
Applicant Eligibility: State governments.
Objective: To train Merchant Marine officers in state marine schools. Funds are used for the operation and maintenance of state marine schools; maintenance and repair of training vessels loaned by federal government; and assistance to students in paying for uniforms, books, and subsistence.
Contact: Director, Office of Maritime Labor and Training, Maritime Administration, Department of Commerce, Washington, DC 20230, 202-377-3018.

11.508   CAPITAL CONSTRUCTION FUND
Type of Assistance: Direct payments in the form of tax benefits.
Applicant Eligibility: Individuals.
Objective: To provide for replacement vessels, additional vessels, or reconstructed vessels, built and documented under the laws of the United States for operation in the United States foreign, Great Lakes, or noncontiguous domestic trades.
Contact: Assistant Administrator for Maritime Aids, Maritime Administration, Department of Commerce, Washington, DC 20230, 202-377-2121.

NATIONAL TELECOMMUNICATIONS AND INFORMATION ADMINISTRATION

11.550   PUBLIC TELECOMMUNICATIONS FACILITIES
Type of Assistance: Grants ranging from $3,000 to $700,000.
Applicant Eligibility: Nonprofit organizations, state and local governments.
Objective: To assist, through matching grants, in the planning and construc-

tion of public telecommunications facilities in order to extend delivery of public telecommunications services to as many citizens of the U.S. and territories as possible by the most efficient and economical means, including the use of broadcast and nonbroadcast technologies; increase public telecommunications services and facilities available to, operated by, and owned by minorities and women; and strengthen the capability of existing public television and radio stations to provide public telecommunications services to the public.

Contact: Director, Public Telecommunications Facilities Division/NTIA, Rm. 298, 1325 G Street, N.W., Washington, DC 20005, 202-724-3307.

11.551 PUBLIC TELECOMMUNICATIONS SERVICE PROGRAM

Type of Assistance: Grants (dollar amount not available).

Applicant Eligibility: Public organizations, private profit and nonprofit telecommunications organizations.

Objective: To develop mechanisms to organize dispersed, low-volume public service satellite users, both federal and non-federal to the point where the public sector can use unsubsidized commercially available satellite services.

Contact: Grants Program Administrators, Office of Telecommunications Applications, National Telecommunications and Information Administration, Department of Commerce, 608 13th Street, N.W., Washington, DC 20004, 202-724-3464.

OFFICE OF PRODUCTIVITY, TECHNOLOGY AND INNOVATION

11.750 COOPERATIVE GENERIC TECHNOLOGY PROGRAM

Type of Assistance: Grants (dollar amount not available).

Applicant Eligibility: Nonprofit organizations.

Objective: To stimulate the development of industrial technology through cooperation between industry and government and to encourage the transfer and commercialization of the technology so that U.S. industries can become more competitive with respect to foreign products.

Contact: Director, Office of Cooperative Generic Technology Program, Department of Commerce, Washington, DC 20230, 202-337-5905.

OFFICE OF MINORITY BUSINESS ENTERPRISE

11.800 MINORITY BUSINESS DEVELOPMENT— MANAGEMENT AND TECHNICAL ASSISTANCE

Type of Assistance: Grants ranging from $10,000 to $3,000,000.

Applicant Eligibility: Individuals, nonprofit organizations, state and local governments.

Objective: To provide free financial, management, and technical assistance to economically and socially disadvantaged individuals who need help in starting and/or operating a business. Primary objectives of the assistance are to increase the gross receipts and decrease the failure rates of the client firms.

Contact: Chief, Grants Administration Division, Minority Business Development Agency, Department of Commerce, Washington, DC 20230, 202-377-3165.

U.S. DEPARTMENT OF DEFENSE

DEFENSE LOGISTICS AGENCY

12.001   INDUSTRIAL EQUIPMENT LOANS TO EDUCATIONAL INSTITUTIONS (TOOLS FOR SCHOOLS)

Type of Assistance: Use of property, facilities, and equipment.
Applicant Eligibility: Nonprofit organizations.
Objective: In order to develop skilled manpower as an industrial preparedness measure, qualified educational institutions and training schools may be loaned idle equipment from the Defense Industrial Reserve.
Contact: Directorate of Technical and Logistics Services, Defense Logistics Agency, Cameron Station, Alexandria, VA 22312, 202-274-6269.

OFFICE OF THE ASSISTANT SECRETARY

12.606   SELECTED RESERVE EDUCATIONAL ASSISTANCE PROGRAM

Type of Assistance: Direct payments up to $2,000.
Applicant Eligibility: Individuals who have never previously served in the Armed Forces of the United States who enlist in the selected reserve for a term of six years.
Objective: To stimulate enlistment of nonprior service individuals into the selected reserve.
Contact: Director, Reserve Affairs, Office of Assistant Secretary of Defense (Manpower, Reserve Affairs and Logistics), Pentagon, Washington, DC 20301, 202-697-4222.

SECRETARIES OF MILITARY DEPARTMENTS

12.700   DONATIONS/LOANS OF DOD SURPLUS PROPERTY

Type of Assistance: Sale, exchange, or donation of property.
Applicant Eligibility: Nonprofit organizations, state and local governments.
Objective: To donate or lend material, surplus to the needs of DOD, to veterans' organizations, soldiers, monument associations, state museums, incorporated museums, and incorporated municipalities.
Contact: Department of Defense, Pentagon, Washington, DC 20301, 202-695-0192.

U.S. DEPARTMENT OF HEALTH AND HUMAN SERVICES

Key to acronyms used in addresses in 13.000 section:

ADAMHA	Alcohol, Drug Abuse, and Mental Health Administration	NINCDS	National Institute of Neurological and Communicative Disorders and Strokes
BHM	Bureau of Health Manpower	OAMS	Office of Administrative Management Services
BHPR	Bureau of Health Professions		
BMS	Bureau of Medical Services	OMCH	Office of Maternal and Child Health
DHHS	Department of Health and Human Services	PHS	Public Health Service
HRA	Health Resources Administration		

PUBLIC HEALTH SERVICE—1

13.103 FOOD AND DRUG ADMINISTRATION—RESEARCH

Type of Assistance: Grants ranging from $5,000 to $125,000.
Applicant Eligibility: Nonprofit organizations, state and local governments.
Objective: To assist public and other nonprofit institutions to establish, expand, and improve research activities concerned with foods, food additives, shellfish sanitation, poison control, drug and cosmetic hazards, human and veterinary drugs, medical devices and diagnostic products, biologics, and radiation-emitting devices and materials.
Contact: Chief, Grants Management Branch, HFA-520, Rm. 12A27, 5600 Fishers Lane, Rockville, MD 20857, 301-443-6170.

13.210 HEALTH INCENTIVE GRANTS FOR COMPREHENSIVE PUBLIC HEALTH SERVICES

Type of Assistance: Grants ranging from $243,100 to $5,139,700.
Applicant Eligibility: State governments.
Objective: To assist state health authorities in meeting the cost of providing comprehensive public health services.

Contact: Center for Disease Control, Rm. 2060, Building 1, 1600 Clifton Road, N.E., Atlanta, GA 30333, 404-329-3243.

13.211   CRIPPLED CHILDREN'S SERVICES
Type of Assistance: Grants ranging from $146,000 to $2,800,000.
Applicant Eligibility: State and local governments.
Objective: To provide financial support to states to extend and improve (especially in rural areas and in areas suffering from severe economic distress) medical and related services to crippled children and children suffering from conditions that lead to crippling; and for special projects of regional or national significance which may contribute to the advancement of services for crippled children.
Contact: Associate Bureau Director for Maternal and Child Health, Health Bureau of Community Health Services, Health Services Administration, Rm. 7-44, Parklawn Building, 5600 Fishers Lane, Rockville, MD 20857, 301-443-2190.

13.217   FAMILY PLANNING PROJECTS
Type of Assistance: Grants ranging from $20,000 to $1,000,000.
Applicant Eligibility: Nonprofit organizations, state and local governments.
Objective: To provide educational, comprehensive medical and social services necessary to enable individuals to freely determine the number and spacing of their children, and by so doing helping to reduce maternal and infant mortality thereby promoting the health of mothers and children. Funds may be used for contraceptive services, infertility services, and special services to adolescents.
Contact: Associate Bureau Director for Family Planning Services, Bureau of Community Health Services, Health Services Administration, DHHS, Rm. 715, 5600 Fishers Lane, Rockville, MD 20857, 301-443-2430.

13.224   COMMUNITY HEALTH CENTERS
Type of Assistance: Grants ranging from $25,000 to $4,000,000.
Applicant Eligibility: Nonprofit organizations, state and local governments.
Objective: To support the development and operation of community health centers which provide primary health services, supplemental health services, and environmental health services to medically underserved populations. Priorities focus on capacity building in medically underserved areas and maintenance of existing centers, expansion of population and service coverage in existing centers, monitoring and assessment of project performance, development and implementation of mechanisms for improving quality of care, and maximizing third party reimbursement levels through improved project administration and management.
Contact: Associate Bureau Director for Community Health Centers, Bureau of Community Health Services, Rm. 7A-55, Parklawn Building, 5600 Fishers Lane, Rockville, MD 20857, 301-443-2260.

13.226 HEALTH SERVICES RESEARCH AND DEVELOPMENT GRANTS

Type of Assistance: Grants ranging from $3,000 to $5,000,000.
Applicant Eligibility: Individuals, nonprofit organizations, state and local governments.
Objective: To support research, development, demonstration, and evaluation activities aimed toward developing new options for health services delivery and health policy; to test the assumptions on which current policies and delivery practices are based; and to develop the means for monitoring the performance of the health care system. Also to support research for the development of useful information to communities that are implementing Emergency Medical Services Systems (EMS). The program supports research studies in many categories of concerns, including cost containment, health insurance, planning and regulation, technology and computer science applications.
Contact: National Center for Health Services Research, Office of Health Research, Statistics and Technology, PHS/DHHS, Rm. 7-41, Center Building, 3700 East-West Highway, Hyattsville, MD 20782, 301-436-6184.

13.228 INDIAN HEALTH SERVICES—HEALTH MANAGEMENT DEVELOPMENT PROGRAM

Type of Assistance: Grants up to $1,000,000.
Applicant Eligibility: Native Americans.
Objective: To raise to the highest possible level the health of American Indians and Alaskan Natives by providing a full range of curative, preventive, and rehabilitative health services that include public health nursing, maternal and child health care, dental and nutrition services, psychiatric care, and health education. Also to increase the Indian communities' capacity to man and manage their health programs, and to build the capability of the American Indian to manage their health programs.
Contact: Contracts and Grants, Indian Health Services, 5600 Fishers Lane, Rockville, MD 20857, 301-443-5204.

13.229 INDIAN HEALTH SERVICES—SANITATION MANAGEMENT DEVELOPMENT PROGRAM

Type of Assistance: Grants up to $1,000,000.
Applicant Eligibility: Native Americans.
Objective: To alleviate unsanitary conditions, lack of safe water supplies, and inadequate waste disposal facilities which contribute to infectious and gastroenteric diseases among Indians and Alaskan Natives, the Indian Health Service engages in environmental health activities, including construction of sanitation facilities for individual homes and communities.
Contact: Contracts and Grants, Indian Health Services, 5600 Fishers Lane, Rockville, MD 20857, 301-443-5204.

13.231 MATERNAL AND CHILD HEALTH RESEARCH

Type of Assistance: Grants ranging from $13,954 to $357,657.

Applicant Eligibility: Nonprofit organizations, state and local governments.

Objective: To provide funds for research projects relating to maternal and child health services or crippled children's services that show promise of substantial contribution to the advancement of such services.

Contact: Bureau of Community Health Services, OMCH, DHHS, Rm. 7-44, 5600 Fishers Lane, Rockville, MD 20857, 301-443-2190.

13.232 MATERNAL AND CHILD HEALTH SERVICES

Type of Assistance: Grants ranging from $160,000 to $18,100,000.

Applicant Eligibility: State and local governments.

Objective: To provide financial support to states to extend and improve services (especially in rural areas and in areas suffering from severe economic distress) for reducing infant mortality and improvement of the health of mothers and children; to help reduce the incidence of mental retardation and other handicapping conditions caused by complications associated with childbearing and of infant and maternal mortality; and promote the physical and dental health of children of school or preschool age; for special projects of regional or national significance which may contribute to the advancement of maternal and child health services.

Contact: Bureau of Community Health Services, OMCH, Rm. 7-44, Parklawn Building, 5600 Fishers Lane, Rockville, MD 20857, 301-443-2170.

13.233 MATERNAL AND CHILD HEALTH TRAINING

Type of Assistance: Grants ranging from $50,000 to $1,000,000.

Applicant Eligibility: Nonprofit organizations, state and local governments.

Objective: To train personnel for health care of, and related services for, mothers and children, particularly mentally retarded children and children with multiple handicaps.

Contact: Office for Maternal and Child Health Services Administration, DHHS, Rm. 7-44, 5600 Fishers Lane, Rockville, MD 20857, 301-443-2340.

13.235 DRUG ABUSE COMMUNITY SERVICE PROGRAMS

Type of Assistance: Grants ranging from $10,000 to $21,000,000.

Applicant Eligibility: Nonprofit organizations, state and local governments.

Objective: To reach, treat, and rehabilitate narcotic addicts, drug abusers, and drug-dependent persons through a wide range of community-based services by the provision of partial support for their operational costs.

Contact: Division of Community Assistance, Director, National Institute on Drug Abuse, ADAMHA, PHS/DHHS, 903 Parklawn Building, 5600 Fishers Lane, Rockville, MD 20857, 301-443-6780.

13.242 MENTAL HEALTH RESEARCH GRANTS

Type of Assistance: Grants ranging from $1,434 to $388,917.

Applicant Eligibility: Individuals, nonprofit organizations, state and local governments.

Objective: To develop new knowledge of and approaches to the causes, diagnoses, treatment, control, and prevention of mental diseases through basic, clinical, and applied research; to develop and test new models and systems for mental health services delivery; and to otherwise develop and improve knowledge relevant to the provision of mental health services through organized systems and networks of services.

Contact: Director, Division of Extramural Research Programs (Behavioral Sciences, Clinical, Applied, and Psychopharmacologic Research and Small Grants), National Institute of Mental Health, 5600 Fishers Lane, Rockville, MD 20857, 301-443-3563.

13.244 MENTAL HEALTH CLINICAL OR SERVICE RELATED TRAINING GRANTS

Type of Assistance: Grants ranging from $4,968 to $346,536.

Applicant Eligibility: Nonprofit organizations, state and local governments.

Objective: To maintain the existing capacity of training institutions to meet mental health manpower needs, while relating the types of personnel trained more closely to service priorities and manpower requirements; to develop and evaluate new training and manpower development models which are responsive to service delivery needs; to strengthen the leadership and capacity of states in regard to mental health services manpower, and build relationships among state mental health service providers and training institutions. Also to support projects in the special mental health areas of crime and delinquency, metropolitan problems, minority groups, mental health education, aging, and rape prevention and control.

Contact: Director, Division of Manpower and Training Programs (Psychiatry, Psychology, Social Work, Psychiatric Nursing, Paraprofessional, State Manpower, Research and Demonstration), National Institute of Mental Health, 5600 Fishers Lane, Rockville, MD 20857, 301-443-4257.

13.246 MIGRANT HEALTH CENTERS GRANT

Type of Assistance: Grants ranging from $30,000 to $1,795,680.

Applicant Eligibility: Nonprofit organizations, state and local governments.

Objective: To support the development and operation of migrant health centers and projects which provide primary, ambulatory, and inpatient health services, supplemental health services, and environmental health services which are accessible to migrant and seasonal farm workers and their families.

Contact: Associate Bureau Director for Migrant Health, Bureau of Community Health Services, Rm. 7A-55, Parklawn Building, 5600 Fishers Lane, Rockville, MD 20857, 301-443-1153.

13.252 ALCOHOLISM TREATMENT AND REHABILITATION/OCCUPATIONAL ALCOHOLISM SERVICES PROGRAMS

Type of Assistance: Grants ranging from $9,997 to $557,116.

Applicant Eligibility: Nonprofit organizations, state and local governments.

Objective: To provide quality alcohol abuse and alcoholism treatment services to persons in need to them; to coordinate alcoholism treatment services within the broader context of community-based resources; to expand the involvement of public agencies (e.g., law enforcement, schools, courts, health agencies) in arranging for, and/or providing alcoholism treatment services; and to enhance the ability of treatment projects to qualify for collection of third-party payments and other nonfederal sources of support. The Occupational Alcoholism Services Program has as its objective to develop and implement within the work place projects to identify for treatment employed people whose work is adversely affected by the abuse of alcohol and aid in the earlier identification and treatment of employed persons with alcohol-related problems.

Contact: Director, Alcoholism Services Development, National Institute on Alcohol Abuse and Alcoholism, ADAMHA, PHS/DHHS, Rm. 1105, 5600 Fishers Lane, Rockville, MD 20857, 301-443-6317.

13.253 MEDICAL FACILITIES CONSTRUCTION—LOANS AND LOAN GUARANTEES

Type of Assistance: Direct loans and guaranteed/insured loans ranging from $75,000 to $17,542,000.

Applicant Eligibility: Nonprofit organizations, state and local governments.

Objective: To assist the states in the provision of medical facility modernization and additional outpatient and inpatient facilities in areas of recent rapid population growth. Funds may be used for the discontinuance of unneeded hospital service facilities and their conversion to needed services or facilities (including outpatient and long-term care), new construction or replacement of facilities, the expansion and/or remodeling of existing facilities or buildings; and equipment necessary for a construction project or for the provision of a new service in a community.

Contact: Bureau of Health Facilities Financing, Compliance, and Conversion, HRA, PHS/DHHS, 6525 Belcrest Road, Hyattsville, MD 20782, 301-436-6880.

13.254 DRUG ABUSE DEMONSTRATION PROGRAMS

Type of Assistance: Grants ranging from $10,000 to $400,000.

Applicant Eligibility: Nonprofit organizations, state and local governments.

Objective: To cover the operational costs of programs for surveys and field trials to evaluate the needs and adequacy of programs for the treatment of narcotic addiction and drug abuse and to determine means of improving such programs; and forms of treatment and rehabilitation of narcotic addicts and

drug abusers of special significance for their new or relatively effective methods of delivery of services, and for the evaluation of such programs.
Contact: Division of Prevention and Treatment Development, National Institute on Drug Abuse, ADAMHA, PHS/DHHS, Parklawn Building, 5600 Fishers Lane, Rockville, MD 20857, 301-443-4060.

13.256   HEALTH MAINTENANCE ORGANIZATIONS
Type of Assistance: Grants, direct loans and loan guarantees up to $4,000,000.
Applicant Eligibility: Nonprofit organizations, state and local governments.
Objective: To stimulate the development and increase the number of various models of prepaid, comprehensive health maintenance organizations throughout the United States and the expansion of federally qualified health maintenance organizations.
Contact: OASH, Office of Health Maintenance Organizations, PHS, 12420 Parklawn Drive, Rockville, MD 20857, 301-443-2560.

13.257   ALCOHOL FORMULA GRANTS
Type of Assistance: Grants ranging from $4,877 to $5,316,546.
Applicant Eligibility: State governments.
Objective: To assist states to plan, establish, maintain, coordinate, and evaluate effective prevention, treatment, and rehabilitation programs to deal with alcohol abuse and alcoholism.
Contact: Grants Management, National Institute on Alcohol Abuse and Alcoholism, ADAMHA, PHS/DHHS, Rm. 14C25, Parklawn Building, 5600 Fishers Lane, Rockville, MD 20857, 301-443-2785.

13.260   FAMILY PLANNING SERVICES
Type of Assistance: Grants ranging from $15,000 to $600,000.
Applicant Eligibility: Nonprofit organizations, state and local governments.
Objective: To provide job-specific training for personnel to improve the delivery of family planning services.
Contact: Health Services Administration, Bureau of Community Health Services, Office for Family Planning, 5600 Fishers Lane, Rockville, MD 20857, 302-443-2430.

13.262   OCCUPATIONAL SAFETY AND HEALTH
   RESEARCH GRANTS
Type of Assistance: Grants ranging from $5,000 to $150,000.
Applicant Eligibility: Individuals, nonprofit organizations, state and local governments.
Objective: To understand the underlying characteristics of occupational safety and health problems; to discover effective solutions in dealing with them; to eliminate or control factors in the work environment which are harmful to the health and safety of workers; and to demonstrate technical

feasibility or application of new or improved occupational safety and health procedures, methods, techniques, or systems.
Contact: Procurement and Grants Management Branch, OAMS, Center for Disease Control, National Institute for Occupational Safety and Health, DHHS, Rm. 8-29, Parklawn Building, 5600 Fishers Lane, Rockville, MD 20857, 301-443-3122.

13.263 OCCUPATIONAL SAFETY AND HEALTH— TRAINING GRANTS

Type of Assistance: Grants ranging from $10,000 to $700,000.
Applicant Eligibility: Nonprofit organizations, state and local governments.
Objective: To develop specialized professional personnel in occupational safety and health problems with training in occupational medicine, nursing, and industrial hygiene and safety.
Contact: Procurement and Grants Management Branch, OAMS, Center for Disease Control, National Institute for Occupational Safety and Health, DHHS, Rm. 8-29, 5600 Fishers Lane, Parklawn Building, Rockville, MD 20857, 301-443-3122.

13.266 CHILDHOOD LEAD-BASED PAINT POISONING PREVENTION

Type of Assistance: Grants ranging from $58,000 to $515,000.
Applicant Eligibility: Nonprofit organizations, state and local governments.
Objective: To stimulate communities in the development of comprehensive lead-based paint poisoning prevention programs, and to assist state agencies in establishing centralized laboratory facilities for analyzing biological and environmental lead specimens obtained from local lead-based paint poisoning detection programs. The funds may be used for educational programs to communicate the health hazard of lead-based paint; intensive community screening programs to detect children with lead toxicity; intensive community follow-up programs to insure that children with evidence of lead toxicity are placed under a program of medical treatment and/or surveillance; and intensive follow-up programs to insure children with undue lead absorption are protected against further exposure.
Contact: Director, Center for Disease Control, PHS/DHHS, 1600 Clifton Road, N.E., Atlanta, GA 30333, 404-329-3291.

13.267 URBAN RAT CONTROL

Type of Assistance: Grants ranging from $57,000 to $2,000,000.
Applicant Eligibility: State and local governments.
Objective: To support comprehensive rat control activities in urban communities by improving the living environment to obviate rat proliferation and to promote the identification of local resources during the project period to sustain the program's achievements.

Contact: Director, Center for Disease Control, PHS/DHHS, 1600 Clifton Road, N.E., Atlanta, GA 30333, 404-329-3291.

13.268 CHILDHOOD IMMUNIZATION GRANTS

Type of Assistance: Grants ranging from $95,000 to $903,000.
Applicant Eligibility: Nonprofit organizations, state and local governments.
Objective: To assist states and communities in establishing and maintaining immunization programs for the control of vaccine-preventable diseases of childhood (including measles, rubella, poliomyelitis, diphtheria, pertussis, tetanus, and mumps).
Contact: Director, Center for Disease Control, PHS/DHHS, 1600 Clifton Road, N.E., Atlanta, GA 30333, 404-329-3291.

13.269 DRUG ABUSE PREVENTION FORMULA GRANTS

Type of Assistance: Grants ranging from $30,000 to $3,945,000.
Applicant Eligibility: State governments.
Objective: To assist the states in the preparation of plans for establishing, conducting, and coordinating projects for the development of more effective drug abuse prevention functions; carrying out projects under such plans; evaluation of such plans; paying the administrative expenses of carrying out such plans.
Contact: Divison of Community Assistance, Director, National Institute on Drug Abuse, ADAMHA, PHS/DHHS, Parklawn Building, 5600 Fishers Lane, Rockville, MD 20857, 301-433-6780.

13.271 ALCOHOL RESEARCH SCIENTIST DEVELOPMENT AND RESEARCH SCIENTIST AWARDS

Type of Assistance: Grants ranging from $32,398 to $46,091.
Applicant Eligibility: Individuals.
Objective: To provide support for research relating to the problems of alcohol abuse and alcoholism prevention, treatment, and rehabilitation, and to raise the level of competence and to increase the number of individuals engaged in such research.
Contact: Division of Extramural Research, Director, National Institute on Alcohol Abuse and Alcoholism, PHS/DHHS, 5600 Fishers Lane, Rockville, MD 20857, 301-443-4223.

13.272 ALCOHOL NATIONAL RESEARCH SERVICE AWARDS FOR RESEARCH TRAINING

Type of Assistance: Grants ranging from $6,900 to $108,806.
Applicant Eligibility: Individuals.
Objective: To provide support to individuals for predoctoral and postdoctoral research training in specific alcohol abuse-related areas via an individual National Research Service Award. An institutional National Research Ser-

vice grant provides support to enable nonprofit institutions to develop research training opportunities for individuals interested in careers in particular specified alcohol abuse-related fields.
Contact: Division of Extramural Research, Director, National Institute on Alcohol Abuse and Alcoholism, PHS/DHHS, 5600 Fishers Lane, Rockville, MD 20857, 301-443-4223.

13.273 ALCOHOL RESEARCH PROGRAMS
Type of Assistance: Grants ranging from $5,000 to $365,355.
Applicant Eligibility: Individuals, nonprofit organizations, state and local governments.
Objective: To develop new knowledge and approaches to the causes, diagnosis, treatment, control, and prevention of alcohol abuse and alcoholism through basic, clinical, and applied research, investigations, experiments, and studies.
Contact: Director, Division of Extramural Research, National Institute on Alcohol Abuse and Alcoholism, PHS/DHHS, 5600 Fishers Lane, Rockville, MD 20857, 301-443-4223.

13.274 ALCOHOL CLINICAL OR SERVICE RELATED TRAINING PROGRAMS
Type of Assistance: Grants ranging from $12,420 to $168,324.
Applicant Eligibility: Individuals, nonprofit organizations, state and local governments.
Objective: To develop human resources for alcoholism services delivery programs through focusing on development of management, administration, planning, and evaluation skills in the alcohol area; provision of training to facilitate the integration of alcoholism treatment into the total health system; and training models and demonstrations.
Contact: Division of Extramural Research, National Institute on Alcohol Abuse and Alcoholism, ADAMHA, PHS/DHHS, 5600 Fishers Lane, Rockville, MD 20857, 301-443-4223.

13.275 DRUG ABUSE PREVENTION/EDUCATION PROGRAMS
Type of Assistance: Grants ranging from $20,000 to $1,164,000.
Applicant Eligibility: Nonprofit organizations, state and local governments.
Objective: To acquire and develop new drug abuse prevention knowledge through evaluative research and to disseminate effective strategies and techniques to the field.
Contact: Prevention Branch, National Institute on Drug Abuse, ADAMHA, PHS/DHHS, Parklawn Building, 5600 Fishers Lane, Rockville, MD 20857, 301-443-2450.

13.277 DRUG ABUSE RESEARCH SCIENTIST DEVELOPMENT AND RESEARCH SCIENTIST AWARDS

Type of Assistance: Grants ranging from $24,000 to $44,000.

Applicant Eligibility: Individuals.

Objective: To provide support for research relating to the problems of narcotic addiction and drug abuse and to raise the level of competence and to increase the number of individuals engaged in such research via special levels of NIDA support.

Contact: Division of Research, National Institute on Drug Abuse, ADAMHA, PHS/DHHS, Rm. 9-36, Parklawn Building, 5600 Fishers Lane, Rockville, MD 20857, 301-443-1887.

13.278 DRUG ABUSE NATIONAL RESEARCH SERVICE AWARDS FOR RESEARCH TRAINING

Type of Assistance: Grants up to $106,000.

Applicant Eligibility: Individuals, nonprofit organizations.

Objective: An Individual National Research Service award provides support to individuals for predoctoral and postdoctoral research training in specified drug-related areas; an institutional National Research Service grant provides support to enable nonprofit institutions to develop research training opportunities for individuals interested in careers in particular specified drug abuse-related fields.

Contact: Division of Training, National Institute on Drug Abuse, ADAMHA, PHS/DHHS, Parklawn Building, 5600 Fishers Lane, Rockville, MD 20857, 301-443-6720.

13.279 DRUG ABUSE RESEARCH PROGRAMS

Type of Assistance: Grants ranging from $11,000 to $1,449,000.

Applicant Eligibility: Individuals, nonprofit organizations, state and local governments.

Objectives: To develop new knowledge and approaches to the epidemiology, etiology, diagnosis, treatment, control, and prevention of narcotic addiction and drug abuse through basic, clinical, and applied research, investigations, experiments, and studies.

Contact: Division of Research, National Institute on Drug Abuse, ADAMHA, PHS/DHHS, Rm. 9-36, Parklawn Building, 5600 Fishers Lane, Rockville, MD 20857, 301-443-1887.

13.280 DRUG ABUSE CLINICAL OR SERVICE RELATED TRAINING PROGRAMS

Type of Assistance: Grants ranging from $10,000 to $1,824,000.

Applicant Eligibility: Nonprofit organizations, state and local governments.

Objective: To support training programs for treatment personnel to work with the drug addict or abuser via multidisciplinary, short-term, and specialized grant and contract programs. Programs may be for professionals, para-professionals, and ex-addicts to work in drug treatment. Also programs are supported for evaluation of teaching methods in order to develop new training methods.

Contact: Division of Training, National Institute on Drug Abuse, ADAMHA, PHS/DHHS, Rm. 10A-46, Parklawn Building, 5600 Fishers Lane, Rockville, MD 20857, 301-443-6720.

13.281 MENTAL HEALTH RESEARCH SCIENTIST DEVELOPMENT AND RESEARCH SCIENTIST AWARDS

Type of Assistance: Grants ranging from $15,000 to $39,852.

Applicant Eligibility: Individuals, nonprofit organizations, state and local governments.

Objective: To provide support for research relating to the problems of mental illness and mental health and to raise the level of competence and increase the number of individuals engaged in such research via special levels of National Institute of Mental Health support.

Contact: Director, Division of Extramural Research Programs, National Institute of Mental Health, Rm. 10104, 5600 Fishers Lane, Rockville, MD 20857, 301-443-4347.

13.282 MENTAL HEALTH NATIONAL RESEARCH SERVICE AWARDS FOR RESEARCH TRAINING

Type of Assistance: Grants up to $14,000.

Applicant Eligibility: Individuals, nonprofit organizations.

Objective: An individual National Research Service award provides support to individuals for predoctoral and postdoctoral research training in specified mental health-related areas; an institutional National Research Service grant provides support and enables nonprofit institutions to develop research training opportunities for individuals interested in careers in a particular specified mental health-related field. The Minority Access to Research Careers programs (MARC) are intended to assist institutions with substantial minority enrollment in the training of greater numbers of scientists and teachers in fields related to mental health, alcoholism, and drug abuse.

Contact: Director, Division of Manpower and Training Programs, National Institute of Mental Health, 5600 Fishers Lane, Rockville, MD 20857, 301-443-4257.

13.284 EMERGENCY MEDICAL SERVICES

Type of Assistance: Grants ranging from $30,000 to $500,000.

Applicant Eligibility: Individuals, nonprofit organizations, state and local governments.

Objective: To provide assistance and encouragement for the development of comprehensive regional emergency medical services systems throughout the country and thereby improve the quality of patient care and reduce morbidity and mortality.

Contact: Division of Emergency Medical Services, Rm. 9A31, 5600 Fishers Lane, Rockville, MD 20857, 301-443-5250.

13.287 GRANTS FOR TRAINING IN EMERGENCY MEDICAL SERVICES

Type of Assistance: Grants ranging from $14,800 to $342,658.

Applicant Eligibility: Nonprofit organizations, state and local governments.

Objective: To assist eligible organizations to meet the cost of training and to aid in the establishment, improvement, or expansion of training programs in the methods of providing emergency medical services.

Contact: Emergency Medical Services, Division of Medicine, BHPR, Federal Building #2, 3700 East-West Highway, Hyattsville, MD 20782, 301-436-6436.

13.288 NATIONAL HEALTH SERVICE CORPS SCHOLARSHIP PROGRAM

Type of Assistance: Grants averaging $12,715 per year.

Applicant Eligibility: Individuals.

Objective: To assure an adequate supply of physicians, dentists, and other health professionals for the National Health Service Corps for service in health manpower shortage areas in the United States. Scholarships are to be used to support students who pursue full-time courses of study in health professions schools.

Contact: National Health Service Corps Scholarship Program, BHM, HRA, PHS/DHHS, Center Building, 3700 East-West Highway, Hyattsville, MD 20782, 800-638-0824. (In Maryland, 301-436-6453.)

13.290 SPECIAL ALCOHOLISM PROJECTS TO IMPLEMENT THE UNIFORM ACT

Type of Assistance: Grants ranging from $71,080 to $1,054,655.

Applicant Eligibility: State governments.

Objective: To assist states in their implementation of the provisions of the Uniform Alcoholism and Intoxication Treatment Act, which facilitates their efforts to approach alcohol abuse and alcoholism from a community care standpoint. Funds may be used to cover the costs of such items as personnel, equipment, supplies, consultant fees for service, travel, curriculum development, and development of and purchase or rental of educational materials.

Contact: State Planning Branch, National Institute on Alcohol Abuse and Alcoholism, ADAMHA, PHS/DHHS, Rm. 14C10, 5600 Fishers Lane, Rockville, MD 20857, 301-443-2570.

13.292 SUDDEN INFANT DEATH SYNDROME INFORMATION AND COUNSELING PROGRAM

Type of Assistance: Grants ranging from $15,000 to $175,000.

Applicant Eligibility: Nonprofit organizations, state and local governments.

Objective: To collect, analyze, and furnish information relating to the causes and other appropriate aspects of Sudden Infant Death Syndrome; to provide information and counseling to families affected by the Sudden Infant Death Syndrome; and to educate health professionals, emergency care providers, and the general public concerning SIDS.

Contact: Director, SIDS Program Office, Bureau of Community Health Services, Health Services Administration, DHHS, Rm. 7-36, 5600 Fishers Lane, Rockville, MD 20857, 301-443-6600.

13.293 STATE HEALTH PLANNING AND DEVELOPMENT AGENCIES

Type of Assistance: Grants ranging from $43,500 to $2,650,227.

Applicant Eligibility: State governments.

Objective: To provide support to the state health planning agencies conducting physical and mental health planning and development functions. Funds may be used by a state health planning and development agency in meeting the cost of its operation, including the administration of the state program and assisting the statewide health coordinating council in the performance of its functions.

Contact: Director, Bureau of Health Planning, HRA, PHS/DHHS, Rm. 622, Center Building, 3700 East-West Highway, Hyattsville, MD 20782, 301-436-6850.

13.294 HEALTH PLANNING—HEALTH SYSTEMS AGENCIES

Type of Assistance: Grants ranging from $175,000 to $3,908,490.

Applicant Eligibility: Nonprofit organizations, state and local governments.

Objective: To provide for effective health resources planning at the area level to meet problems in health care delivery systems, maldistribution of health care facilities and manpower, and increasing cost of health care.

Contact: Director, Bureau of Health Planning, HRA, PHS/DHHS, Center Building, 3700 East-West Highway, Hyattsville, MD 20782, 301-436-6850.

13.295 COMMUNITY MENTAL HEALTH CENTERS— COMPREHENSIVE SERVICES SUPPORT

Type of Assistance: Grants ranging from $13,506 to $1,666,563.

Applicant Eligibility: Nonprofit organizations, state and local governments.

Objective: To provide comprehensive mental health services through a community mental health center via six grant programs: staffing grants; planning grants; grants for initial operations; consultation and education service grants; conversion grants; and financial distress grants.

Contact: Community Mental Health Services Support Branch, National Institute of Mental Health, ADAMHA, PHS/DHHS, 5600 Fishers Lane, Rockville, MD 20857, 301-443-3623.

13.296 COMPREHENSIVE HEMOPHILIA DIAGNOSTIC AND TREATMENT CENTERS

Type of Assistance: Grants ranging from $50,000 to $300,000.
Applicant Eligibility: Nonprofit organizations, state and local governments.
Objective: To expand the nationwide availability of comprehensive ambulatory diagnostic and treatment centers for persons with hemophilia, particularly in areas where there are the greatest number with severe or moderate cases of the condition.
Contact: Habilitative Branch Maternal and Child Health, Bureau of Community Health Services, Health Services Administration, Rm. 7-22, Parklawn Building, 5600 Fishers Lane, Rockville, MD 20857, 301-443-2350.

13.297 NATIONAL RESEARCH SERVICE AWARDS

Type of Assistance: Grants ranging from $8,040 to $55,500 per year.
Applicant Eligibility: Individuals.
Objective: To prepare qualified professional nurses to conduct nursing research, collaborate in interdisciplinary research, and function as faculty in schools of nursing at the graduate level. To provide up to five years of support in the aggregate for full-time predoctoral study, and three years for postdoctoral study.
Contact: Chief, Research Training Section, Division of Nursing, BHM, HRA, DHHS, Rm. 3-50, Center Building, 3700 East-West Highway, Hyattsville, Md 20782, 301-436-6204.

13.298 NURSE PRACTITIONER TRAINING PROGRAM AND NURSE PRACTITIONER TRAINEESHIPS

Type of Assistance: Grants ranging from $3,725 to $396,754; students may receive stipends up to $5,040 plus tuition and other expenses.
Applicant Eligibility: Nonprofit organizations, state and local governments.
Objective: To educate registered nurses who will be qualified to provide primary health care.
Contact: Division of Nursing, BHM, HRA, PHS/DHHS, Center Building, 3700 East-West Highway, Hyattsville, MD 20782, 301-436-6681.

13.299 ADVANCED NURSE TRAINING PROGRAM

Type of Assistance: Grants ranging from $19,405 to $334,909.
Applicant Eligibility: Nonprofit organizations, state and local governments.
Objective: To prepare registered nurses at the master's and doctoral levels to teach in the various fields of nurse training and to serve in administrative or supervisory capacities, in nursing specialties, and as nurse clinicians.
Contact: Division of Nursing, BHM, HRA, PHS/DHHS, Rm. 3-46, Center Building, 3700 East-West Highway, Hyattsville, MD 20782, 301-436-6627.

13.306   LABORATORY ANIMAL SCIENCES
AND PRIMATE RESEARCH

Type of Assistance: Grants ranging from $5,475 to $2,863,285.

Applicant Eligibility: Individuals, nonprofit organizations, state and local governments.

Objective: To provide animal resources with which the biomedical scientist can develop knowledge for prevention and control of disease in man through experimentation with animal models.

Contact: Animal Resources Branch, Division of Research Resources, National Institutes of Health, Rm. 5B59, Building 31, Bethesda, MD 20205, 301-496-5175.

13.319   DENTAL TEAM PRACTICE

Type of Assistance: Grants ranging from $83,498 to $312,810.

Applicant Eligibility: Nonprofit organizations and local governments.

Objective: To teach dental students how to function effectively as managers and organizers in multiple auxiliary dental health care delivery teams.

Contact: Professional Education Branch, Division of Dentistry, BHM, HRA, PHS/DHHS, Center Building, 3700 East-West Highway, Hyattsville, MD 20782, 301-436-6510.

13.333   CLINICAL RESEARCH

Type of Assistance: Grants ranging from $196,752 to $1,502,270.

Applicant Eligibility: Nonprofit organizations and local governments.

Objective: To create and sustain on a stable basis, highly specialized institutional resources in which clinical investigators can observe and study human disease.

Contact: General Clinical Research Centers Program Branch, Division of Research Resources, National Institutes of Health, Rm. 5B59, Building 31, Bethesda, MD 20205, 301-496-6595.

13.337   BIOMEDICAL RESEARCH SUPPORT

Type of Assistance: Grants ranging from $14,441 to $201,413.

Applicant Eligibility: Nonprofit organizations and local governments.

Objective: To strengthen, balance, and stabilize Public Health Service-supported biomedical and behavioral research; enable quick and effective response to emerging opportunities and unpredictable requirements; enhance creativity, encourage innovation, and improve the quality of project grant proposals; develop and maintain physical and human research resources; strengthen and/or expand health-related research in eligible institutions to improve the training of manpower for clinical professions or health-related research.

Contact: Biomedical Research Support Program, Division of Research Resources, National Institutes of Health, Rm. 5B35, Building 31, Bethesda, MD 20205, 301-496-6743.

13.339 HEALTH PROFESSIONS—CAPITATION GRANTS
Type of Assistance: Grants ranging from $12,417 to $1,504,672.
Applicant Eligibility: Nonprofit organizations and local governments.
Objective: To provide financial assistance to schools of medicine, osteopathy, dentistry, public health, veterinary medicine, optometry, pharmacy, and podiatry in return for addressing geographic specialty requirements for enrollment goals.
Contact: BHM, HRA, PHS/DHHS, Rm. 4-27, Center Building, 3700 East-West Highway, Hyattsville, MD 20782, 301-436-6564.

13.342 HEALTH PROFESSIONS—STUDENT LOANS
Type of Assistance: Grants ranging from $3,500 to $224,752.
Applicant Eligibility: Nonprofit organizations, state and local governments.
Objective: To increase educational opportunities for students in need of financial assistance to pursue a course of study in specified health professions by providing long-term low-interest loans.
Contact: Division of Manpower Training Support, BHM, HRA, PHS/DHHS, Rm. G23, Center Building, 3700 East-West Highway, Hyattsville, MD 20782, 301-436-6310.

13.358 PROFESSIONAL NURSE TRAINEESHIPS
Type of Assistance: Grants ranging from $8,799 to $609,502; students may receive stipends up to $5,040 plus tuition and other expenses.
Applicant Eligibility: Nonprofit organizations, state and local governments.
Objective: To prepare registered nurses as administrators, supervisors, teachers, nursing specialists, and nurse practitioners for positions in hospitals and related institutions, in public health agencies, in schools of nursing, and in other roles requiring advanced training.
Contact: Division of Nursing, BHM, HRA, PHS/DHHS, Rm. 3-50, Center Building, 3700 East-West Highway, Hyattsville, MD 20782, 301-436-6681.

13.359 NURSE TRAINING IMPROVEMENT— SPECIAL PROJECTS
Type of Assistance: Grants ranging from $7,142 to $233,064.
Applicant Eligibility: Nonprofit organizations, state and local governments.
Objective: To help schools of nursing and other institutions improve the quality and availability of nursing education through projects for specified purposes, such as opportunities for individuals from disadvantaged backgrounds.
Contact: Division of Nursing, BHM, HRA, PHS/DHHS, Rm. 3-50, Center Building, 3700 East-West Highway, Hyattsville, MD 20783, 301-436-6690.

13.361 NURSING RESEARCH PROJECT GRANTS
Type of Assistance: Grants ranging from $11,878 to $394,649.
Applicant Eligibility: Individuals, nonprofit organizations, state and local governments.

Objective: To support basic and applied research activities in nursing education, practice, and administration.
Contact: Division of Nursing, BHM, HRA, PHS/DHHS, Center Building, 3700 East-West Highway, Hyattsville, MD 20782, 301-436-6204.

13.363 NURSING SCHOLARSHIPS
Type of Assistance: Grants ranging from $256 to $54,329.
Applicant Eligibility: Nonprofit organizations and local governments.
Objective: To enable students with exceptional financial need to pursue a course of study in nursing by providing scholarship aid.
Contact: Student and Institutional Assistance Branch, Division of Manpower Training Support, BHM, HRA, PHS/DHHS, Rm. G-23, Center Building, 3700 East-West Highway, Hyattsville, MD 20782, 301-436-6310.

13.364 NURSING STUDENT LOANS
Type of Assistance: Grants ranging from $920 to $135,046.
Applicant Eligibility: Nonprofit organizations and local governments.
Objective: To assist students in need of financial assistance to pursue a course of study in professional nursing education by providing long-term, low-interest loans.
Contact: Student and Institutional Assistance Branch, Division of Manpower Training Support, BHM, HRA, PHS/DHHS, Rm. G-23, Center Building, 3700 East-West Highway, Hyattsville, MD 20782, 301-436-6310.

13.371 BIOTECHNOLOGY RESEARCH
Type of Assistance: Grants ranging from $53,996 to $2,087,389.
Applicant Eligibility: Nonprofit organizations and local governments.
Objective: To assist academic and other nonprofit institutions in developing and sustaining sophisticated teachnological capabilities, such as computer centers, biological structure resources, and biomedical engineering resources which are vital to modern biomedical research.
Contact: Biotechnology Resources Branch, Division of Research Resources, National Institutes of Health, Rm. 5B-41, Building 31, Bethesda, MD 20205, 301-496-5411.

13.375 MINORITY BIOMEDICAL SUPPORT
Type of Assistance: Grants ranging from $100,000 to $300,000.
Applicant Eligibility: Nonprofit organizations, state and local governments.
Objective: To increase the numbers of ethnic minority faculty, students, and investigators engaged in biomedical research, and to broaden the opportunities for participation in biomedical research of ethnic minority faculty, students, and investigators by providing support for biomedical research programs at eligible institutions.
Contact: Minority Biomedical Support Program Branch, Division of Re-

search Resources, National Institutes of Health, Rm. 5B-35, Building 31, Bethesda, MD 20205, 301-496-6743.

13.379 GRANTS FOR GRADUATE TRAINING IN FAMILY MEDICINE

Types of Assistance: Grants ranging from $15,000 to $1,154,351.
Applicant Eligibility: Nonprofit organizations, state and local governments.
Objective: To increase the number of physicians practicing family medicine. Funds are used to cover the cost of developing and operating approved (or provisionally approved) residency training programs, and to provide financial assistance to participants in approved residency programs in the field of family medicine.
Contact: Director, Division of Medicine, BHM, HRA, PHS/DHHS, Rm. 3-30, Center Building, 3700 East-West Highway, Hyattsville, MD 20782, 301-436-6583.

13.381 HEALTH PROFESSIONS— FINANCIAL DISTRESS GRANTS

Type of Assistance: Grants ranging from $15,000 to $2,753,349.
Applicant Eligibility: Nonprofit organizations, state and local governments.
Objective: To assist schools of medicine, osteopathy, dentistry, optometry, pharmacy, podiatry, public health, and veterinary medicine which are in serious financial distress to meet costs of operation or have special financial need to meet accreditation requirements or to carry out appropriate operational, managerial, and financial reforms.
Contact: BHM, HRA, PHS/DHHS, Rm. 427, Center Building, 3700 East-West Highway, Hyattsville, MD 20782, 301-436-6564.

13.384 HEALTH PROFESSIONS—START-UP ASSISTANCE

Type of Assistance: Grants ranging from $180,000 to $583,990.
Applicant Eligibility: Nonprofit organizations and local governments.
Objective: To assist new schools of medicine, osteopathy, dentistry, public health, veterinary medicine, optometry, pharmacy, and podiatry to accelerate start of instruction or increase size of entering class.
Contact: BHM, HRA, PHS/DHHS, Rm. 427, Center Building, 3700 East-West Highway, Hyattsville, MD 20782, 301-436-6564.

13.386 NURSING CAPITATION GRANTS

Type of Assistance: Grants ranging from $1,109 to $197,876.
Applicant Eligibility: Nonprofit organizations, state and local governments.
Objective: To support the educational programs of nursing schools. Applicants must assure that they will increase first-year enrollment of nursing students or carry out projects to improve nursing education and the utilization of nursing skills.

Contact: Division of Nursing, BHM, HRA, PHS/DHHS, Rm. 3-50, Center Building, 3700 East-West Highway, Hyattsville, MD 20782, 301-436-6674.

13.392 CANCER—CONSTRUCTION
Type of Assistance: Grants ranging from $589,000 to $3,175,259.
Applicant Eligibility: Nonprofit organizations, state and local governments.
Objective: To provide new cancer research facilities and expand and upgrade existing ones to meet laboratory safety and animal care standards, in order to achieve a geographic distribution of cancer research facilities and centers.
Contact: Grants Administration Branch, Division of Cancer Research Resources and Centers, National Cancer Institute, Westwood 8A18, Bethesda, MD 20205, 301-496-7753.

13.393 CANCER CAUSE AND PREVENTION RESEARCH
Type of Assistance: Grants ranging from $10,870 to $2,717,133.
Applicant Eligibility: Individuals, nonprofit organizations, state and local governments.
Objective: Cause and prevention research is concerned with identification of those factors which cause cancer in man, and with the development of mechanisms for preventing cancer in man.
Contact: Chief, Grants Administration Branch, Division of Cancer Research Resources and Centers, National Cancer Institute, Westwood 8A18, Bethesda, MD 20205, 301-496-7753.

13.394 CANCER DETECTION AND DIAGNOSIS RESEARCH
Type of Assistance: Grants ranging from $14,209 to $500,000.
Applicant Eligibility: Nonprofit organizations, state and local governments.
Objective: To identify cancer in patients early enough and precisely enough so that the latest methods of treatment can be applied toward control of the disease.
Contact: Chief, Grants Administration Branch, Division of Cancer Research Resources and Centers, National Cancer Institute, Westwood 8A18, Bethesda, MD 20205, 301-496-7753.

13.395 CANCER TREATMENT RESEARCH
Type of Assistance: Grants ranging from $10,000 to $3,063,635.
Applicant Eligibility: Individuals, nonprofit organizations, state and local governments.
Objective: To develop the means to cure as many cancer patients as possible and to control the disease in those patients who are not cured.
Contact: Chief, Grants Administration Branch, Division of Cancer Research Resources and Centers, National Cancer Institute, Westwood 8A18, Bethesda, MD 20205, 301-496-7753.

13.396 CANCER BIOLOGY RESEARCH

Type of Assistance: Grants ranging from $3,308 to $1,170,739.
Applicant Eligibility: Individuals, nonprofit organizations, state and local governments.
Objective: To provide fundamental information on the cause and nature of cancer in man, with the expectation that this will result in better methods of prevention, detection and diagnosis, and treatment of neoplastic diseases.
Contact: Chief, Grants Administration Branch, Division of Cancer Research Resources and Centers, National Cancer Institute, Westwood 8A18, Bethesda, MD 20205, 301-496-7753.

13.397 CANCER CENTERS SUPPORT

Type of Assistance: Grants ranging from $16,000 to $6,492,620.
Applicant Eligibility: Nonprofit organizations, state and local governments.
Objective: To provide core funds to assist in the development and maintenance of multidisciplinary cancer centers for laboratory and clinical research, as well as training in and demonstration of the latest diagnostic and treatment techniques.
Contact: Chief, Grants Administration Branch, Division of Cancer Research Resources and Centers, National Cancer Institute, Westwood 8A18, Bethesda, MD 20205, 301-496-7753.

13.398 CANCER RESEARCH MANPOWER

Type of Assistance: Grants ranging from $10,000 to $550,000.
Applicant Eligibility: Nonprofit organizations, state and local governments.
Objective: To make available support for nonprofit institutions interested in providing biomedical training opportunities for individuals pursuing careers in basic and clinical research which support important areas of the National Cancer Program.
Contact: Chief, Research Manpower Branch, Division of Cancer Research Resources and Centers, National Cancer Institute, Blair 727, Bethesda, MD 20205, 301-427-8866.

13.399 CANCER CONTROL

Type of Assistance: Grants ranging from $6,552 to $1,301,115.
Applicant Eligibility: Nonprofit organizations, state and local governments.
Objective: To establish and support demonstration, education and other programs for the detection, diagnosis, prevention, and treatment of cancer and for rehabilitation and counseling related to cancer.
Contact: Grants Inquiry Office, Division of Research Grants, National Cancer Institute, 5333 Westbard Avenue, Bethesda, MD 20205, 301-496-7441.

OFFICE OF HUMAN DEVELOPMENT SERVICES

13.600 ADMINISTRATION FOR CHILDREN, YOUTH AND FAMILIES—HEAD START

Type of Assistance: Grants ranging from $60,000 to $15,000,000.
Applicant Eligibility: Nonprofit organizations, state and local governments.
Objective: To provide comprehensive health, educational, nutritional, social, and other services primarily to economically disadvantaged preschool children and their families, and to involve parents in activities with their children so that the children will attain overall social competence.
Contact: Administration for Children, Youth and Families—Head Start, Office of Human Development Services, DHHS, P.O. Box 1182, Washington, DC 20013, 202-755-7790.

13.608 ADMINISTRATION FOR CHILDREN, YOUTH AND FAMILIES—CHILD WELFARE RESEARCH AND DEMONSTRATION

Type of Assistance: Grants ranging from $10,000 to $500,000.
Applicant Eligibility: Nonprofit organizations, state and local governments.
Objective: To provide financial support for research and demonstration projects in the area of child and family development and welfare.
Contact: Grants Coordinator, Research and Evaluation Division, Administration for Children, Youth and Families, Office of Human Development Services, DHHS, P.O. Box 1182, Washington, DC 20013, 202-755-7755.

13.612 NATIVE AMERICAN PROGRAMS

Type of Assistance: Grants ranging from $40,000 to $5,000,000.
Applicant Eligibility: Nonprofit organizations, state and local governments.
Objective: To promote the economic and social self-sufficiency of American Indians, Native Hawaiians, and Alaskan Natives.
Contact: Administration for Native Americans, DHHS, 200 Independence Avenue, S.W., Washington, DC 20201, 202-245-7776.

13.623 ADMINISTRATION FOR CHILDREN, YOUTH AND FAMILIES—RUNAWAY YOUTH

Type of Assistance: Grants ranging from $25,000 to $75,000.
Applicant Eligiblity: Nonprofit organizations, state and local governments.
Objective: To develop local facilities to address the immediate needs of runaway youth.
Contact: Director, Youth Development Bureau, Administration for Children, Youth and Families, Office of Human Development Services, DHHS, Washington, DC, 20201, 202-755-0590.

13.628   CHILD ABUSE AND NEGLECT PREVENTION AND TREATMENT

Type of Assistance: Grants ranging from $30,000 to $300,000.

Applicant Eligibility: Nonprofit organizations, state and local governments.

Objective: To assist state, local, and voluntary agencies and organizations to strengthen their capacities to develop programs that will prevent, identify, and treat child abuse and neglect.

Contact: National Center on Child Abuse and Neglect, Children's Bureau, P.O. Box 1182, Washington, DC 20013, 202-245-2840.

13.630   ADMINISTRATION FOR DEVELOPMENTAL DISABILITIES—BASIC SUPPORT AND ADVOCACY GRANTS

Type of Assistance: Grants ranging from $30,000 to $3,581,000.

Applicant Eligibility: State governments.

Objective: To assist states in the provision of comprehensive services to assure that developmentally disabled persons receive services necessary to enable them to achieve their maximum potential to insure the protection of their legal and human rights.

Contact: Director, Bureau of Developmental Disabilities, Rehabilitation Services Administration, Office of Human Development Services, Office of the Secretary, DHHS, Washington, DC 20201, 202-472-7214.

13.631   ADMINISTRATION FOR DEVELOPMENTAL DISABILITIES—SPECIAL PROJECTS

Type of Assistance: Grants ranging from $25,000 to $561,700.

Applicant Eligibility: Nonprofit organizations, state and local governments.

Objective: To provide support for projects to improve the quality of service to the developmentally disabled, public awareness and informational programs, demonstration of new or improved service delivery, training, coordination of available community resources, and technical assistance.

Contact: Deputy Assistant Secretary, Office of Human Development Services, DHHS, Washington, DC 20201, 202-472-7213.

13.632   DEVELOPMENTAL DISABILITIES— UNIVERSITY-AFFILIATED FACILITIES

Type of Assistance: Grants ranging from $92,100 to $348,200.

Applicant Eligibility: Nonprofit organizations, state and local governments.

Objective: To assist with the cost of administration and operation of facilities for interdisciplinary training of personnel concerned with developmental disabilities, the demonstration of the provision of exemplary services for the developmentally disabled, and the demonstration of findings related to the provision of those services.

Contact: Commissioner, Rehabilitation Services Administration, Office of Human Development Services, DHHS, Washington, DC 20201, 202-472-7213.

13.633 SPECIAL PROGRAMS FOR THE AGING— GRANTS FOR STATES AND COMMUNITY PROGRAMS ON AGING

Type of Assistance: Grants ranging from $121,875 to $22,094,560.

Applicant Eligibility: State governments.

Objective: To provide assistance to state and area agencies for the statewide planning of programs for older persons and for area planning and provision of social services, including multipurpose senior centers.

Contact: Associate Commissioner, Office of Program Operations, Administration on Aging, Office of Human Development Services, DHHS, Washington, DC 20201, 202-472-3057.

13.634 SPECIAL PROGRAMS FOR THE AGING— DISCRETIONARY PROJECTS AND PROGRAMS

Type of Assistance: Grants ranging from $50,000 to $250,000.

Applicant Eligibility: Nonprofit organizations, state and local governments.

Objective: To demonstrate new approaches, techniques, and methods to improve or expand social, nutritional, or other services to promote the well-being of older individuals.

Contact: Office of Research Demonstration and Evaluation, Administration on Aging, Office of Human Development Services, DHHS, Washington, DC 20201, 202-472-7225.

13.635 SPECIAL PROGRAMS FOR THE AGING— NUTRITION SERVICES

Type of Assistance: Grants ranging from $157,500 to $22,602,884.

Applicant Eligibility: State governments.

Objective: To provide older Americans with low-cost, nutritious meals, appropriate nutrition education, and other appropriate nutrition services. Meals may be served in a congregate setting or delivered to the home.

Contact: Associate Commissioner, Office of Program Operations, Administration on Aging, Office of Human Development Services, DHHS, Washington, DC 20201, 202-245-0011.

13.636 SPECIAL PROGRAMS FOR THE AGING—RESEARCH AND DEVELOPMENT

Type of Assistance: Grants ranging from $35,000 to $400,000.

Applicant Eligibility: Nonprofit organizations, state and local governments.

Objective: To support research and development on the needs and services of the vulnerable elderly living in the community; on various aspects of the organization, operation, and changes of the social services delivery systems; and on policy areas such as income, health, and housing.

Contact: Office of Research Demonstration and Evaluation Resources, Administration on Aging, Office of Human Development Services, DHHS, Washington, DC 20201, 202-472-7225.

13.637 SPECIAL PROGRAMS FOR THE AGING—TRAINING

Type of Assistance: Grants ranging from $23,000 to $218,000.
Applicant Eligibility: Nonprofit organizations, state and local governments.
Objective: To support activities that attract qualified persons to the field of care of the aging and train persons employed or preparing for employment in care of the aging and related fields.
Contact: Office of Education and Training, Administration on Aging, Office of Human Development Services, DHHS, Washington, DC 20201, 202-472-4683.

13.638 SPECIAL PROGRAMS FOR THE AGING— MULTIDISCIPLINARY CENTERS OF GERONTOLOGY

Type of Assistance: Grants ranging from $50,000 to $200,000.
Applicant Eligibility: Nonprofit organizations, state and local governments.
Objective: To establish new, and support existing, multidisciplinary centers of gerontology.
Contact: Office of Education and Training, Administration on Aging, Office of Human Development Services, DHHS, Washington, DC 20201, 202-472-4683.

13.640 ADMINISTRATION FOR CHILDREN, YOUTH AND FAMILIES—YOUTH RESEARCH AND DEVELOPMENT

Type of Assistance: Grants ranging from $15,000 to $400,000.
Applicant Eligibility: Nonprofit organizations, state and local governments.
Objective: To support research, development, and evaluation efforts in the area of runaway youth and in broader youth development issues.
Contact: Director, Youth Development Branch, Administration for Children, Youth and Families, Office of Human Development Services, DHHS, Washington, DC 20201, 202-245-2840.

13.642 SOCIAL SERVICES FOR LOW-INCOME AND PUBLIC ASSISTANCE RECIPIENTS

Type of Assistance: Grants ranging from $25,000 to $282,730,000.
Applicant Eligibility: State governments.
Objective: To enable states to provide necessary social services to public assistance recipients and other low-income persons.
Contact: Director, Office of Policy Control, Interpretation and Coordination, Administration for Public Services, Office of Human Development Services, DHHS, 330 C Street, S.W., Washington, DC 20201, 202-245-9415.

13.644 SOCIAL SERVICES TRAINING GRANTS

Type of Assistance: Grants ranging from $13,000 to $11,461,000.
Applicant Eligibility: State governments.
Objective: To provide training and retraining of staff and volunteers of a

state's social services agency, as well as of students preparing for employment in a social services agency.

Contact: Director, Division of Program Management, Administration for Public Services, Office of Human Development Services, DHHS, 330 C Street, S.W., Washington, DC 20201, 202-245-6461.

13.645 CHILD WELFARE SERVICES—STATE GRANTS

Type of Assistance: Grants ranging from $112,530 to $4,420,291.

Applicant Eligibility: State governments.

Objective: To establish, extend, and strengthen preventive or protective services provided by state and local public welfare programs which will prevent the neglect, abuse, exploitation, or delinquency of children.

Contact: Children's Bureau, Administration for Children, Youth and Families, Office of Human Development Services, DHHS, P.O. Box 1182, Washington, DC 20013, 202-755-8888.

13.646 WORK INCENTIVE PROGRAM

Type of Assistance: Grants (dollar amount not available).

Applicant Eligibility: State governments.

Objective: To move men, women, and out-of-school youth age 16 or older from dependence on Aid to Families with Dependent Children grants to economic independence through permanent, productive employment by providing appropriate employment training, job placement, and other related services, supplemented by child care and other social services when needed to enable a person to participate or secure employment.

Contact: Executive Director, National Coordination Committee, Work Incentive Program, Washington, DC 20213, 202-376-7030.

13.647 SOCIAL SERVICES RESEARCH AND DEMONSTRATION

Type of Assistance: Grants ranging from $50,000 to $250,000.

Applicant Eligibility: Nonprofit organizations, state and local governments.

Objective: To discover, test, demonstrate, and promote new social service concepts concerning dependent and vulnerable populations such as the poor, the aging, children and youth, Native Americans, and the handicapped.

Contact: Director, Division of Research, Demonstration and Evaluation, Administration for Public Services, DHHS, 330 C Street, S.W., Washington, DC 20201, 202-245-6296.

13.648 CHILD WELFARE SERVICES TRAINING GRANTS

Type of Assistance: Grants averaging $50,000.

Applicant Eligibility: Nonprofit organizations and local governments.

Objective: To develop and maintain an adequate supply of qualified and trained personnel for the field of services to children and their families, and

to improve educational programs and resources for preparing personnel for this field.
Contact: Children's Bureau, DHHS, P.O. Box 1182, Washington, DC 20013, 202-755-7820.

13.652   ADMINISTRATION FOR CHILDREN, YOUTH AND FAMILIES—ADOPTION OPPORTUNITIES
Type of Assistance: Grants ranging from $50,000 to $500,000.
Applicant Eligibility: Nonprofit organizations, state and local governments.
Objective: To provide financial support for demonstration projects to improve adoption practices. To gather information on adoptions and to provide training and technical assistance to provide improved adoption services.
Contact: Grants Coordinator, Training and Technical Assistance Division, Children's Bureau, Administration for Children, Youth and Families, DHHS, P.O. Box 1182, Washington, DC 20013, 202-755-7820.

13.655   SPECIAL PROGRAMS FOR THE AGING—GRANTS TO INDIAN TRIBES
Type of Assistance: Grants (dollar amount not available).
Applicant Eligibility: Native Americans.
Objective: To promote the delivery of services to older Indians.
Contact: Chief, Division of State and Community Programs, Administration on Aging, Office of Human Development Services, DHHS, Washington, DC 20201, 202-472-3057.

OFFICE OF THE SECRETARY

13.679   CHILD SUPPORT ENFORCEMENT
Type of Assistance: Grants ranging from $117,000 to $44,317,000.
Applicant Eligibility: State governments.
Objective: To enforce the support obligations owed by absent parents to their children, locate absent parents, establish paternity, and obtain child support.
Contact: Deputy Director, Office of Child Support Enforcement, DHHS, 6110 Executive Boulevard, Rockville, MD 20852, 301-443-4442.

HEALTH CARE FINANCING ADMINISTRATION

13.714   MEDICAL ASSISTANCE PROGRAM
Type of Assistance: Grants ranging from $900,000 to $2,054,860,000.
Applicant Eligibility: State and local governments.
Objective: To provide financial assistance to states for payments of medical

assistance on behalf of cash assistance recipients and, in certain states, on behalf of other medically needy, who, except for income and resources, would be eligible for cash assistance.

Contact: Director, Bureau of Program Operations, Health Care Financing Administration, DHHS, Rm. 300, East High Rise Building, 6401 Security Boulevard, Baltimore, MD 21235, 301-594-9000.

13.766 HEALTH CARE FINANCING RESEARCH, DEMONSTRATIONS AND EXPERIMENTS

Type of Assistance: Grants ranging from $25,000 to $6,000,000.

Applicant Eligibility: Nonprofit organizations, state and local governments.

Objective: To discover, test, demonstrate, and promote utilization of health care financing concepts that will provide service to beneficiary population while at the same time providing incentives for efficient use of services and resources by provider and beneficiaries.

Contact: Office of Policy, Planning and Research, Health Care Financing Administration, DHHS, 330 C Street, S.W., Washington, DC 20201, 202-245-2184.

13.773 MEDICARE—HOSPITAL INSURANCE

Type of Assistance: Direct payments to cover most inpatient hospital services and posthospital extended care services.

Applicant Eligibility: Individuals.

Objective: To provide hospital insurance protection for covered services to any person 65 or above and to certain disabled persons.

Contact: Medicare Bureau, Health Care Financing Administration, Rm. 700, East High Rise Building, 6401 Security Boulevard, Baltimore, MD 21235, 301-594-9000.

13.774 MEDICARE—SUPPLEMENTARY MEDICAL INSURANCE

Type of Assistance: Direct payments to cover charges of physicians and other suppliers of medical services.

Applicant Eligibility: Individuals.

Objective: To provide medical insurance protection for covered services to persons 65 or over and certain disabled persons who elect this coverage.

Contact: Medicare Bureau, Health Care Financing Administration, Rm. 700, East High Rise Building, 6401 Security Boulevard, Baltimore, MD 21235, 301-594-9000.

SOCIAL SECURITY ADMINISTRATION

13.802   SOCIAL SECURITY—DISABILITY INSURANCE

Type of Assistance: Direct payments up to $989.30 monthly. .
Applicant Eligibility: Individuals.
Objective: To replace part of the earnings lost because of a physical or mental impairment severe enough to prevent a person from working.
Contact: Office of Information, Social Security Administration, Rm. 124, Altmeyer Building, Baltimore, MD 21235, 301-592-3000.

13.803   SOCIAL SECURITY—RETIREMENT INSURANCE

Type of Assistance: Direct payments up to $1,000.60 monthly.
Applicant Eligibility: Individuals.
Objective: To replace part of the earnings lost because of retirement.
Contact: Office of Information, Social Security Administration, Rm. 124, Altmeyer Building, Baltimore, MD 21235, 301-592-3000.

13.804   SOCIAL SECURITY—SPECIAL BENEFITS FOR PERSONS AGE 72 AND OVER.

Type of Assistance: Direct payments up to $138.10 monthly.
Applicant Eligibility: Individuals.
Objective: To assure some regular income to certain persons age 72 and over who had little or no opportunity to earn Social Security protection during their working years.
Contact: Office of Information, Social Security Administration, Rm. 124, Altmeyer Building, Baltimore, MD 21235, 301-592-3000.

13.805   SOCIAL SECURITY—SURVIVORS INSURANCE

Type of Assistance: Direct payments up to $1,000.60 monthly.
Applicant Eligibility: Individuals.
Objective: To replace part of earnings lost to dependents because of worker's death.
Contact: Office of Information, Social Security Administration, Rm. 124, Altmeyer Building, Baltimore, MD 21235, 301-592-3000.

13.806   SPECIAL BENEFITS FOR DISABLED COAL MINERS ("BLACK LUNG" BENEFITS)

Type of Assistance: Direct payments up to $508 monthly.
Applicant Eligibility: Individuals.
Objective: To pay benefits to coal miners who have become disabled due to pneumoconiosis (black lung disease) and their dependents or survivors.
Contact: Office of Information, Social Security Administration, Rm. 124, Altmeyer Building, Baltimore, MD 21235, 301-592-3000.

13.807 SUPPLEMENTAL SECURITY INCOME
Type of Assistance: Direct payments up to $312.30 monthly.
Applicant Eligibility: Individuals.
Objective: To provide supplemental income to persons age 65 and over and to persons blind or disabled whose income and resources are below specified levels.
Contact: Office of Information, Social Security Administration, Rm. 124, Altmeyer Building, Baltimore, MD 21235, 301-592-3000.

13.808 ASSISTANCE PAYMENTS—MAINTENANCE ASSISTANCE (STATE AID)
Type of Assistance: Grants ranging from $1,413,000 to $1,020,168,000.
Applicant Eligibility: Local governments.
Objective: To set general standards for state administration; to provide the federal financial share to states for aid to families with dependent children, emergency assistance to families with children, assistance to repatriated U.S. nationals, and aid to the aged, blind, permanently and totally disabled; in Guam, Puerto Rico, and the Virgin Islands and the administration of these welfare programs and monitoring of their performance.
Contact: Office of Family Assistance, Social Security Administration, DHHS, 330 C Street, S.W., Washington, DC 20201, 202-245-2528.

13.810 ASSISTANCE PAYMENTS— STATE AND LOCAL TRAINING
Type of Assistance: Grants up to $6,020,163.
Applicant Eligibility: State governments.
Objective: To train personnel employed or preparing for employment in state agencies or in local agencies administering approved public assistance plans.
Contact: Director, Office of Procedures, Office of Family Assistance, Social Security Administration, DHHS, 330 C Street, S.W., Washington, DC 20201, 202-245-0361.

13.812 ASSISTANCE PAYMENTS—RESEARCH
Type of Assistance: Grants ranging from $10,000 to $300,000.
Applicant Eligibility: Nonprofit organizations, state and local governments.
Objective: To experiment with, pilot, demonstrate, and research new public assistance concepts to reduce dependency and to improve living conditions of recipients of public assistance.
Contact: Director of the Family Assistance Studies Staff, Office of Research and Statistics, Social Security Administration, 1875 Connecticut Avenue, N.W., Washington, DC 20009, 202-673-5747.

13.813   REFUGEE ASSISTANCE—CUBAN REFUGEES

Type of Assistance: Direct payments (dollar amount not available).
Applicant Eligibility: State governments.
Objective: To assist Cuban refugees with problems such as finding homes, training, and job opportunities; and to help alleviate fiscal impact on state and local resources for welfare and medical assistance to needy eligible refugees, and in Dade County for public education.
Contact: Director, Office of Refugee Resettlement, DHHS, Rm. 1229, 330 C Street, S.W., Washington, DC 20201, 202-245-0418.

13.814   REFUGEE ASSISTANCE— STATE-ADMINISTERED PROGRAMS

Type of Assistance: Direct payments up to $66,000,000.
Applicant Eligibility: State governments.
Objective: To help refugees resettle throughout the country, by funding, through state and local public assistance agencies, maintenance and medical assistance and social services for needy refugees; and to provide grants for training, services, and related projects. Currently assists refugees from Cambodia, Vietnam, and Laos.
Contact: Director, Office of Refugee Resettlement, DHHS, Rm. 1229, 330 C Street, S.W., Washington, DC 20201, 202-245-0418.

13.815   REFUGEE ASSISTANCE— VOLUNTARY AGENCY PROGRAMS

Type of Assistance: Grants ranging from $60,000 to $15,000,000.
Applicant Eligibility: State governments.
Objective: To assist Soviet and other refugees to become self-supporting and independent members of American society by providing grant funds to voluntary resettlement agencies currently resettling these refugees in the United States. Currently assists agencies resettling Soviet-Jewish refugees.
Contact: Director, Office of Refugee Resettlement, DHHS, Rm. 1229, 330 C Street, S.W., Washington, DC 20201, 202-245-0418.

13.816   LOW-INCOME ENERGY ASSISTANCE PROGRAM

Type of Assistance: Grants (dollar amount not available).
Applicant Eligibility: State governments.
Objective: To make funds available to states to provide eligible low-income individuals money to offset their rising costs of home energy consumption.
Contact: Office of Family Assistance, Social Security Administration, DHHS, Rm. B428, Trans Point Building, 2100 Second Street, Washington, DC 20024, 202-245-2015.

PUBLIC HEALTH SERVICE-2

13.820 SCHOLARSHIPS FOR FIRST-YEAR STUDENTS OF EXCEPTIONAL FINANCIAL NEED

Type of Assistance: Grants averaging $10,000 a year.
Applicant Eligibility: Nonprofit organizations and local governments.
Objective: To make funds available to authorized health professions schools to award scholarships to full-time first-year health professions students of exceptional financial need.
Contact: Student and Institutional Assistance Branch, Division of Manpower Training Support, BHM, HRA, PHS/DHHS, Rm. 5-50, Center Building, 3700 East-West Highway, Hyattsville, MD 20782, 301-436-6310.

13.821 PHYSIOLOGY AND BIOMEDICAL ENGINEERING

Type of Assistance: Grants ranging from $3,900 to $1,342,000.
Applicant Eligibility: Individuals, nonprofit organizations, state and local governments.
Objective: To support the basic research that applies concepts from mathematics, physics, and engineering to biological systems, uses engineering principles in the development of computers for patient monitoring, or is related to physiology, anesthesiology, trauma and burn studies, and related areas.
Contact: Director, Physiology and Biomedical Engineering, National Institute of General Medical Sciences, National Institutes of Health, Bethesda, MD 20014, 301-496-7891.

13.822 HEALTH CAREERS OPPORTUNITY PROGRAM

Type of Assistance: Grants ranging from $17,957 to $651,234.
Applicant Eligibility: Nonprofit organizations, state and local governments.
Objective: To identify, recruit, and select individuals from disadvantaged backgrounds for education and training in a health profession; to facilitate their entry into such a school; to provide counseling or other needed services to assist such individuals to successfully complete their education; to provide preliminary education designed to assist them to successfully complete their course of education; and to publicize existing sources of financial aid.
Contact: Grants Management Office, BHM, HRA, DHHS, Rm. 4-27, Center Building, 3700 East-West Highway, Hyattsville, MD 20782, 301-436-7481.

13.823 PRIMARY CARE RESEARCH AND DEMONSTRATION PROJECTS

Type of Assistance: Grants ranging from $20,000 to $433,000.
Applicant Eligibility: Nonprofit organizations, state and local governments.
Objective: To provide grants to and enter into contracts with public and private entities which provide health service in order to demonstrate new and

innovative methods for the provision of primary health and dental services, or to conduct research on such methods or on existing ones.
Contact: Director, Program Office for Rural Health, Bureau of Community Health Services, DHHS, Rm. 7A-55, Parklawn Building, 5600 Fishers Lane, Rockville, MD 20857, 301-443-2220.

13.837   HEART AND VASCULAR DISEASES RESEARCH
Type of Assistance: Grants ranging from $13,000 to $4,411,667.
Applicant Eligibility: Individuals, nonprofit organizations, and local governments.
Objective: To foster research, prevention, education, and control activities related to heart and vascular diseases, and to develop young science investigators in these areas.
Contact: Director, Division of Heart and Vascular Diseases, National Heart, Lung, and Blood Institute, Bethesda, MD 20014, 301-496-5595.

13.838   LUNG DISEASES RESEARCH
Type of Assistance: Grants ranging from $13,000 to $1,233,333.
Applicant Eligibility: Individuals, nonprofit organizations, and local governments.
Objective: To use available knowledge and technology to solve specific disease problems of the lungs; to promote further studies on the structure and function of the lung; and to achieve improvement in prevention and treatment of lung diseases.
Contact: Director, Division of Lung Diseases, National Heart, Lung, and Blood Institute, Bethesda, MD 20014, 301-496-7208.

13.839   BLOOD DISEASES AND RESOURCES RESEARCH
Type of Assistance: Grants ranging from $13,000 to $1,435,653.
Applicant Eligibility: Individuals, nonprofit organizations, and local governments.
Objective: To further the development of blood resources and coordinate national and regional activities of blood centers; to promote research on blood diseases including sickle cell disease; and to develop new scientists for such research.
Contact: Director, Division of Blood Diseases, National Heart, Lung, and Blood Institute, Bethesda, MD 20014, 301-496-3533.

13.840   CARIES RESEARCH
Type of Assistance: Grants ranging from $5,000 to $300,000.
Applicant Eligibility: Individuals, nonprofit organizations, and local governments.
Objective: To develop methods to eliminate dental caries as a major health problem.
Contact: Grants and NRSA's: Extramural Programs, National Institute of

Dental Research, National Institutes of Health, Bethesda, MD 20014, 301-496-7884.

13.841   PERIODONTAL DISEASES RESEARCH

Type of Assistance: Grants ranging from $5,000 to $300,000.

Applicant Eligibility: Individuals, nonprofit organizations, and local governments.

Objective: To develop new knowledge which may lead to the prevention and eradication of periodontal diseases.

Contact: Grants and NRSA's: Extramural Programs, National Institute of Dental Research, National Institutes of Health, Bethesda, MD 20014, 301-496-7784.

13.842   CRANIOFACIAL ANOMALIES RESEARCH

Type of Assistance: Grants ranging from $5,000 to $300,000.

Applicant Eligibility: Individuals, nonprofit organizations, state and local governments.

Objective: To acquire new knowledge toward the prevention and treatment of malformations such as cleft lip/palate; acquired malformations from surgery or accident; and malocclusion of teeth and jaws.

Contact: Grants and NRSA's: Extramural Programs, National Institute of Dental Research, National Institutes of Health, Bethesda, MD 20014, 301-496-7807.

13.843   RESTORATIVE MATERIALS RESEARCH

Type of Assistance: Grants ranging from $5,000 to $300,000.

Applicant Eligibility: Individuals, nonprofit organizations, state and local governments.

Objective: To provide better dental care by fostering the development of improved materials and methods to restore lost oral tissues to normal form and function.

Contact: Grants and NRSA's: Extramural Programs, National Institute of Dental Research, National Institutes of Health, Bethesda, MD 20014, 301-496-7492.

13.844   PAIN CONTROL AND BEHAVIORAL STUDIES

Type of Assistance: Grants ranging from $5,000 to $300,000.

Applicant Eligibility: Individuals, nonprofit organizations, state and local governments.

Objective: To increase knowledge concerning the nature, etiology, pathophysiology, diagnosis, and treatment of oral pain problems; and to achieve greater utilization of behavioral sciences knowledge in dental and oral problems.

Contact: Grants and NRSA's: Extramural Programs, National Institute of

Dental Research, National Institutes of Health, Bethesda, MD 20014, 301-496-7491.

13.845 DENTAL RESEARCH INSTITUTES

Type of Assistance: Grants ranging from $1,000,000 to $1,500,000.
Applicant Eligibility: Nonprofit organizations, state and local governments.
Objective: To develop institutes or centers to focus resources on the problems of oral health in ideal research and training environments.
Contact: Extramural Programs, National Institute of Dental Research, National Institutes of Health, Bethesda, MD 20014, 301-496-7748.

13.846 ARTHRITIS, BONE, AND SKIN DISEASES RESEARCH

Type of Assistance: Grants ranging from $25,000 to $1,041,000.
Applicant Eligibility: Individuals, nonprofit organizations, state and local governments.
Objective: To support basic laboratory research and clinical investigations and to provide postdoctoral biomedical research training for individuals interested in careers in health sciences and fields related to these programs.
Contact: Associate Director for Extramural Program Activities, National Institute of Arthritis, Metabolism and Digestive Diseases, National Institutes of Health, Rm. 607A, Westwood Building, Bethesda, MD 20014, 301-496-7277.

13.847 DIABETES, ENDOCRINOLOGY AND METABOLISM RESEARCH

Type of Assistance: Grants ranging from $25,000 to $1,448,191.
Applicant Eligibility: Individuals, nonprofit organizations, state and local governments.
Objective: To support basic laboratory research and clinical investigations and to provide postdoctoral biomedical research training for individuals interested in careers in health sciences and fields related to these programs.
Contact: Associate Director for Extramural Program Activities, National Institute of Arthritis, Metabolism and Digestive Diseases, National Institutes of Health, Rm. 607A, Westwood Building, Bethesda, MD 20014, 301-496-7277.

13.848 DIGESTIVE DISEASES AND NUTRITION RESEARCH

Type of Assistance: Grants ranging from $25,000 to $1,069,000.
Applicant Eligibility: Individuals, nonprofit organizations, and local governments.
Objective: To support basic laboratory research and clinical investigations and to provide postdoctoral biomedical research training for individuals interested in careers in health sciences and fields related to these programs.
Contact: Associate Director for Extramural Program Activities, National In-

stitute of Arthritis, Metabolism and Digestive Diseases, National Institutes of Health, Rm. 603A, Westwood Building, Bethesda, MD 20014, 301-496-7277.

13.849 KIDNEY DISEASES, UROLOGY AND HEMATOLOGY RESEARCH

Type of Assistance: Grants ranging from $25,000 to $650,000.
Applicant Eligibility: Individuals, nonprofit organizations, and local governments.
Objective: To support basic laboratory research and clinical investigations and to provide postdoctoral biomedical research training for individuals interested in careers in health sciences and fields related to these programs.
Contact: Associate Director for Extramural Program Activities, National Institute of Arthritis, Metabolism and Digestive Diseases, National Institutes of Health, Rm. 603A, Westwood Building, Bethesda, MD 20014, 301-496-7277.

13.851 COMMUNICATIVE DISORDERS RESEARCH

Type of Assistance: Grants ranging from $6,000 to $910,000.
Applicant Eligibility: Individuals, nonprofit organizations, state and local governments.
Objective: To support specific research and research training directed toward understanding the causes, prevention, diagnoses, and treatment of communicative disorders.
Contact: Extramural Activities Program, NINCDS, National Institutes of Health, Bethesda, MD 20205, 301-496-9248.

13.852 NEUROLOGICAL DISORDERS RESEARCH

Type of Assistance: Grants ranging from $5,000 to $2,177,800.
Applicant Eligibility: Nonprofit organizations, state and local governments.
Objective: To support specific research and research training directed toward understanding the causes, prevention, diagnoses, and treatment of neurological disorders.
Contact: Extramural Activities Program, NINCDS, National Institutes of Health, Bethesda, MD 20205, 301-496-9248.

13.853 STROKE, NERVOUS SYSTEM TRAUMA RESEARCH

Type of Assistance: Grants ranging from $8,000 to $1,565,000.
Applicant Eligibility: Individuals, nonprofit organizations, state and local governments.
Objective: To support specific research and research training directed toward understanding the causes, prevention, diagnoses, and treatment of stroke and nervous system trauma.
Contact: Extramural Activities Program, NINCDS, National Institutes of Health, Bethesda, MD 20205, 301-496-9248.

13.854 FUNDAMENTAL NEUROSCIENCES RESEARCH

Type of Assistance: Grants ranging from $10,000 to $443,500.

Applicant Eligibility: Individuals, nonprofit organizations, state and local governments.

Objective: To support specific research and research training in the fundamental neurosciences to elucidate the mechanism responsible for normal function of the human nervous system and to understand the nature of its diseases and disorders.

Contact: Extramural Activities Program, NINCDS, National Institutes of Health, Bethesda, MD 20205, 301-496-1447.

13.855 IMMUNOLOGY, ALLERGIC AND IMMUNOLOGIC DISEASES RESEARCH

Type of Assistance: Grants ranging from $6,000 to $1,878,000.

Applicant Eligibility: Individuals, nonprofit organizations, state and local governments.

Objective: To assist public and private nonprofit institutions and individuals to establish, expand, and improve biomedical research and research training in allergic and immunologic diseases and related areas; and to assist public, private, and commercial institutions to conduct developmental research, to produce and test research materials, and to provide research services as required by the agency for research programs in allergic and immunologic diseases.

Contact: Grants Management Branch, National Institute of Allergy and Infectious Diseases, National Institutes of Health, Bethesda, MD 20205, 301-496-7075.

13.856 MICROBIOLOGY AND INFECTIOUS DISEASES RESEARCH

Type of Assistance: Grants ranging from $4,000 to $451,000.

Applicant Eligibility: Individuals, nonprofit organizations, state and local governments.

Objective: To assist public and private nonprofit institutions and individuals to establish, expand, and improve biomedical research and research training in infectious diseases and related areas; and to assist public, private, and commercial institutions to conduct developmental research, produce and test research materials, and provide research services as required by the agency for research programs in infectious diseases.

Contact: Grants Management Branch, National Institute of Allergy and Infectious Diseases, National Institutes of Health, Bethesda, MD 20205, 301-496-7075.

13.859 PHARMACOLOGICAL SCIENCES

Type of Assistance: Grants ranging from $3,900 to $1,311,000.

Applicant Eligibility: Nonprofit organizations, state and local governments.

Objective: To improve medical therapy through acquisition of increased knowledge of the mechanisms of drug action and of ways to increase efficacy and safety and diminish toxicity.

Contact: Program Director, Pharmacological Sciences, National Institute of General Medical Sciences, National Institutes of Health, Bethesda, MD 20014, 301-496-7707.

13.862   GENETICS RESEARCH

Type of Assistance: Grants ranging from $3,900 to $1,399,000.

Applicant Eligibility: Individuals, nonprofit organizations, state and local governments.

Objective: To support basic research ultimately aimed at the prevention, therapy, and control of genetic diseases in man, including those multifactorial illnesses with a strong hereditary component.

Contact: Program Director, Genetics, National Institute of General Medical Sciences, National Institutes of Health, Bethesda, MD 20014, 301-496-7087.

13.863   CELLULAR AND MOLECULAR BASIS
OF DISEASE RESEARCH

Type of Assistance: Grants ranging from $3,900 to $672,000.

Applicant Eligibility: Individuals, nonprofit organizations, state and local governments.

Objective: To support research on the structure and function of cells and their component parts, with the expectation that a greater understanding of these aspects will contribute to ultimate control of all forms and manifestations of human disease.

Contact: Program Director, Cellular and Molecular Basis of Disease, National Institute of General Medical Sciences, National Institutes of Health, Bethesda, MD 20014, 301-496-7021.

13.864   POPULATION RESEARCH

Type of Assistance: Grants ranging from $1,458 to $788,229.

Applicant Eligibility: Individuals, nonprofit organizations, state and local governments.

Objective: To seek solutions to the fundamental problems of the reproductive processes; to develop and evaluate safer and more effective and convenient contraceptives; and to understand how population dynamics affects the health and well-being of individuals and society.

Contact: Office of Grants and Contracts, National Institute of Child Health and Human Development, National Institutes of Health, Bethesda, MD 20014, 301-496-5001.

13.865 RESEARCH FOR MOTHERS AND CHILDREN
Type of Assistance: Grants ranging from $1,405 to $732,633.
Applicant Eligibility: Individuals, nonprofit organizations, state and local governments.
Objective: To improve the health and well-being of mothers, children, and families as the key to assuring a healthy adult population. Research in this field studies the health problems of the period of life from conception through adolescence and centers on the major problems of pregnancy and infancy, developmental biology and nutrition, human learning and behavior, and mental retardation and developmental disabilities.
Contact: Office of Grants and Contracts, National Institute of Child Health and Human Development, National Institutes of Health, Bethesda, MD 20014, 301-496-5001.

13.866 AGING RESEARCH
Type of Assistance: Grants ranging from $5,000 to $398,222.
Applicant Eligibility: Individuals, nonprofit organizations, state and local governments.
Objective: To be responsible for biomedical, social, and behavioral research and research training directed toward greater understanding of the aging process, and the needs and problems of the elderly. The primary goal is to improve the health and well-being of the elderly through the development and application of new knowledge.
Contact: National Institute on Aging, National Institutes of Health, Bethesda, MD 20205, 301-496-5534.

13.867 RETINAL AND CHOROIDAL DISEASES RESEARCH
Type of Assistance: Grants ranging from $10,000 to $300,000.
Applicant Eligibility: Individuals, nonprofit organizations, state and local governments.
Objective: To support research and training to study how the retina responds to light and converts it into electrical signals that travel to the brain resulting in sight; to advance understanding of how the retina is damaged by diseases; to develop methods of prevention, early detection, and treatment of retinal diseases; and to develop animal models of various retinal diseases to facilitate laboratory and clinical research.
Contact: Associate Director for Extramural and Collaborative Programs, National Eye Institute, National Institutes of Health, Bethesda, MD 20014, 301-496-4903.

13.868 CORNEAL DISEASES RESEARCH
Type of Assistance: Grants ranging from $6,000 to $300,000.
Applicant Eligibility: Individuals, nonprofit organizations, state and local governments.

Objective: To reduce the impact of this leading cause of visual disability through improved methods of treatment, prevention, and diagnosis; to develop and test drugs and improve corneal surgery, and develop means for delivery of nutrients and medication to the cornea; and to provide base research on the structure and function of the cornea.

Contact: Director for Extramural and Collaborative Programs, National Eye Institute, National Institutes of Health, Bethesda, MD 20014, 301-496-4903.

13.869 CATARACT RESEARCH

Type of Assistance: Grants ranging from $10,000 to $300,000.

Applicant Eligibility: Individuals, nonprofit organizations, state and local governments.

Objective: To support research and training to identify the causes of cataract disorders and develop methods for its prevention and improved treatment.

Contact: Director for Extramural and Collaborative Programs, National Eye Institute, National Institutes of Health, Bethesda, MD 20014, 301-496-4903.

13.870 GLAUCOMA RESEARCH

Type of Assistance: Grants ranging from $10,000 to $300,000.

Applicant Eligibility: Individuals, nonprofit organizations, state and local governments.

Objective: To support research and training to determine the cause of glaucoma, develop techniques for prevention and detection of the disease, and improve methods of treatment.

Contact: Director for Extramural and Collaborative Programs, National Eye Institute, National Institutes of Health, Bethesda, MD 20014, 301-496-4903.

13.871 SENSORY AND MOTOR DISORDERS OF VISION RESEARCH

Type of Assistance: Grants ranging from $10,000 to $300,000.

Applicant Eligibility: Individuals, nonprofit organizations, state and local governments.

Objective: To support laboratory and clinical investigations of the optic nerve and the development and function of those activities of the brain and the eye muscles which make vision possible. Support is also provided for the development of rehabilitation techniques and vision substitution devices.

Contact: Director for Extramural and Collaborative Programs, National Eye Institute, National Institutes of Health, Bethesda, MD 20014, 301-496-4903.

13.878 SOFT TISSUE STOMATOLOGY AND NUTRITION RESEARCH

Type of Assistance: Grants ranging from $5,000 to $300,000.

Applicant Eligibility: Individuals, nonprofit organizations, and local governments.

Objective: To develop new knowledge that may lead to improved treatment and/or prevention of oral soft tissue diseases and conditions; to determine the effect of nutritional variation on development, function, and health of the oralfacial complex; to provide a better understanding of the structure and function of salivary glands and their secretions; and to determine the physiology, metabolism, and morphology of the mineralization process.

Contact: Extramural Programs, National Institute of Dental Research, National Institutes of Health, Bethesda, MD 20014, 301-496-7808.

13.879 MEDICAL LIBRARY ASSISTANCE

Type of Assistance: Grants ranging from $4,000 to $200,000.

Applicant Eligibility: Nonprofit organizations, state and local governments.

Objective: To improve health information services by providing funds to train professional personnel, strengthen library resources, support biomedical publications, and conduct research in ways of improving information transfer.

Contact: Extramural Programs, National Library of Medicine, Bethesda, MD 20209, 301-496-6131.

13.880 MINORITY ACCESS TO RESEARCH CAREERS

Type of Assistance: Grants ranging from $3,900 to $100,000.

Applicant Eligibility: Individuals, nonprofit organizations, state and local governments.

Objective: To assist minority institutions to train larger numbers of scientists and teachers in health-related fields; and to increase the number of minority students who can compete successfully for entry into graduate programs which lead to the Ph.D. degree in biomedical science fields.

Contact: Program Director, MARC Program, National Institute of General Medical Sciences, National Institutes of Health, Bethesda, MD 20014, 301-496-7941.

13.882 HYPERTENSION PROGRAM

Type of Assistance: Grants ranging from $16,000 to $1,079,977.

Applicant Eligibility: State governments.

Objective: To assist state health authorities in establishing and maintaining programs for screening, detection, diagnosis, prevention, and referral for treatment of hypertension, and follow-up on compliance with treatment prescribed.

Contact: Bureau of Community Health Services, Rm. 7A-42, Parklawn Building, 5600 Fishers Lane, Rockville, MD 20857, 301-443-2270.

13.884 GRANTS FOR RESIDENCY TRAINING IN GENERAL INTERNAL MEDICINE AND/OR GENERAL PEDIATRICS

Type of Assistance: Grants ranging from $54,000 to $517,004.
Applicant Eligibility: Nonprofit organizations, state and local governments.
Objective: Grants are made to promote the graduate education of physicians who plan to enter the practice of general internal medicine or general pediatrics.
Contact: Director, Division of Medicine, BHM, HRA, PHS/DHHS, Center Building, 3700 East-West Highway, Hyattsville, MD 20782, 301-436-6418.

13.886 GRANTS FOR PHYSICIAN ASSISTANT TRAINING PROGRAMS

Type of Assistance: Grants ranging from $37,453 to $437,117.
Applicant Eligibility: Nonprofit organizations, state and local governments.
Objective: To enable public or nonprofit private health or educational entities to meet the cost of projects; to plan, develop, and operate or maintain programs for the training of physician assistants.
Contact: Director, Division of Medicine, BHM, HRA, PHS/DHHS, Center Building, 3700 East-West Highway, Hyattsville, MD 20782, 301-436-6418.

13.887 MEDICAL FACILITIES CONSTRUCTION— PROJECT GRANTS

Type of Assistance: Grants ranging from $50,000 to $5,223,905.
Applicant Eligibility: Nonprofit organizations, state and local governments.
Objective: To assist projects to prevent or eliminate safety hazards in publicly or nonprofit privately owned or operated medical facilities, or to avoid noncompliance by such facilities with licensing or accreditation standards.
Contact: Division of Facilities, Financing, Bureau of Health Facilities, Financing, Compliance, and Conversion, HRA, PHS/DHHS, Center Building, 3700 East-West Highway, Hyattsville, MD 20782, 301-436-6880.

13.888 HOME HEALTH SERVICES AND TRAINING GRANT PROGRAM

Type of Assistance: Grants ranging from $10,000 to $200,000.
Applicant Eligibility: Nonprofit organizations, state and local governments.
Objective: To expand and develop home health agencies and services as defined under the Medicare programs, and to provide funds for the training of professional and paraprofessional personnel to provide home health services.
Contact: Home Health Care Administrator, Bureau of Community Health Services, Health Services Administration, DHHS, Rm. 7A-42, Parklawn Building, 5600 Fishers Lane, Rockville, MD 20857, 301-443-1360.

13.889 EXPANDED FUNCTION DENTAL AUXILIARY TRAINING PROGRAM

Type of Assistance: Grants ranging from $24,000 to $100,000.

Applicant Eligiblity: Nonprofit organizations, state and local governments.

Objective: To plan, develop and operate, or maintain programs for the training of expanded function dental facilities.

Contact: Professional Education Branch, Division of Dentistry, BHM, HRA, Rm. 1-16, Center Building, 3700 East-West Highway, Hyattsville, MD 20782, 301-436-6510.

13.890 GENETIC DISEASES TESTING AND COUNSELING SERVICES

Type of Assistance: Grants ranging from $10,000 to $400,000.

Applicant Eligibility: Nonprofit organizations, state and local governments.

Objective: To establish and operate voluntary genetic testing and counseling programs primarily in conjunction with other existing health programs.

Contact: Genetic Diseases Services Branch, MCH, Bureau of Community Health Services, Health Services Administration, PHS/DHHS, 5600 Fishers Lane, Rockville, MD 20857, 301-443-1080.

13.891 ALCOHOL RESEARCH CENTER GRANTS

Type of Assistance: Grants ranging from $177,524 to $716,642.

Applicant Eligibility: Nonprofit organizations, state and local governments.

Objective: To provide long-term support for multidisciplinary research efforts into the problems of alcohol use and alcoholism by coordinating the activities of investigators from biomedical, behavioral, and social science disciplines.

Contact: Division of Extramural Research, National Institute on Alcohol Abuse and Alcoholism, ADAMHA, DHHS, 5600 Fishers Lane, Rockville, MD 20857, 301-443-4375.

13.892 PREDICTION, DETECTION AND ASSESSMENT OF ENVIRONMENTALLY CAUSED DISEASES AND DISORDERS

Type of Assistance: Grants ranging from $20,000 to $1,283,000.

Applicant Eligibility: Nonprofit organizations, state and local governments.

Objective: To provide the scientific basis for effective forecasting technology. Identification of sources and understanding of the dynamics of transport and conversion of contaminants are key factors in the development of new knowledge necessary for the resolution of present and future environmentally induced health problems. New technologies, new chemical substances, and changing human exposure patterns must be identified and evaluated as rapidly and accurately as possible in order to protect the health of this and future generations. Technology surveillance and disease forecasting capabilities are an essential ingredient in this effort.

Contact: Director for Extramural Programs, National Institute of Environmental Health Sciences, P.O. Box 12233, Research Triangle Park, NC 27711, 919-755-4015.

13.893 MECHANISMS OF ENVIRONMENTAL DISEASES AND DISORDERS

Type of Assistance: Grants ranging from $17,000 to $1,036,000.

Applicant Eligibility: Individuals, nonprofit organizations, state and local governments.

Objective: To gain a thorough understanding of the mechanisms involved in environmental disease processes and to prevent or reduce disease caused by environmental agents. Developing an understanding of the biochemical and biological mechanisms of disease will contribute to the most efficient means of disease prevention; provide information regarding the relative susceptibility of people who are at higher risks by virtue of their genetic background, nutritional status, pre-existing disease state, or lifestyle; improve the ability to predict long-term chronic effects; contribute to the development of sensitive assay systems; improve the ability to extrapolate reliably the results of laboratory animal studies to man; and improve the capability of regulatory agencies to control general exposure to known hazards.

Contact: Director for Extramural Programs, National Institute of Environmental Health Sciences, P.O. Box 12233, Research Triangle Park, NC 27711, 919-755-4015.

13.894 ENVIRONMENTAL HEALTH RESEARCH AND MANPOWER DEVELOPMENT RESOURCES

Type of Assistance: Grants ranging from $92,000 to $1,879,000.

Applicant Eligibility: Nonprofit organizations, state and local governments.

Objective: To provide long-term support for broadly based multidisciplinary research and training in environmental health problems in Environmental Health Sciences Centers (EHS Centers), and Marine and Freshwater Biomedical Centers (MFB Centers). Overall, these centers are to serve as national focal points and resources for research and manpower development in health problems related to air, water, and food pollution; occupational and industrial neighborhood health and safety; heavy metal toxicity; agricultural chemicals hazards; the relationships of the environment to cancer, birth defects, behavioral anomalies, respiratory and cardiovascular diseases, and diseases of other specific organs; basic aspects of toxicity mechanisms, body defense mechanisms, and the influence of age, nutrition, and other factors in chemically induced injury and disease; and to increase the pool of trained research manpower in the environmental health sciences through support of individual and institutional National Research Service Awards. (NRSA).

Contact: Director for Extramural Programs, National Institute of Environmental Health Sciences, P.O. Box 12233, Research Triangle Park, NC 27711, 919-755-4015.

13.895 GRANTS FOR FACULTY DEVELOPMENT IN FAMILY MEDICINE

Type of Assistance: Grants ranging from $16,063 to $282,636.
Applicant Eligibility: Nonprofit organizations, state and local governments.
Objective: To increase the supply of physician faculty available to teach in family medicine programs and to enhance the pedagogical skills of faculty currently teaching in family medicine.
Contact: Director, Division of Medicine, BHM, HRA, PHS/DHHS, Center Building, 3700 East-West Highway, Hyattsville, MD 20782, 301-436-6418.

13.896 GRANTS FOR PREDOCTORAL TRAINING IN FAMILY MEDICINE

Type of Assistance: Grants ranging from $34,560 to $323,827.
Applicant Eligibility: Nonprofit organizations, state and local governments.
Objective: To assist schools of medicine and osteopathy in meeting the costs of projects to plan, develop, and operate (or participate in) professional pre-doctoral training programs in the field of family medicine.
Contact: Director, Division of Medicine, BHM, HRA, PHS, DHHS, Center Building, 3700 East-West Highway, Hyattsville, MD 20782, 301-436-6418.

13.897 RESIDENCY TRAINING IN THE GENERAL PRACTICE OF DENTISTRY

Type of Assistance: Grants ranging from $20,000 to $250,000.
Applicant Eligibility: Nonprofit organizations, state and local governments.
Objective: To plan, develop, and operate an approved residency program in the general practice of dentistry.
Contact: Professional Education Branch, Division of Dentistry, BHM, HRA, PHS/DHHS, Center Building, 3700 East-West Highway, Hyattsville, MD 20782, 301-436-6510.

13.898 ALCOHOLISM DEMONSTRATION/EVALUATION

Type of Assistance: Grants ranging from $49,918 to $274,326.
Applicant Eligibility: Nonprofit organizations, state and local governments.
Objective: To support exploratory studies and to gather, analyze, and evaluate information regarding the effectiveness of innovative or standard alcoholism prevention or treatment.
Contact: Division of Special Treatment and Rehabilitation Programs, National Institute on Alcohol Abuse and Alcoholism, ADAMHA, DHHS, 5600 Fishers Lane, Rockville, MD 20857, 301-443-6317.

13.899 ALCOHOL ABUSE PREVENTION DEMONSTRATION/EVALUATION

Type of Assistance: Grants ranging from $45,833 to $215,136.
Applicant Eligibility: Nonprofit organizations, state and local governments.

Objective: To support exploratory studies to gather, analyze, and evaluate information regarding the effectiveness of innovative or standard prevention projects and policies to reduce the occurrence of alcohol-related problems through means other than direct treatment or rehabilitation services.

Contact: Director, Division of Prevention, National Institute on Alcohol Abuse and Alcoholism, ADAMHA, PHS/DHHS, 5600 Fishers Lane, Rockville, MD 20857, 301-443-4733.

PUBLIC HEALTH SERVICE-3

13.961   PUBLIC HEALTH SPECIAL PROJECT GRANTS

Type of Assistance: Grants ranging from $4,023 to $205,848.

Applicant Eligibility: Nonprofit organizations and local governments.

Objective: To develop, strengthen, revise, or expand graduate public health programs in biostatistics or epidemiology, health administration, health planning, or health policy analysis and planning, environmental or occupational health, dietetics and nutrition, and maternal and child health.

Contact: Grants Management Officer, BHM, HRA, DHHS, Rm. 4-27, Center Building, 3700 East-West Highway, Hyattsville, MD 20782, 301-436-6564.

13.962   HEALTH ADMINISTRATION GRADUATE TRAINEESHIPS

Type of Assistance: Grants ranging from $27,720 to $326,770.

Applicant Eligibility: Nonprofit organizations and local governments.

Objective: To support eligible students enrolled in accredited graduate degree programs in health administration, hospital administration, or health policy analysis and planning.

Contact: Grants Management Officer, BHM, HRA, DHHS, Rm. 4-27, Center Building, 3700 East-West Highway, Hyattsville, MD 20782, 302-436-6564.

13.963   GRADUATE PROGRAMS IN HEALTH ADMINISTRATION

Type of Assistance: Grants averaging $123,750.

Applicant Eligibility: Nonprofit organizations and local governments.

Objective: To support accredited graduate educational programs in health administration, hospital administration, and health planning.

Contact: Grants Management Officer, BHM, HRA, DHHS, Rm. 4-27, Center Building, 3700 East-West Highway, Hyattsville, MD 20782, 301-436-6564.

13.964 TRAINEESHIPS FOR STUDENTS IN SCHOOLS OF PUBLIC HEALTH AND OTHER GRADUATE PUBLIC HEALTH PROGRAMS

Type of Assistance: Grants ranging from $9,730 to $613,675.
Applicant Eligibility: Nonprofit organizations, state and local governments.
Objective: To support traineeships for students in graduate educational programs in schools of public health or other public or nonprofit educational entities.
Contact: BHM, HRA, DHHS, Rm. 4-27, Center Building, 3700 East-West Highway, Hyattsville, MD 20782, 301-436-6564.

13.965 COAL MINERS' RESPIRATORY IMPAIRMENT TREATMENT, CLINICS AND SERVICES

Type of Assistance: Grants ranging from $30,000 to $150,000.
Applicant Eligibility: Nonprofit organizations, state and local governments.
Objective: To develop in areas high quality-oriented, integrated systems of care where there are significant numbers of active and inactive miners; to emphasize patient and family-member education to maximize the patient's ability for self-care; and to expand the local capacity to perform examination of miners seeking eligibility for black lung benefits.
Contact: Director, Regional Commissions Health Programs, Health Services Administration, Bureau of Community Health Services, DHHS, Rm. 7A-55, Parklawn Building, 5600 Fishers Lane, Rockville, MD 20857, 301-443-5033.

13.966 ALLIED HEALTH TRAINEESHIP GRANTS FOR ADVANCED TRAINING INSTITUTES (SHORT-TERM)

Type of Assistance: Grants ranging from $3,980 to $278,699.
Applicant Eligibility: Nonprofit organizations, state and local governments.
Objective: To provide support to public and nonprofit private entities which offer advanced training for allied health professions personnel to increase their preparedness for teaching, administrative, or supervisory positions in the field of allied health.
Contact: Grants Management Officer, BHM, HRA, DHHS, Rm. 4-27, Center Building, 3700 East-West Highway, Hyattsville, MD 20782, 301-436-6564.

13.967 ALLIED HEALTH TRAINEESHIP GRANTS FOR ADVANCED TRAINING (LONG-TERM)

Type of Assistance: Grants ranging from $2,627 to $146,678.
Applicant Eligibility: State and local governments.
Objective: To provide support for traineeship grants to public and nonprofit private colleges and universities which offer graduate programs to prepare allied health professionals as teachers, administrators, or supervisors.
Contact: Grants Management Officer, BHM, HRS, DHHS, Rm. 4-27, Cen-

ter Building, 3700 East-West Highway, Hyattsville, MD 20782, 301-436-6564.

13.968 ALLIED HEALTH PROFESSIONS POLICY GRANTS

Type of Assistance: Grants ranging from $655 to $399,919.
Applicant Eligibility: Nonprofit organizations, state and local governments.
Objective: To establish or improve recruitment, training, and retraining of allied health personnel; to establish state or regional systems to assure that allied health and nursing needs are met; and to establish career ladders and advancement programs for practicing allied health personnel.
Contact: Grants Management Officer, BHM, HRA, DHHS, Rm. 4-27, Center Building, 3700 East-West Highway, Hyattsville, MD 20782, 301-436-6564.

13.969 CURRICULUM DEVELOPMENT GRANTS

Type of Assistance: Grants ranging from $23,301 to $193,420.
Applicant Eligibility: Nonprofit organizations and local governments.
Objective: To assist health profession schools, allied health and nurse training institutions, or other public or nonprofit entities in the development and implementation of new course materials in applied nutrition, environmental health, geriatrics, and humanistic health care.
Contact: DHHS, Rm. 4-27, Center Building, 3700 East-West Highway, Hyattsville, MD 20782, 301-436-6564.

13.970 HEALTH PROFESSIONS RECRUITMENT PROGRAM FOR INDIANS

Type of Assistance: Grants ranging from $10,000 to $80,000.
Applicant Eligibility: Native Americans.
Objective: To identify Indians with a potential for education or training in the health professions and encouraging and assisting them to enroll in health or allied health profession schools.
Contact: Office of Grants and Contracts, Indian Health Service, Health Services Administration, PHS/DHHS, 5600 Fishers Lane, Rockville, MD 20857, 301-443-5204.

13.971 HEALTH PROFESSIONS PREPARATORY SCHOLARSHIP PROGRAM FOR INDIANS

Type of Assistance: Grants ranging from $5,000 to $12,000.
Applicant Eligibility: Native Americans.
Objective: To make scholarship grants to Indians for the purpose of completing compensatory preprofessional education to enable the recipient to qualify for enrollment or re-enrollment in a health profession school.
Contact: Office of Grants and Contracts, Indian Health Service, Health Services Administration, PHS, DHHS, 5600 Fishers Lane, Rockville, MD 20856, 301-443-5204.

13.972 HEALTH PROFESSIONS SCHOLARSHIP PROGRAM FOR INDIANS

Type of Assistance: Grants ranging from $25,000 to $100,000.
Applicant Eligibility: Native Americans.
Objective: To make scholarship grants to Indians and others for the purposes of completing health profession education. Upon completion, grantees are required to fulfill an obligated service payback requirement.
Contact: Office of Grants and Contracts, Indian Health Service, Health Services Administration, PHS/DHHS, 5600 Fishers Lane, Rockville, MD 20857, 301-443-5204.

13.973 SPECIAL GRANTS FOR FORMER NATIONAL HEALTH SERVICE CORPS MEMBERS TO ENTER PRIVATE PRACTICE

Type of Assistance: Grants up to $25,000.
Applicant Eligibility: Individuals.
Objective: To assist former National Health Service Corps members establish their own private practice in a health manpower shortage area.
Contact: National Health Service Corps, DHHS, P. O. Box 1838, Presidential Building, 6525 Bellcrest Road, Hyattsville, MD 20782, 301-436-5661.

13.974 FAMILY PLANNING SERVICES DELIVERY IMPROVEMENT RESEARCH GRANTS

Type of Assistance: Grants ranging from $15,000 to $200,000.
Applicant Eligibility: Local governments.
Objective: To provide techniques for service delivery improvement through demonstration projects, operational research, or technology development and technical assistance.
Contact: Health Services Administration, Bureau of Community Health Services, Office for Family Planning, DHHS, 5600 Fishers Lane, Rockville, MD 20857, 301-443-2430.

13.975 ADOLESCENT PREGNANCY PREVENTION AND SERVICES

Type of Assistance: Grants ranging from $10,000 to $1,000,000.
Applicant Eligibility: Nonprofit organizations, state and local governments.
Objective: To establish networks of community-based health, education, and social services for adolescents at risk of unintended pregnancies, for pregnant adolescents, and for adolescent parents.
Contact: Office of Adolescent Pregnancy Programs, Office of the Assistant Secretary for Health, DHHS, Rm. 725-H, 200 Independence Avenue, S.W., Washington, DC 20201, 202-472-9093.

13.976 HOSPITAL-AFFILIATED PRIMARY CARE CENTERS

Type of Assistance: Grants up to $150,000.

Applicant Eligibility: Nonprofit organizations, state and local governments.

Objective: To provide funds for the planning, development, and operation of hospital-affiliated primary care centers.

Contact: Associate Bureau Director, Home Health Services Program and Hospital-Affiliated Primary Care Centers, Rm. 7A-42, Parklawn Building, 5600 Fishers Lane, Rockville, MD 20857, 301-443-1360.

13.977 PREVENTIVE HEALTH SERVICE—VENEREAL DISEASE CONTROL GRANTS

Type of Assistance: Grants ranging from $30,000 to $2,340,000.

Applicant Eligibility: Nonprofit organizations and state governments.

Objective: The purpose of the venereal disease control program is to reduce morbidity and mortality by preventing cases and complications of these diseases. Project grants emphasize the development and implementation of national uniform control programs which focus on intervention activities to reduce the incidence of these diseases.

Contact: Director, Center for Disease Control, PHS/DHHS, 1600 Clifton Road, N.E., Atlanta, GA 30333, 404-329-3291.

13.978 PREVENTIVE HEALTH SERVICE—VENEREAL DISEASE RESEARCH, DEMONSTRATION, AND PUBLIC INFORMATION AND EDUCATION GRANTS

Type of Assistance: Grants ranging from $20,000 to $150,000.

Applicant Eligibility: Nonprofit organizations, state and local governments.

Objective: The purpose of the venereal disease research, demonstrations, and public information and education grants is to provide assistance to programs designed for the conduct of research, demonstrations, and public information and education for the prevention and control of venereal disease.

Contact: Director, Center for Disease Control, PHS/DHHS, 1600 Clifton Road, N.E., Atlanta, GA 30333, 404-329-3291.

13.980 PREVENTIVE HEALTH SERVICE— FLUORIDATION GRANTS

Type of Assistance: Grants ranging from $5,000 to $250,000.

Applicant Eligibility: Nonprofit organizations, state and local governments.

Objective: The purpose of the fluoridation grant program is to assist states and communities in promoting, implementing, and maintaining fluoridated water systems on a national basis.

Contact: Director, Center for Disease Control, PHS, DHHS, 1600 Clifton Road, N.E., Atlanta, GA 30333, 404-329-3291.

13.981 GRANTS FOR HEALTH EDUCATION—RISK REDUCTION

Type of Assistance: Grants ranging from $15,000 to $150,000.
Applicant Eligibility: State and local governments.
Objective: To assist state and local health agencies to plan, coordinate, and evaluate health education programs that emphasize personal choice in reducing the health risks of preventable conditions and certain chronic diseases.
Contact: Director, Bureau of Health Education, Center for Disease Control, PHS, DHHS, 1600 Clifton Road, N.E., Building 14, Rm. 1, Atlanta, GA 30333, 404-329-3111.

13.982 MENTAL HEALTH DISASTER ASSISTANCE AND EMERGENCY MENTAL HEALTH

Type of Assistance: Grants ranging from $7,000 to $462,000.
Applicant Eligibility: Nonprofit organizations, state and local governments.
Objective: Provision of supplemental emergency mental health counseling to individuals affected by major disasters, including the training of volunteers to provide such counseling.
Contact: Disaster Assistance and Emergency Mental Health Section, National Institute of Mental Health, 5600 Fishers Lane, Rockville, MD 20857, 301-443-4283.

13.984 GRANTS FOR ESTABLISHMENT OF DEPARTMENTS OF FAMILY MEDICINE

Type of Assistance: Grants (dollar amount not available).
Applicant Eligibility: Nonprofit organizations, state and local governments.
Objective: To assist in establishing and/or maintaining family medicine academic administrative units that are comparable in status, faculty, and curriculum to those of other clinical units at the applying school.
Contact: Director, Division of Medicine, BHM, HRA, PHS/DHHS, Center Building, 3700 East-West Highway, Hyattsville, MD 20782, 301-436-6418.

13.985 EYE RESEARCH—FACILITY CONSTRUCTION

Type of Assistance: Grants ranging from $75,000 to $500,000.
Applicant Eligibility: Nonprofit organizations.
Objective: To carry out a program of grants for public, nonprofit, vision research facilities.
Contact: Associate Director for Extramural and Collaborative Programs, National Eye Institute, National Institutes of Health, Bethesda, MD 20205, 301-496-4903.

13.986 HEALTH CARE TECHNOLOGY RESEARCH

Type of Assistance: Grants ranging from $35,000 to $250,000.
Applicant Eligibility: State and local governments, nonprofit organizations, and individuals.

Objective: To support research, demonstration, and evaluation activities designed to increase knowledge concerning the safety, effectiveness, efficiency, cost effectiveness, and social, ethical, and economical impacts of health care technologies.

Contact: Associate Director for Extramural Programs, National Center for Health Care Technology, Office of Health Research, Statistics and Technology, Public Health Service, DHHS, Rm. 17A-29, Parklawn Building, Rockville, MD 20587, 301-443-1820.

13.987 HEALTH PROGRAMS FOR REFUGEES

Type of Assistance: Grants (dollar amount not known).

Applicant Eligibility: State and local health agencies.

Objective: To assist states and localities in meeting the public needs of their refugee population and in providing general health assessments of refugees when necessary.

Contact: Associate Director, Bureau of State Agencies, Center for Disease Control, PHS, DHHS, Atlanta, GA 30333, 404-329-3773.

U.S. DEPARTMENT OF HOUSING AND URBAN DEVELOPMENT

HOUSING—FEDERAL HOUSING COMMISSIONER

14.103   INTEREST REDUCTION PAYMENTS— RENTAL AND COOPERATIVE HOUSING FOR LOWER-INCOME FAMILIES

Type of Assistance: Direct payments and guaranteed/insured loans up to $42,756.

Applicant Eligibility: Nonprofit organizations.

Objective: To provide good quality rental and cooperative housing for persons of low- and moderate-income by providing interest reduction payments in order to lower their housing costs.

Contact: Director, Multifamily Development Division, Office of Multifamily Housing Development, Department of Housing and Urban Development, Washington, DC 20410, 202-755-9280.

14.105   INTEREST REDUCTION—HOMES FOR LOWER-INCOME FAMILIES

Type of Assistance: Direct payments and guaranteed/insured loans up to $1,013 per year in interest subsidy payments per unit.

Applicant Eligibility: Individuals.

Objective: To make home ownership more readily available to lower-income families by providing interest reduction payments on a monthly basis to lenders on behalf of the lower-income families.

Contact: Director, Single Family Development Division, Office of Single Family Housing, Department of Housing and Urban Development, Washington, DC 20410, 202-755-6720.

14.108   REHABILITATION MORTGAGE INSURANCE

Type of Assistance: Guaranteed/insured loans up to $92,000.

Applicant Eligibility: Individuals.

Objective: To help families repair or improve, purchase and improve, or refinance and improve existing residential structures more than one year old.

Contact: Director, Single Family Development Division, Office of Single Family Housing, Department of Housing and Urban Development, Washington, DC 20410, 202-755-6720.

14.110   MOBILE HOME LOAN INSURANCE—FINANCING PURCHASE OF MOBILE HOMES AS PRINCIPAL RESIDENCES OF BORROWERS

Type of Assistance: Guaranteed/insured loans up to $18,000.

Applicant Eligibility: Individuals.

Objective: To make possible reasonable financing of mobile home purchases.

Contact: Director, Title I Insured and 312 Loan Servicing Division, Office of Single Family Housing, Department of Housing and Urban Development, Washington, DC 20410, 202-755-6880.

14.112   MORTGAGE INSURANCE— CONSTRUCTION OR SUBSTANTIAL REHABILITATION OF CONDOMINIUM PROJECTS

Type of Assistance: Guaranteed/insured loans up to $36,000.

Applicant Eligibility: Individuals.

Objective: To enable sponsors to develop condominium projects in which individual units will be sold to home buyers.

Contact: Office of Multifamily Housing Development, Department of Housing and Urban Development, Washington, DC 20410, 202-755-5720.

14.115   MORTGAGE INSURANCE—DEVELOPMENT OF SALES-TYPE COOPERATIVE PROJECTS

Type of Assistance: Guaranteed/insured loans (dollar amount not available).

Applicant Eligibility: Nonprofit organizations.

Objective: To make it possible for nonprofit cooperative ownership housing corporations or trusts to sponsor the development of new housing that will be sold to individual cooperative members.

Contact: Director, Elderly, Cooperatives and Health Facilities Division, Office of Multifamily Housing Development, Department of Housing and Urban Development, Washington, DC 20410, 202-755-6513.

14.116   MORTGAGE INSURANCE GROUP PRACTICE FACILITIES

Type of Assistance: Guaranteed/insured loans (dollar amount not available).

Applicant Eligibility: Nonprofit organizations.

Objective: To help develop group health practice facilities, and to insure lenders against loss on mortgage loans. These loans may be used to finance the construction or rehabilitation of facilities, including major movable equipment, for the provision of preventive, diagnostic, and treatment services by a medical, dental, optometric, osteopathic, or podiatric group.

Contact: Office of Multifamily Housing Development, Department of Housing and Urban Development, Washington, DC 20410, 202-755-5720.

14.117 MORTGAGE INSURANCE—HOMES

Type of Assistance: Guaranteed/insured loans up to $107,000.

Applicant Eligibility: Individuals.

Objective: To help families undertake home ownership, and to insure lenders against loss on mortgage loans. These loans may be used to finance the purchase of proposed, under-construction, or existing one to four-family housing, as well as to refinance debts on existing housing.

Contact: Director, Single Family Development Division, Office of Single Family Housing, Department of Housing and Urban Development, Washington, DC 20410, 202-755-6720.

14.118 MORTGAGE INSURANCE— HOMES FOR CERTIFIED VETERANS

Type of Assistance: Guaranteed/insured loans up to $67,000.

Applicant Eligibility: Individuals.

Objective: To help veterans undertake home ownership on a sound basis, and to insure lenders against loss on mortgage loans. These loans may be used to finance the purchase of proposed, under-construction, or existing single family housing, as well as to refinance debts on existing housing.

Contact: Director, Single Family Development Division, Office of Single Family Housing, Department of Housing and Urban Development, Washington, DC 20410, 202-755-6720.

14.119 MORTGAGE INSURANCE— HOMES FOR DISASTER VICTIMS

Type of Assistance: Guaranteed/insured loans up to $14,400.

Applicant Eligibility: Individuals.

Objective: To help victims of a major disaster undertake home ownership on a sound basis, and to insure lenders against loss on mortgage loans. These loans may be used to finance the purchase of proposed, under-construction, or existing single family housing for the occupant-mortgager who is a victim of a major disaster.

Contact: Director, Single Family Development Division, Office of Single Family Housing, Department of Housing and Urban Development, Washington, DC 20410, 202-755-6720.

14.120 MORTGAGE INSURANCE—HOMES FOR LOW- AND MODERATE-INCOME FAMILIES

Type of Assistance: Guaranteed/insured loans up to $42,000.

Applicant Eligibility: Individuals.

Objective: To make home ownership more readily available to families displaced by urban renewal or other government actions as well as other low-income and moderate-income families, and to insure lenders against loss on mortgage loans. These loans may be used to finance the purchase of proposed or existing low-cost one- to four-family housing or the rehabilitation of such housing.

Contact: Director, Single Family Development Division, Office of Single Family Housing, Department of Housing and Urban Development, Washington, DC 20410, 202-755-6720.

14.121   MORTGAGE INSURANCE—HOMES IN OUTLYING AREAS

Type of Assistance: Guaranteed/insured loans up to $75,000.

Applicant Eligibility: Individuals.

Objective: To help families purchase homes in outlying areas, and to insure lenders against loss on mortgage loans. These loans may be used to finance the purchase of proposed, under-construction, or existing one-family nonfarm housing, or new farm housing on five or more acres adjacent to a highway.

Contact: Director, Single Family Development Division, Office of Single Family Housing, Department of Housing and Urban Development, Washington, DC 20410, 202-755-6720.

14.122   MORTGAGE INSURANCE—HOMES IN URBAN RENEWAL AREAS

Type of Assistance: Guaranteed/insured loans up to $107,000.

Applicant Eligibility: Individuals.

Objective: To help families purchase or rehabilitate homes in urban renewal areas, and to insure lenders against loss on mortgage loans. These loans may be used to finance acquisition or rehabilitation of one- to eleven-family housing in approved urban renewal or code enforcement areas.

Contact: Director, Single Family Development Division, Office of Single Family Housing, Department of Housing and Urban Development, Washington, DC 20410, 202-755-6720.

14.123   MORTGAGE INSURANCE—HOUSING IN OLDER, DECLINING AREAS

Type of Assistance: Guaranteed/insured loans averaging $9,400.

Applicant Eligibility: Individuals.

Objective: To help families purchase or rehabilitate housing in older, declining urban areas, and to insure lenders against loss on mortgage loans. These loans may be used to finance the purchase, repair, rehabilitation, and construction of housing in older, declining urban areas where conditions are such that certain normal eligibility requirements for mortgage insurance under a particular program cannot be met. The property must be an acceptable risk, giving consideration to the need for providing adequate housing for low- and moderate-income families.

Contact: Director, Single Family Development Division, Office of Single

Family Housing, Department of Housing and Urban Development, Washington, DC 20410, 202-755-6720.

14.124 MORTGAGE INSURANCE—INVESTOR-SPONSORED COOPERATIVE HOUSING

Type of Assistance: Guaranteed/insured loans up to $36,000.
Applicant Eligibility: Individuals.
Objective: To provide good quality multifamily housing to be sold to nonprofit cooperatives, ownership housing corporations, or trusts, and to insure lenders against loss on mortgage loans. Insured mortgages may be used to finance the construction or rehabilitation of detached, semidetached, row, walk-up, or elevator-type structures with five or more units.
Contact: Office of Multifamily Housing Development, Department of Housing and Urban Development, Washington, DC 20410, 202-755-5720.

14.125 MORTGAGE INSURANCE—LAND DEVELOPMENT AND NEW COMMUNITIES

Type of Assistance: Guaranteed/insured loans (dollar amount not available).
Applicant Eligibility: Individuals.
Objective: To assist the development of large subdivisions or new communities on a sound economic basis, and to insure lenders against loss on mortgage loans. These loans may be used to assist in financing the purchase of land and the development of building sites for subdivisions or new communities including water and sewer systems, streets and lighting, and other installations needed for residential communities.
Contact: Director, Single Family Development Division, Office of Single Family Housing, Department of Housing and Urban Development, Washington, DC 20410, 202-755-6720.

14.126 MORTGAGE INSURANCE—MANAGEMENT-TYPE COOPERATIVE PROJECTS

Type of Assistance: Guaranteed/insured loans up to $36,000.
Applicant Eligibility: Nonprofit organizations.
Objective: To make it possible for nonprofit cooperative ownership housing corporations or trusts to acquire housing projects to be operated as management-type cooperatives, and to insure lenders against loss on mortgage loans. Insured mortgages may be used to finance construction, acquisition of existing, or rehabilitation of detached, semidetached, row, walk-up, or elevator-type housing consisting of five or more units.
Contact: Co-op and Condominium Branch, Department of Housing and Urban Development, Washington, DC 20410, 202-426-7191.

14.127   MORTGAGE INSURANCE—MOBILE HOME PARKS

Type of Assistance: Guaranteed/insured loans up to $14,000 per mobile home space.

Applicant Eligibility: Individuals.

Objective: To make possible the financing of construction or rehabilitation of mobile home parks, and to insure lenders against loss on mortgage loans. Insured mortgages may be used to finance the construction or rehabilitation of mobile home parks consisting of five or more spaces.

Contact: Multifamily Development Division, Office of Multifamily Housing Development, Department of Housing and Urban Development, Washington, DC 20410, 202-755-9280.

14.128   MORTGAGE INSURANCE—HOSPITALS

Type of Assistance: Guaranteed/insured loans (dollar amount not available).

Applicant Eligibility: Nonprofit organizations.

Object: To make possible the financing of hospitals, and to insure lenders against loss on mortgage loans. The loans may be used to finance the construction or rehabilitation of private nonprofit and proprietary hospitals including major movable equipment.

Contact: Office of Multifamily Housing Development, Department of Housing and Urban Development, Washington, DC 20410, 202-755-5720.

14.129   MORTGAGE INSURANCE—NURSING HOMES AND INTERMEDIATE CARE FACILITIES

Type of Assistance: Guaranteed/insured loans (dollar amount not available).

Applicant Eligibility: Individuals and nonprofit organizations.

Objective: To make possible financing for construction or rehabilitation of nursing homes and intermediate care facilities, to provide loan insurance to install fire safety equipment, and to insure lenders against loss on mortgage loans. Insured mortgages may be used to finance construction or renovation of facilities to accommodate 20 or more patients requiring skilled nursing care and related medical services, or those while not in need of nursing home care are in need of minimum but continuous care provided by licensed or trained personnel.

Contact: Office of Multifamily Housing Development, Department of Housing and Urban Development, Washington, DC 20410, 202-755-5720.

14.130   MORTGAGE INSURANCE— PURCHASE BY HOMEOWNERS OF FEE-SIMPLE TITLE FROM LESSORS

Type of Assistance: Guaranteed/insured loans up to $30,000 per family.

Applicant Eligibility: Individuals.

Objective: To help homeowners obtain fee-simple title to the property that they hold under long-term leases and on which their homes are located, and to insure lenders against loss on mortgage loans. These loans may be used to finance the purchase from lessors by homeowners of fee-simple title to property that is held under long-term leases and on which their homes are located.

Contact: Director, Single Family Development Division, Office of Single Family Housing, Department of Housing and Urban Development, Washington, DC 20410, 202-755-6720.

14.132 MORTGAGE INSURANCE—PURCHASE OF SALES-TYPE COOPERATIVE HOUSING UNITS

Type of Assistance: Guaranteed/insured loans up to $67,500.
Applicant Eligibility: Nonprofit organizations.
Objective: To make available good quality new housing for purchase by individual members of a housing cooperative, and to insure lenders against loss on mortgage loans. Insured mortgages may be used to finance purchase by a cooperative member of single family detached, semidetached, or row housing constructed under the sponsorship of a nonprofit cooperative with five or more units.
Contact: Co-op and Condominium Branch, Department of Housing and Urban Development, Washington, DC 20410, 207-426-7191.

14.133 MORTGAGE INSURANCE— PURCHASE OF UNITS IN CONDOMINIUMS

Type of Assistance: Guaranteed/insured loans up to $67,500.
Applicant Eligibility: Individuals.
Objective: To enable families to purchase units in condominium projects, and to insure lenders against loss on mortgage loans. These loans may be used to finance the acquisition of individual units in proposed or existing condominium projects containing four or more units.
Contact: Director, Single Family Development Division, Office of Single Family Housing, Department of Housing and Urban Development, Washington, DC 20410, 202-755-6720.

14.134 MORTGAGE INSURANCE—RENTAL HOUSING

Type of Assistance: Guaranteed/insured loans up to $36,000.
Applicant Eligibility: Individuals.
Objective: To provide good quality rental housing, and to insure lenders against loss on mortgage loans. Insured mortgages may be used to finance the construction or rehabilitation of rental detached, semidetached, row, walk-up, or elevator-type structures with five or more units.
Contact: Director, Multifamily Development Division, Office of Multifamily Housing Development, Department of Housing and Urban Development, Washington, DC 20410, 202-755-9280.

14.135 MORTGAGE INSURANCE—RENTAL HOUSING FOR MODERATE-INCOME FAMILIES

Type of Assistance: Guaranteed/insured loans up to $37,870.

Applicant Eligibility: Nonprofit organizations.

Objective: To provide good quality rental housing within the price range of low- and moderate-income families, and to insure lenders against loss on mortgage loans. Insured mortgages may be used to finance construction or rehabilitation of detached, semidetached, row, walk-up, or elevator-type rental housing containing five or more units.

Contact: Director, Multifamily Development Division, Office of Multifamily Housing Development, Department of Housing and Urban Development, Washington, DC 20410, 202-755-9280.

14.137 MORTGAGE INSURANCE—RENTAL AND COOPERATIVE HOUSING FOR LOW- AND MODERATE-INCOME FAMILIES, MARKET INTEREST RATE

Type of Assistance: Guaranteed/insured loans up to $35,480.

Applicant Eligibility: Individuals and nonprofit organizations.

Objective: To provide good quality rental or cooperative housing within the price range of low- and moderate-income families.

Contact: Director, Multifamily Development Division, Office of Multifamily Housing Development, Department of Housing and Urban Development, Washington, DC 20410, 202-755-9280.

14.138 MORTGAGE INSURANCE—RENTAL HOUSING FOR THE ELDERLY

Type of Assistance: Guaranteed/insured loans up to $34,846.

Applicant Eligibility: Individuals and nonprofit corporations.

Objective: To provide good quality rental housing for the elderly, and to insure lenders against loss on mortgages. Insured mortgages may be used to finance construction or rehabilitation of detached, semidetached, walk-up, or elevator-type rental housing designed for occupancy by elderly or handicapped individuals and consisting of eight or more units.

Contact: Director, Multifamily Development Division, Office of Multifamily Housing Development, Department of Housing and Urban Development, Washington, DC 20410, 202-755-9280.

14.139 MORTGAGE INSURANCE—RENTAL HOUSING IN URBAN RENEWAL AREAS

Type of Assistance: Guaranteed/insured loans up to $36,000.

Applicant Eligibility: Individuals.

Objective: To provide good quality rental housing in urban renewal areas, and to insure lenders against loss on mortgage loans. Insured mortgages may be used to finance proposed construction or rehabilitation of detached, semi-

detached, row, walk-up, or elevator-type rental housing, or finance purchase of properties which have been rehabilitated by a local public agency.
Contact: Director, Multifamily Development Division, Office of Multifamily Housing Development, Department of Housing and Urban Development, Washington, DC 20410, 202-755-9280.

14.140 MORTGAGE INSURANCE—SPECIAL CREDIT RISKS
Type of Assistance: Guaranteed/insured loans up to $18,000.
Applicant Eligibility: Individuals.
Objective: To make home ownership possible for low- and moderate-income families who cannot meet normal HUD requirements, and to insure lenders against loss on mortgage loans. These loans may be used to finance the purchase of new, existing, or substantially rehabilitated single family homes.
Contact: Director, Single Family Development Division, Office of Single Family Housing, Department of Housing and Urban Development, Washington, DC 20410, 202-755-6720.

14.141 NONPROFIT SPONSOR ASSISTANCE PROGRAM
Type of Assistance: Direct loans (dollar amount not available).
Applicant Eligibility: Nonprofit organizations.
Objective: To assist and stimulate prospective nonprofit sponsors to develop sound housing projects for the elderly or handicapped, and to make interest-free loans to nonprofit sponsors to cover 80 percent of preconstruction expenses for planning housing projects for the elderly or handicapped.
Contact: Director, Elderly, Cooperatives and Health Facilities Division, Office of Multifamily Housing Development, Department of Housing and Urban Development, Washington, DC 20410, 202-755-6142.

14.142 PROPERTY IMPROVEMENT LOAN INSURANCE FOR IMPROVING ALL EXISTING STRUCTURES AND BUILDING OF NEW NONRESIDENTIAL STRUCTURES
Type of Assistance: Guaranteed/insured loans up to $37,500.
Applicant Eligibility: Individuals.
Objective: To facilitate the financing of improvements to homes and other existing structures and the erection of new nonresidential structures, and to insure lenders against losses on loans. Insured loans may be used to finance alterations, repairs, and improvements for existing structures, and the erection of new nonresidential structures which substantially protect or improve the basic livability or utility of the properties.
Contact: Director, Title I Insured and 312 Loan Servicing Division, Office of Single Family Housing, Department of Housing and Urban Development, Washington, DC 20410, 202-755-6880.

14.146 LOW-INCOME HOUSING—ASSISTANCE PROGRAM (PUBLIC HOUSING)

Type of Assistance: Direct payments averaging $2,500 per unit.
Applicant Eligibility: Local governments.
Objective: To provide decent, safe, and sanitary housing and related facilities for families of low income through an authorized public housing agency.
Contact: Deputy Assistant Secretary for Public Housing and Indian Programs, Housing, Department of Housing and Urban Development, Washington, DC 20410, 202-755-6522.

14.147 LOW-INCOME HOUSING—HOME OWNERSHIP OPPORTUNITIES FOR LOW-INCOME FAMILIES

Type of Assistance: Direct payments (dollar amount not available).
Applicant Eligibility: Local governments.
Objective: To provide low-income families with the opportunity of owning their own homes through local public housing agencies.
Contact: Public Housing and Indian Programs, Housing, Department of Housing and Urban Development, Washington, DC 20410, 202-755-6522.

14.149 RENT SUPPLEMENTS—RENTAL HOUSING FOR LOWER-INCOME FAMILIES

Type of Assistance: Direct payments (dollar amount not available).
Applicant Eligibility: Individuals and nonprofit organizations.
Objective: To make good quality rental housing available to low-income families at a cost they can afford, and to make payments to owners of approved multifamily rental housing projects to supplement the partial rental payments of eligible tenants.
Contact: Director, Office of Multifamily Housing Management and Occupancy, Housing, Department of Housing and Urban Development, Washington, DC 20410, 202-755-5866.

14.151 SUPPLEMENTAL LOAN INSURANCE—MULTIFAMILY RENTAL HOUSING

Type of Assistance: Guaranteed/insured loans (dollar amount not available).
Applicant Eligibility: Individuals.
Objective: To finance additions and improvements to any multifamily project, group practice facility, hospital, or nursing home insured or held by HUD. Major movable equipment for nursing homes, or group practice facilities or hospitals may be covered by a mortgage under this program.
Contact: Director, Multifamily Development Division, Office of Multifamily Housing Development, Housing, Department of Housing and Urban Development, Washington, DC 20410, 202-755-9280.

14.152 MORTGAGE INSURANCE—EXPERIMENTAL HOMES

Type of Assistance: Guaranteed/insured loans ranging from $30,000 to $35,000.

Applicant Eligibility: Individuals.

Objective: To help finance, by providing mortgage insurance, the development of homes that incorporate new or untried construction concepts designed to reduce housing costs, raise living standards, and improve neighborhood design.

Contact: Assistant Secretary for Policy Development and Research, Department of Housing and Urban Development, 451 7th Street, S.W., Washington, DC 20410, 202-755-5544.

14.153 MORTGAGE INSURANCE—EXPERIMENTAL PROJECTS OTHER THAN HOUSING

Type of Assistance: Guaranteed/insured loans (dollar amount not available).

Applicant Eligibility: Individuals.

Objective: To provide mortgage insurance to help finance the development of group medical facilities or subdivisions or new communities that incorporate new or untried construction concepts intended to reduce construction costs, raise living standards, and improve neighborhood design.

Contact: Assistant Secretary for Policy Development and Research, Department of Housing and Urban Development, 415 7th Street, S.W., Washington, DC 20410, 202-755-0640.

14.154 MORTGAGE INSURANCE— EXPERIMENTAL RENTAL HOUSING

Type of Assistance: Guaranteed/insured loans averaging $2,314,814.

Applicant Eligibility: Individuals.

Objective: To provide mortgage insurance to help finance the development of multifamily housing that incorporates new or untried construction concepts designed to reduce housing costs, raise living standards, and improve neighborhood design.

Contact: Secretary for Policy Development and Research, Department of Housing and Urban Development, 451 7th Street, S.W., Washington, DC 20410, 202-755-5544.

14.155 MORTGAGE INSURANCE FOR THE PURCHASE OR REFINANCING OF EXISTING MULTIFAMILY HOUSING PROJECTS

Type of Assistance: Guaranteed/insured loans (dollar amount not available).

Applicant Eligibility: Individuals.

Objective: To provide mortgage insurance for the purchase or refinancing of existing multifamily housing projects, whether conventionally financed or subject to federally insured mortgages at the time of application for mortgage insurance.

Contact: Director, Office of Multifamily Housing Development, Multifamily Housing Development Division, Housing, Department of Housing and Urban Development, Washington, DC 20410, 202-755-9280.

14.156   LOWER-INCOME HOUSING ASSISTANCE PROGRAM (SECTION 8)

Type of Assistance: Direct payments (dollar amount not available).

Applicant Eligibility: Individuals, nonprofit organizations, state and local governments.

Objective: To aid lower-income families in obtaining decent, safe, and sanitary housing in private accommodations and to promote economically mixed existing, newly constructed, and substantially and moderately rehabilitated housing. Payments are used to make up the difference between the maximum approved rent due to the owner for the dwelling unit which is reasonable in relation to comparable market units and the occupant family's required contribution toward rent. Assisted families are required to contribute not less than 15 nor more than 25 percent of their adjusted family income toward rent.

Contact: Public Housing and Indian Programs, Department of Housing and Urban Development, Washington, DC 20410, 202-755-6522.

14.157   HOUSING FOR THE ELDERLY OR HANDICAPPED

Type of Assistance: Direct loans averaging $4,661,200.

Applicant Eligibility: Nonprofit organizations.

Objective: To provide for rental or cooperative housing and related facilities (such as central dining) for the elderly or handicapped. Loans may be used to finance the construction or rehabilitation of rental or cooperative detached, semidetached, row, walk-up or elevator-type structures.

Contact: Director, Elderly, Cooperative and Health Facilities Division, Office of Multifamily Housing Development, Department of Housing and Urban Development, Washington, DC 20410, 202-755-6142.

14.158   PUBLIC HOUSING—MODERNIZATION OF PROJECTS

Type of Assistance: Direct loans and direct payments (dollar amount not available).

Applicant Eligibility: State governments.

Objective: To provide annual contributions to modernize existing public housing projects to upgrade living conditions, correct physical deficiencies, and achieve operating efficiency and economy.

Contact: Public Housing and Indian Programs, Department of Housing and Urban Development, Washington, DC 20410, 202-755-6522.

14.159 SECTION 245 GRADUATED PAYMENT MORTGAGE PAYMENTS

Type of Assistance: Guaranteed/insured loans up to $67,500.
Applicant Eligibility: Individuals.
Objective: To facilitate early home ownership for households that expect their incomes to rise. Program allows homeowners to make smaller monthly payments initially and to increase their size gradually over time.
Contact: Director, Single Family Development Division, Office of Single Family Housing, Department of Housing and Urban Development, Washington, DC 20410, 202-755-6720.

14.161 SINGLE FAMILY HOME MORTGAGE COINSURANCE

Type of Assistance: Guaranteed/insured loans up to $67,500.
Applicant Eligibility: Individuals.
Objective: To help families undertake home ownership. Loans may be used to finance the purchase of proposed, under-construction, or existing one- to four-family housing, as well as to refinance debts on existing housing.
Contact: Director, Single Family Development Division, Office of Single Family Housing, Department of Housing and Urban Development, Washington, DC 20410, 202-755-6720.

14.162 MORTGAGE INSURANCE—COMBINATION AND MOBILE HOME LOT LOANS

Type of Assistance: Guaranteed/insured loans up to $36,500.
Applicant Eligibility: Individuals.
Objective: To make possible reasonable financing of mobile home purchase and the lot to place it on.
Contact: Director, Title I Insured and 312 Loan Servicing Division, Office of Single Family Housing, Department of Housing and Urban Development, Washington, DC 20410, 202-755-6880.

14.163 MORTGAGE INSURANCE—COOPERATIVE FINANCING

Type of Assistance: Guaranteed/insured loans up to $67,500.
Applicant Eligibility: Individuals.
Objective: To provide insured financing for the purchase of shares of stock in a cooperative project. Ownership of the shares carries the right to occupy a unit located within the cooperative project.
Contact: Director, Single Family Development Division, Office of Single Family Housing, Department of Housing and Urban Development, Washington, DC 20410, 202-755-6720.

14.164 OPERATING ASSISTANCE FOR TROUBLED MULTIFAMILY HOUSING PROJECTS

Type of Assistance: Grants and direct payments ranging from $20,000 to $1,700,000.

Objective: To provide assistance to restore or maintain the financial soundness, assist in the management, and maintain the low- to moderate-income character of certain projects assisted or approved for assistance under the National Housing Act or under the Housing and Urban Development Act of 1965.

Contact: Director, Management Operations Division, Office of Multifamily Housing Management and Occupancy, Department of Housing and Urban Development, Washington, DC 20410, 202-755-5866.

14.165 MORTGAGE INSURANCE—HOMES IN MILITARY IMPACTED AREAS

Type of Assistance: Guaranteed/insured loans up to $107,000.

Applicant Eligibility: Individuals.

Objective: To help families undertake home ownership in military impacted areas.

Contact: Director, Single Family Development Division, Office of Single Family Housing, Department of Housing and Urban Development, Washington, DC 20410, 202-755-7620.

COMMUNITY PLANNING AND DEVELOPMENT

14.203 COMPREHENSIVE PLANNING ASSISTANCE

Type of Assistance: Grants (dollar amount not available).

Applicant Eligibility: State and local governments.

Objective: To assist recipients to undertake comprehensive planning and management strategies which further the following national policy objectives: conservation and improvement of existing communities; expansion of housing, employment opportunities, and choices for the poor, minorities, and disadvantaged; and promotion of efficient and orderly growth and development that will prevent future conditions of distress.

Contact: Director, Office of Planning and Program Coordination, Community Planning and Development, Department of Housing and Urban Development, 451 7th Street, S.W., Washington, DC 20410, 202-755-6290.

14.207 NEW COMMUNITIES—LOAN GUARANTEES

Type of Assistance: Loan guarantees and grants ranging from $7,500,000 to $50,000,000.

Applicant Eligibility: State and local governments.

Objective: To encourage the development of well planned, diversified, and economically sound new communities, including major additions to existing communities.

Contact: General Manager, New Community Development Corporation, Department of Housing and Urban Development, 451 7th Street, S.W., Washington, DC 20410, 202-755-7920.

14.211 SURPLUS LAND FOR LOW- AND MODERATE-INCOME HOUSING

Type of Assistance: Sale, exchange, or donation of property.
Applicant Eligibility: State and local governments.
Objective: To make federal surplus land and/or property available at fair value that will be used predominately for low- or moderate-income housing and related commercial and industrial use.
Contact: Director, Office of Surplus Land and Housing, New Community Development Corporation, Department of Housing and Urban Development, 451 7th Street, S.W., Washington, DC 20410, 202-755-1862.

14.218 COMMUNITY DEVELOPMENT BLOCK GRANTS/ENTITLEMENT GRANTS

Type of Assistance: Grants (dollar amount not available).
Applicant Eligibility: State and local governments.
Objective: To develop viable urban communities, including decent housing and a suitable living environment, and expand economic opportunities, principally for persons of low and moderate income.
Contact: Community Planning and Development, Department of Housing and Urban Development, 451 7th Street, S.W., Washington, DC 20410, 202-755-6587.

14.219 COMMUNITY DEVELOPMENT BLOCK GRANTS/SMALL CITIES PROGRAM

Type of Assistance: Grants ranging from $100,000 to $1,600,000.
Applicant Eligibility: State and local governments.
Objective: To assist communities in providing decent housing and a suitable living environment, and expanded economic opportunities, principally for persons of low and moderate income.
Contact: Community Planning and Development, Department of Housing and Urban Development, 451 7th Street, S.W., Washington, DC 20410, 202-755-6587.

14.220 SECTION 312 REHABILITATION LOANS

Type of Assistance: Direct loans up to $200,000.
Applicant Eligibility: Individuals.
Objective: To promote the revitalization of neighborhoods by providing funds for rehabilitation of residential, commercial and other nonresidential properties.
Contact: Community Planning and Development, Office of Urban Rehabilitation, Department of Housing and Urban Development, 451 7th Street, S.W., Washington, DC 20410, 202-755-5970 or -5324.

14.221   URBAN DEVELOPMENT ACTION GRANTS

Type of Asistance: Grants ranging from $35,000 to $14,233,000.
Applicant Eligibility: State and local governments.
Objective: To assist severely distressed cities and urban counties in alleviating physical and economic deterioration through economic development, neighborhood revitalization, job creation, and strengthening of the tax base; and to assist cities and urban counties containing severely distressed pockets of poverty.
Contact: Office of Urban Development Action Grants, Community Planning and Development, Department of Housing and Urban Development, 451 7th Street, S.W., Washington, DC 20410, 202-472-3947.

14.222   URBAN HOMESTEADING

Type of Assistance: Sale, exchange, or donation of property.
Applicant Eligibility: State and local governments.
Objective: To provide home ownership to individuals and families and revitalize neighborhoods, and to provide one- to four-unit properties to units of general local government, states, or their designated public agencies, for use in an Urban Homesteading program. Homestead properties received from HUD must be conditionally conveyed without substantial consideration.
Contact: Director, Urban Homesteading Division, Office of Urban Rehabilitation and Community Reinvestment, Department of Housing and Urban Development, 451 7th Street, S.W., Washington, DC 20410, 202-755-5324.

14.223   INDIAN COMMUNITY DEVELOPMENT BLOCK GRANT PROGRAM

Type of Assistance: Grants ranging from $43,000 to $1,714,532.
Applicant Eligibility: Native Americans.
Objective: To assist Indian tribes and Alaskan Natives in the development of viable Indian communities principally for persons of low and moderate income.
Contact: Office of Policy Planning, Community Planning and Development, Department of Housing and Urban Development, 451 7th Street, S.W., Washington, DC 20410, 202-755-6092.

14.224   SECRETARY'S DISCRETIONARY FUND/COMMUNITY DEVELOPMENT DISASTER ASSISTANCE

Type of Assistance: Grants (dollar amount not available).
Applicant Eligibility: State and local governments.
Objective: To meet emergency community development needs caused by federally recognized disasters.
Contact: Office of Policy Planning, Community Planning and Development, Department of Housing and Urban Development, 451 7th Street, S.W., Washington, DC 20410, 202-755-6092.

14.225 SECRETARY'S DISCRETIONARY FUND/TERRITORIES PROGRAM

Type of Assistance: Grants (dollar amount not available).

Applicant Eligibility: U.S. Territories.

Objective: To provide assistance to Guam, the Virgin Islands, American Samoa, the Trust Territory of the Pacific Islands, and the Commonwealth of the Northern Marianas.

Contact: Office of Policy Planning, Community Planning and Development, Department of Housing and Urban Development, 451 7th Street, S.W., Washington, DC 20410, 202-755-6093.

14.226 SECRETARY'S DISCRETIONARY FUND/INNOVATIVE GRANTS PROGRAM

Type of Assistance: Grants (dollar amount not available).

Applicant Eligibility: State and local governments.

Objective: To provide an opportunity for HUD to award grants to states and units of local government for projects that test or demonstrate exemplary community development activities or techniques.

Contact: Office of Policy Planning, Community Planning and Development, Department of Housing and Urban Development, 451 7th Street, S.W., Washington, DC 20410, 202-755-6092.

14.227 SECRETARY'S DISCRETIONARY FUND/COMMUNITY DEVELOPMENT TECHNICAL ASSISTANCE GRANTS

Type of Assistance: Grants and direct payments ranging from $2,000 to $1,400,000.

Applicant Eligibility: States, local governments, profit and nonprofit organizations.

Objective: To help states, units of local government, Indian tribes, and areawide planning organizations to plan, develop, and administer block grant and urban development action grant programs.

Contact: Office of Policy Planning, Community Planning and Development, Department of Housing and Urban Development, 451 7th Street, S.W., Washington, DC 20410, 202-755-6092.

14.401 FAIR HOUSING ASSISTANCE PROGRAM

Type of Assistance: Grants up to $200,000.

Applicant Eligibility: State and local governments.

Objective: To provide to those agencies to whom HUD must refer Title VIII complaints both the incentives and resources required to develop an effective work force to handle complaints and provide technical assistance and training to assure that HUD-referred complaints are properly and efficiently handled.

Contact: Office of Fair Housing Enforcement and Section 3 Compliance, Department of Housing and Urban Development, 451 7th Street, S.W., Washington, DC 20410, 202-755-5518.

OFFICE OF POLICY DEVELOPMENT AND RESEARCH

14.506 GENERAL RESEARCH AND TECHNOLOGY ACTIVITY

Type of Assistance: Grants ranging from $150 to $500,000.

Applicant Eligibility: Nonprofit organizations, state and local governments.

Objective: To carry out applied research and demonstration projects of high priority and preselected by the Department to serve the needs of housing and community development groups and to improve the operations of the Department's programs.

Contact: Assistant Secretary for Policy Development and Research, Department of Housing and Urban Development, 451 7th Street, S.W., Washington, DC 20410, 202-755-8238.

NEIGHBORHOODS, VOLUNTARY ASSOCIATIONS AND CONSUMER PROTECTION

14.800 NEIGHBORHOOD SELF-HELP DEVELOPMENT

Type of Assistance: Grants ranging from $50,000 to $125,000.

Applicant Eligibility: State governments.

Objective: To assist neighborhood organizations to undertake specific housing, economic or community development, and other appropriate neighborhood conversion and revitalization projects in low- and moderate-income neighborhoods, and to increase the capacity of neighborhood organizations to utilize and coordinate resources available from the public and private sectors and from the residents and neighborhoods themselves.

Contact: Program Support Division, Office of Neighborhood Development, Department of Housing and Urban Development, 451 7th Street, S.W., Washington, DC 20410, 202-755-7970.

14.802 HOUSING COUNSELING PROGRAM

Type of Assistance: Grants ranging from $12,500 to $62,500.

Applicant Eligibility: State and local governments, and nonprofit organizations.

Objective: To counsel homeowners, homebuyers, and tenants under HUD-assisted, -owned and -insured housing programs in order to assure successful home ownership and rentership, and thereby prevent and reduce delinquencies, defaults, and foreclosures.

Contact: Housing Counseling Branch, Housing Consumer Programs Division, Office of Consumer Affairs, NVACP, Department of Housing and Urban Development, 451 7th Street, S.W., Washington, DC 20410, 202-755-6473.

14.803 CONGREGATE HOUSING SERVICES PROGRAM

Type of Assistance: Grants ranging from $50 to $80,000.

Applicant Eligibility: Public housing projects.

Objective: To prevent premature or unnecessary institutionalization of the elderly, elderly-handicapped, nonelderly-handicapped, and temporarily disabled; to provide a variety of innovative approaches that will improve the delivery of meals and nonmedical supportive services while utilizing existing service programs; and to fill gaps in existing service systems and insure availability of funding for meals and appropriate services needed to maintain independent living.

Contact: Community Services Branch, Office of Consumer Affairs, Department of Housing and Urban Development, Rm. 4140, 451 7th Street, S.W., Washington, DC 20410, 202-755-5356.

U.S. DEPARTMENT OF THE INTERIOR

BUREAU OF INDIAN AFFAIRS

15.103 INDIAN SOCIAL SERVICES— CHILD WELFARE ASSISTANCE

Type of Assistance: Direct payments ranging from $100 to $800 per child per month.

Applicant Eligibility: Native Americans.

Objective: To provide foster home care and appropriate institutional care for dependent, neglected, and handicapped Indian children residing on or near reservations, including those children living in jurisdictions under the Bureau of Indian Affairs in Alaska and Oklahoma, when these services are not available from state or local public agencies.

Contact: Division of Social Services, Office of Indian Services, Bureau of Indian Affairs, 18th and C Streets, N.W., Washington, DC 20245, 202-343-6434.

15.108 INDIAN EMPLOYMENT ASSISTANCE

Type of Assistance: Grants ranging from $800 to $5,500.

Applicant Eligibility: Native Americans.

Objective: To provide vocational training and employment opportunities for Indians.

Contact: Office of Tribal Resources Development, Division of Job Placement and Training, Bureau of Indian Affairs, Rm. 4659, 18th and C Streets, N.W., Washington, DC 20245, 703-235-8355.

15.113 INDIAN SOCIAL SERVICES—GENERAL ASSISTANCE

Type of Assistance: Direct payments up to $300 monthly.

Applicant Eligibility: Native Americans.

Objective: To provide assistance for living needs to needy Indians on or near reservations, including those Indians living in jurisdictions under the Bureau of Indian Affairs in Alaska and Oklahoma, when such assistance is not available from state or local public agencies.

Contact: Division of Social Services, Office of Indian Services, Bureau of Indian Affairs, 18th and C Streets, N.W., Washington, DC 20245, 202-343-6434.

15.114 HIGHER EDUCATION GRANT—COLLEGES AND UNIVERSITIES

Type of Assistance: Grants ranging from $200 to $7,000.
Applicant Eligibility: Native Americans.
Objective: To encourage Indian students to continue their education and training beyond high school.
Contact: Office of Indian Education Programs, Bureau of Indian Affairs, 18th and C Streets, N.W., Washington, DC 20245, 202-343-7387.

15.123 INDIAN LOANS—CLAIMS ASSISTANCE

Type of Assistance: Direct loans ranging from $500 to $250,000.
Applicant Eligibility: Native Americans.
Objective: To enable Indian tribes or identifiable groups of Indians without available funds to obtain expert assistance in the preparation and processing of claims pending before the U.S. Court of Claims.
Contact: Director, Office of Tribal Resources Development, Bureau of Indian Affairs, 19th Street and Constitution Avenue, N.W., Washington, DC 20245, 202-343-5324.

15.124 INDIAN LOANS—ECONOMIC DEVELOPMENT

Type of Assistance: Grants, direct loans, and guaranteed/insured loans ranging from $100 to $1,000,000.
Applicant Eligibility: Native Americans.
Objective: To provide assistance to Indians, Alaskan Natives, tribes, and Indian organizations to obtain financing from private and governmental sources which serve other citizens. When otherwise unavailable, financial assistance through the Bureau of Indian Affairs is provided to eligible applicants for any purpose that will promote the economic development of a federal Indian reservation.
Contact: Director, Office of Tribal Resources Development, Bureau of Indian Affairs, 19th Street and Constitution Avenue, N.W., Washington, DC 20245, 202-343-5324.

15.130 INDIAN EDUCATION—ASSISTANCE TO SCHOOLS

Type of Assistance: Direct payments ranging from $10,000 to $7,000,000.
Applicant Eligibility: Native Americans.
Objective: To assure adequate educational opportunities for Indian children attending public schools and tribally operated previously private schools.
Contact: Division of Elementary and Secondary Education, Office of Indian Education Programs, Bureau of Indian Affairs, 18th and C Streets, N.W., Washington, DC 20245, 202-343-8657.

15.142 SELF-DETERMINATION GRANTS—INDIAN TRIBAL GOVERNMENTS

Type of Assistance: Grants (dollar amount not available).

Applicant Eligibility: Native Americans.

Objective: To improve tribal governing capabilities; to prepare tribes for contracting of Bureau programs; to enable tribes to provide direction to the Bureau, and to have input to other federal programs intended to serve Indian people.

Contact: Division of Self-Determination Services, Office of Indian Services, Bureau of Indian Affairs, 18th and C Streets, N.W., Washington, DC 20245, 202-343-2706.

15.143 TRAINING AND TECHNICAL ASSISTANCE—INDIAN TRIBAL GOVERNMENTS

Type of Assistance: Grants (dollar amount not available).

Applicant Eligibility: Native Americans.

Objective: To aid Indian tribes to exercise self-determination; to provide training and technical assistance options; to help develop skills needed to utilize options; to enhance capability to contract for Bureau and other federal programs; to strengthen tribal government; to encourage personnel use options; and to improve capabilities to direct Bureau and other federal programs.

Contact: Division of Self-Determination Services, Office of Indian Services, Bureau of Indian Affairs, 18th and C Streets, N.W., Washington, DC 20245, 202-343-2706.

15.144 INDIAN CHILD WELFARE ACT—TITLE II GRANTS

Type of Assistance: Grants from $15,000 upward.

Applicant Eligibility: Local governments.

Objective: To promote the stability and security of Indian tribes and families by the establishment of minimum federal standards for the removal of Indian children from their families and the placement of such children in foster or adoptive homes; and to provide assistance to Indian tribes in the operation of child and family service programs.

Contact: Division of Social Services, Office of Indian Services, Bureau of Indian Affairs, 1951 Constitution Avenue, N.W., Washington, DC 20245, 202-343-6434.

OFFICE OF SURFACE MINING RECLAMATION AND ENFORCEMENT

15.250 REGULATION OF SURFACE COAL MINING AND SURFACE EFFECTS OF UNDERGROUND COAL MINING

Type of Assistance: Grants and direct payments ranging from $26,240 to $5,078,000.

Applicant Eligibility: State governments.

Objective: To protect society and the environment from the adverse effects of surface coal mining operations consistent with assuring the coal supply essential to the nation's energy requirements.

Contact: State Grants and Small Operator Assistance, State and Federal Programs, Office of Surface Mining Reclamation and Enforcement, Department of the Interior, 1951 Constitution Avenue, N.W., Washington, DC 20240, 202-343-5361.

15.251 GRANTS FOR MINING AND MINERAL RESOURCES AND RESEARCH INSTITUTES, MINERAL RESEARCH PROJECTS, SCHOLARSHIPS AND FELLOWSHIPS

Type of Assistance: Grants up to $270,000.

Applicant Eligibility: State governments.

Objective: To support research and training in mining and mineral resource problems related to the mission of the Department of the Interior; to contribute to a comprehensive nationwide program of mining and mineral research, with due regard for the protection and conservation of the environment; to support specific mineral research and demonstration projects of industrywide application; to assist the states in carrying on the work of competent and qualified mining and mineral resources research institutes; and to provide scholarships, graduate fellowships, and postdoctoral fellowships in mining and mineral resources, and allied fields.

Contact: Office of Surface Mining Reclamation and Enforcement, Department of the Interior, South Building, 1900 Constitution Avenue, N.W., Washington, DC 20240, 202-343-6912.

15.252 ABANDONED MINE LAND RECLAMATION PROGRAM

Type of Assistance: Grants (dollar amount not available).

Applicant Eligibility: State and local governments.

Objective: To protect the public and correct the environmental damage caused by coal- and noncoal-mining practices that occurred before August 3, 1977.

Contact: Office of Surface Mining, Division of Abandoned Mined Lands, Department of the Interior, 1951 Constitution Avenue, N.W., Washington, DC 20240, 202-343-4012.

HERITAGE CONSERVATION AND RECREATION SERVICE

15.400 OUTDOOR RECREATION—ACQUISITION, DEVELOPMENT AND PLANNING

Type of Assistance: Grants ranging from $150 to $5,450,000.
Applicant Eligibility: State governments.
Objective: To provide financial assistance to the states and their political subdivisions for the preparation of comprehensive statewide outdoor recreation plans and acquisition and development of outdoor recreation areas and facilities for the general public, to meet current and future needs.
Contact: Heritage Conservation and Recreation Service, State, Local and Urban Program, Department of the Interior, Washington, DC 20243, 202-343-5971.

15.411 HISTORIC PRESERVATION GRANTS-IN-AID

Type of Assistance: Grants ranging from $500 to $500,000.
Applicant Eligibility: State governments.
Objective: To expand and maintain the National Register of Historic Places—the nation's listing of districts, sites, buildings, structures, and objects significant in American history, architecture, archeology, and culture at the national, state, and local levels; to provide matching survey and planning grants-in-aid to assist in the identification, evaluation, and protection of historic properties; to provide matching acquisition and development grants-in-aid, through the states, to public and private parties for preservation for public benefit of National Register-listed properties; to provide matching grants-in-aid to the National Trust for Historic Preservation to assist in the accomplishment of its congressionally chartered responsibilities (63 Stat. 927) to preserve historic resources.
Contact: Chief, Grants Administration, Heritage Conservation and Recreation Service, Department of the Interior, Washington, DC 20243, 202-343-4941.

15.417 URBAN PARK AND RECREATION RECOVERY PROGRAM

Type of Assistance: Grants ranging from $12,500 to $2,100,000.
Applicant Eligibility: Local governments.
Objective: Federal grants to economically hard pressed communities specifically for the rehabilitation of critically needed recreation areas, facilities, and development of improved recreation programs for a period of five years.
Contact: Heritage Conservation and Recreation Service, State, Local and Urban Program, Department of the Interior, 440 G Street, N.W., Washington, DC 20243, 202-343-5971.

WATER AND POWER RESOURCES SERVICE

15.501 IRRIGATION DISTRIBUTION SYSTEM LOANS
Type of Assistance: Direct loans ranging from $3,760,000 to $7,980,000.
Applicant Eligibility: State governments.
Objective: To provide fully reimbursable federal loans to organized irrigation districts with lands included within congressionally authorized reclamation projects to plan, design, and construct irrigation and municipal and industrial water distribution or drainage systems in lieu of federal construction.
Contact: Bureau of Reclamation, Department of the Interior, Washington, DC 20240, 202-343-3125.

15.502 IRRIGATION SYSTEMS REHABILITATION AND BETTERMENT
Type of Assistance: Direct loans ranging from $1,900,000 to $8,300,000.
Applicant Eligibility: State governments.
Objective: To rehabilitate and improve irrigation facilities on projects governed by reclamation law.
Contact: Commissioner, Water and Power Resources Service, Department of the Interior, Washington, DC 20240, 202-343-5471.

15.503 SMALL RECLAMATION PROJECTS
Type of Assistance: Grants and direct loans ranging from $700,000 to $18,000,000.
Applicant Eligibility: State governments.
Objective: To provide fully reimbursable federal loans and possible grants to public nonfederal organizations for rehabilitation and betterment or construction of water resource development projects located in the 17 western-most contiguous states and Hawaii.
Contact: Bureau of Reclamation, Department of the Interior, Washington, DC 20240, 202-343-3125.

U.S. FISH AND WILDLIFE SERVICE

15.600 ANADROMOUS FISH CONSERVATION
Type of Assistance: Grants ranging from $6,000 to $632,800.
Applicant Eligibility: Individuals, nonprofit organizations, state and local governments.
Objective: To conserve, develop, and enhance the anadromous fish resources of the nation and the fish of the Great Lakes and Lake Champlain that ascend streams to spawn.
Contact: Fish and Wildlife Service, Department of the Interior, Washington, DC 20240, 202-343-6394.

15.603 FARM FISH POND MANAGEMENT (FARM POND STOCKING)

Type of Assistance: Donation of property and goods.
Applicant Eligibility: Individuals.
Objective: To serve as an impetus to farm pond construction and water conservation, to supply high-protein food, and to supply fish to stock new or reclaimed farm and ranch ponds.
Contact: Chief, Division of National Fish Hatcheries, Fish and Wildlife Service, Department of the Interior, Washington, DC 20240, 202-343-2197.

15.605 FISH RESTORATION

Type of Assistance: Grants ranging from $280,000 to $1,400,000.
Applicant Eligibility: State governments.
Objective: To support projects designed to restore and manage sport fish population for the preservation and improvement of sport fishing and related uses of these fisheries resources.
Contact: Division of Hatcheries and Fishery Resource Management, Fish and Wildlife Service, Department of the Interior, Washington, DC 20240, 202-343-2197.

15.611 WILDLIFE RESTORATION

Type of Assistance: Grants ranging from $501,440 to $3,998,480.
Applicant Eligibility: State governments.
Objective: To support projects to restore or manage wildlife populations and the provision of public use of these resources; and to provide facilities and services for conducting a hunter safety program.
Contact: Fish and Wildlife Service, Department of the Interior, Washington, DC 20240, 703-235-1526.

15.612 ENDANGERED SPECIES CONSERVATION

Type of Assistance: Grants ranging from $10,600 to $1,630,000.
Applicant Eligibility: State governments.
Objective: To provide federal financial assistance to any state, through its respective state agency, which has entered into a cooperative agreement to assist in the development of programs for the conservation of endangered and threatened species.
Contact: Fish and Wildlife Service, Department of the Interior, Washington, DC 20240, 703-235-1526.

15.613 MARINE MAMMAL GRANT PROGRAM

Type of Assistance: Grants (dollar amount not available).
Applicant Eligibility: State governments.
Objective: To provide financial assistance to states in development and implementation of programs for protection and management of marine mammals that inhabit a state's waters.

Contact: Division of Wildlife Management, Fish and Wildlife Service, Department of the Interior, Washington, DC 20240, 202-632-2202.

GEOLOGICAL SURVEY

15.802 MINERALS DISCOVERY LOAN PROGRAM
Type of Assistance: Direct loans up to $25,000.
Applicant Eligibility: Individuals.
Objective: To encourage exploration for specified minerals within the United States, its territories and possessions; and to contribute to the total allowable costs of exploration to a maximum of 75 percent for nine specified mineral commodities, and to a maximum of 50 percent for 27 others. Funds must be spent for the exploration of geologic targets considered to be favorable for the occurrence of deposits of ore of the specified commodities.
Contact: U.S. Geological Survey, Box 25046, MS 933, Denver, CO 80225, 303-234-2451.

NATIONAL PARK SERVICE

15.900 DISPOSAL OF SURPLUS WILDLIFE
Type of Assistance: Sale, exchange, or donation of property and goods.
Applicant Eligibility: Nonprofit organizations, state and local governments.
Objective: To obtain the maximum public benefit of animals surplus to agency needs by providing animals for restocking of wildlife ranges, zoo display animals, scientific specimens, and meat.
Contact: Chief, Division of Natural Resources, National Park Service, Department of the Interior, 18th and C Streets, N.W., Washington, DC 20240, 202-523-5127.

U.S. DEPARTMENT OF JUSTICE

LAW ENFORCEMENT ASSISTANCE ADMINISTRATION

16.534   LAW ENFORCEMENT ASSISTANCE—TRAINING

Type of Assistance: Grants ranging from $10,000 to $400,000.

Applicant Eligibility: Individuals, nonprofit organizations, state and local governments.

Objective: To upgrade the professionalism of criminal justice practitioners through training.

Contact: Office of Criminal Education and Training, Law Enforcement Assistance Administration, Department of Justice, Washington, DC 20531, 202-724-7677.

16.538   PUBLIC SAFETY OFFICERS' BENEFITS PROGRAM

Type of Assistance: Direct payment up to $50,000.

Applicant Eligibility: Individuals.

Objective: To provide a $50,000 death benefit to the eligible survivors of state and local public safety officers whose death is the direct and proximate result of a personal injury sustained in the line of duty on or after September 29, 1976.

Contact: Director, Public Safety Officers' Benefits Program, Law Enforcement Assistance Administration, Department of Justice, Washington, DC 20531, 202-724-7620.

16.540   JUVENILE JUSTICE AND DELINQUENCY PREVENTION—ALLOCATION TO STATES

Type of Assistance: Grants ranging from $6,250 to $225,000.

Applicant Eligibility: State governments.

Objective: To increase the capacity of state and local governments to conduct effective juvenile justice and delinquency prevention programs by providing matching grants to each state and territory; to develop guidelines for state plans that meet the requirements set forth in the Juvenile Justice and Delinquency Prevention Act of 1974 as amended, and to assist states in developing such plans.

Contact: Office of Juvenile Justice and Delinquency Prevention, Law Enforcement Assistance Administration, Department of Justice, Washington, DC 20531, 202-724-7753.

16.541 JUVENILE JUSTICE AND DELINQUENCY PREVENTION—SPECIAL EMPHASIS AND TECHNICAL ASSISTANCE PROGRAMS

Type of Assistance: Grants (dollar amount not available).

Applicant Eligibility: Individuals, nonprofit organizations, state and local governments.

Objective: To develop and implement programs that support effective approaches to preventing and controlling juvenile delinquency through community-based alternatives to traditional forms of official justice system processing; to improve the capability of public and private agencies to provide delinquency prevention services to youth and their families; to develop new approaches to reducing school dropouts, unwarranted suspensions and expulsions; to support groups and organizations committed to the legal rights and welfare of youth; to provide technical assistance to federal, state, and local governments, courts, public and private agencies, institutions, and individuals, in the planning, establishment, operation, or evaluation of juvenile delinquency programs; and to assist operating agencies having direct responsibilities for prevention and treatment of juvenile delinquency in meeting standards established through the Office of Juvenile Justice and Delinquency Prevention and the priorities for formula grant programs.

Contact: Office of Juvenile Justice and Delinquency Prevention, Law Enforcement Assistance Administration, Department of Justice, Washington, DC 20531, 202-724-7753.

16.542 NATIONAL INSTITUTE FOR JUVENILE JUSTICE AND DELINQUENCY PREVENTION

Type of Assistance: Grants (dollar amount not available).

Applicant Eligibility: Individuals and nonprofit organizations.

Objective: To encourage, coordinate, and conduct research and evaluation of juvenile justice and delinquency prevention activities; to provide a clearinghouse and information center for collecting, publishing, and distributing information on juvenile delinquency; to conduct a national training program; and to establish standards for the administration of juvenile justice.

Contact: Director, National Institute for Juvenile Justice and Delinquency Prevention, Law Enforcement Assistance Administration, Department of Justice, Washington, DC 20531, 202-724-7753.

BUREAU OF JUSTICE STATISTICS

16.553 PRIVACY AND SECURITY OF CRIMINAL JUSTICE SYSTEMS

Type of Assistance: Dissemination of technical information and grants ranging from $84,000 to $255,000.

Applicant Eligibility: Nonprofit organizations, state and local governments.

Objective: To provide assistance to criminal justice agencies in achieving compliance with federal and state privacy and security requirements, and to further the administration of criminal justice through assistance in the specific area of computer crime.

Contact: Privacy and Security Staff, Bureau of Justice Statistics, Department of Justice, Washington, DC 20531, 301-492-9036.

NATIONAL INSTITUTE OF JUSTICE

16.560   JUSTICE RESEARCH AND DEVELOPMENT PROJECT GRANTS

Type of Assistance: Dissemination of technical information and grants (dollar amount not available).

Applicant Eligibility: Individuals.

Objective: To encourage and support research and development to further understanding of the causes of crime and to improve the criminal justice system.

Contact: National Institute of Justice, Department of Justice, Washington, DC 20531, 301-492-9133.

16.561   NATIONAL INSTITUTE OF JUSTICE VISITING FELLOWSHIPS

Type of Assistance: Grants (dollar amount not available).

Applicant Eligibility: Individuals.

Objective: To provide opportunities for experienced criminal justice professionals to pursue promising new ideas for improved understanding of crime, delinquency, and criminal justice administration by sponsoring research projects of their own creation and design.

Contact: National Institute of Justice, Department of Justice, Washington, DC 20531, 301-492-9126.

15.562   LAW ENFORCEMENT RESEARCH AND DEVELOPMENT—GRADUATE RESEARCH FELLOWSHIPS

Type of Assistance: Grants up to $5,600 per year.

Applicant Eligibility: Local governments.

Objective: To enhance the criminal justice system by providing support to doctoral students engaged in dissertation research and writing.

Contact: National Institute of Justice, Department of Justice, Washington, DC 20531, 301-492-9104.

BUREAU OF PRISONS

16.601 CORRECTIONS—
TRAINING AND STAFF DEVELOPMENT

Type of Assistance: Dissemination of technical information and grants ranging from $1,500 to $300,000.

Applicant Eligibility: Individuals, nonprofit organizations, state and local governments.

Objective: To devise and conduct in various geographical locations, seminars, workshops, and training programs for law enforcement officers, judges and judicial personnel, probation and parole personnel, correctional personnel, welfare workers and other personnel, including lay ex-offenders and paraprofessionals, connected with the treatment and rehabilitation of criminal and and juvenile offenders; and to develop technical training teams to aid in the development of seminars, workshops, and training programs with the state and local agencies that work with prisoners, parolees, probationers, and other offenders.

Contact: Staff Development Branch, National Institute of Corrections, Department of Justice, Rm. 970, 320 First Street, N.W., Washington, DC 20534, 202-724-3106.

16.602 CORRECTIONS—RESEARCH AND EVALUATION

Type of Assistance: Specialized services and grants ranging from $1,500 to $200,000.

Applicant Eligibility: Individuals, nonprofit organizations, state and local governments.

Objective: To conduct, encourage, and coordinate research relating to corrections, including the causes, prevention, diagnosis, and treatment of criminal offenders; and to conduct evaluation programs that study the effectiveness of new approaches to improve the correction system.

Contact: Chief, Correctional Services Branch, National Institute of Corrections, Department of Justice, Rm. 970, 320 First Street, N.W., Washington, DC 20534, 202-724-3106.

16.603 CORRECTIONS—TECHNICAL ASSISTANCE

Type of Assistance: Specialized services and grants ranging from $1,500 to $50,000.

Applicant Eligibility: Individuals, nonprofit organizations, state and local governments.

Objective: To encourage and assist federal, state, and local government programs and services, and programs and services of other public and private agencies in their efforts to develop and implement improved corrections programs; and to serve in a consulting capacity to federal, state, and local courts, departments, and agencies in the development, maintenance, and coordination of programs, facilities, and services for training, treatment, and rehabilitation of criminal and juvenile offenders.

Contact: Administrative Assistant, National Institute of Corrections, Department of Justice, 320 First Street, N.W., Washington, DC 20534, 202-724-3106.

16.604 CORRECTIONS—POLICY FORMULATION

Type of Assistance: Specialized services and grants ranging from $1,500 to $75,000.

Applicant Eligibility: Individuals, nonprofit organizations, state and local governments.

Objective: To formulate and disseminate correctional policy, goals, standards, and recommendations for federal, state, and local correctional agencies, organizations, institutions, and personnel.

Contact: Director, National Institute of Corrections, Department of Justice, 320 First Street, N.W., Washington, DC 20534, 202-724-3106.

16.605 CORRECTIONS—CLEARINGHOUSE

Type of Assistance: Specialized services and grants ranging from $1,500 to $25,000.

Applicant Eligibility: Individuals, nonprofit organizations, state and local governments.

Objective: To serve as a clearinghouse and information center for the collection, preparation, and dissemination of information on corrections including, but not limited to, programs for the prevention of crime and recidivism, training of corrections personnel, and rehabilitation and treatment of criminal and juvenile offenders.

Contact: National Institute of Corrections, Department of Justice, Rm. 920, 320 First Street, N.W., Washington, DC 20534, 202-724-3106.

U.S. DEPARTMENT OF LABOR

EMPLOYMENT AND TRAINING ADMINISTRATION

17.207 EMPLOYMENT SERVICE
Type of Assistance: Specialized services and grants ranging from $1,151,575 to $42,075,242.
Applicant Eligibility: State governments.
Objective: To place persons in employment by providing a variety of placement-related services to job seekers and to employers seeking qualified individuals to fill job openings.
Contact: Director, Office of Plans, Policies, and Design, United States Employment Service, Employment and Training Administration, Department of Labor, Washington, DC 20213, 202-376-6650.

17.211 JOB CORPS
Type of Assistance: Grants ranging from $500,000 to $12,500,000.
Applicant Eligibility: Nonprofit organizations, state and local governments.
Objective: To assist young men and women who need and can benefit from an intensive educational and vocational training program in order to become more responsible, employable, and productive citizens. Operated in a residential group setting.
Contact: Director, Job Corps, Employment and Training Administration, Department of Labor, 601 D Street, N.W., Washington, DC 20213, 202-376-6995.

17.218 DOCTORAL DISSERTATION PROGRAM
Type of Assistance: Grants ranging from $2,500 to $26,000.
Applicant Eligibility: Nonprofit organizations.
Objective: To provide financial support for doctoral dissertation research in the employment and training field; and to assure the availability of manpower experts, specialists, and scholars to provide research and technical support as may be required at the national, state, and local level and for the development of policy and programs.
Contact: Social Science Research Council, Employment and Training Administration, Department of Labor, 1755 Massachusetts Avenue, N.W., #410, Washington, DC 20036, 202-376-7243.

17.219   INSTITUTIONAL GRANT PROGRAM
Type of Assistance: Grants ranging from $100,000 to $130,000.
Applicant Eligibility: Nonprofit organizations and state governments.
Objective: To assist academic institutions in developing human resources educational programs aimed at professionalizing state- and local-level employment and training staff, and assuring a future source of skilled planners, evaluators, and administrators.
Contact: Director, Office of Research and Development, Employment and Training Administration, Department of Labor, 601 D Street, N.W., Washington, DC 20213, 202-376-7335.

17.225   UNEMPLOYMENT INSURANCE
Type of Assistance: Grants and direct payments ranging from $754,404 to $120,139,683.
Applicant Eligibility: State governments.
Objective: To administer program of unemployment insurance for eligible workers through federal and state cooperation; to administer payment of worker adjustment assistance.
Contact: Administrator, Unemployment Insurance Service, Employment and Training Administration, Department of Labor, 601 D Street, N.W., Washington, DC 20210, 202-376-7032.

17.230   MIGRANT AND SEASONAL FARM WORKERS
Type of Assistance: Grants ranging from $100,000 to $3,000,000.
Applicant Eligibility: Nonprofit organizations, state and local governments.
Objective: To provide necessary employment, training, and supportive services to help migrant and seasonal farm workers and their families find economically viable alternatives to seasonal agricultural labor, and improve the lifestyle of seasonal agricultural workers who remain in the agricultural labor market.
Contact: Office of National Programs, Employment and Training Administration, Department of Labor, 601 D Street, N.W., Washington, DC 20213, 202-376-6128.

17.232   COMPREHENSIVE EMPLOYMENT
AND TRAINING PROGRAMS
Type of Assistance: Grants (dollar amount not available).
Applicant Eligibility: State and local governments.
Objective: To provide job training and employment opportunities for economically disadvantaged, unemployed, and underemployed persons, and to assure that training and other services lead to increased earnings and enhanced self-sufficiency by establishing a flexible decentralized system of federal, state, and local programs.
Contact: Employment and Training Administration, Department of Labor, 601 D Street, N.W., Washington, DC 20213, 202-376-6366.

17.233 EMPLOYMENT AND TRAINING RESEARCH AND DEVELOPMENT PROJECTS

Type of Assistance: Grants ranging from $1,000 to $1,000,000.

Applicant Eligibility: Individuals, nonprofit organizations, state and local governments.

Objective: To support employment and training studies to develop policy and programs for achieving the fullest utilization of the nation's human resources; to improve and strengthen the functioning of the nation's employment and training system; to develop new approaches to facilitate employment of the difficult to employ; and to conduct research and development addressing the employment implications of long-term social and economic trends and forces.

Contact: Director, Office of Research and Development, Employment and Training Administration, Department of Labor, 601 D Street, N.W., Washington, DC 20213, 202-376-7335.

17.234 EMPLOYMENT AND TRAINING— INDIANS AND NATIVE AMERICANS

Type of Assistance: Grants ranging from $50,000 to $7,500,000.

Applicant Eligibility: Native Americans.

Objective: To reduce the economic disadvantages among Indians and others of Native American descent and to advance the economic and social development of such people in accordance with their goals and lifestyles.

Contact: Office of Indian and Native American Programs, Employment and Training Administration, Department of Labor, 601 D Street, N.W., Washington, DC 20213, 202-376-6102.

17.235 SENIOR COMMUNITY SERVICE EMPLOYMENT PROGRAM

Type of Assistance: Grants (dollar amount not available).

Applicant Eligibility: Nonprofit organizations and state governments.

Objective: To provide, foster, and promote useful part-time work opportunities up to 20 hours per week in community service activities for low-income persons who are 55 years old and older and who have poor employment records.

Contact: Administrator, Office of National Programs for Older Workers, Employment and Training Administration, Department of Labor, Rm. 6122, 601 D Street, N.W., Washington, DC 20213, 202-376-6232.

17.241 YOUTH INCENTIVE ENTITLEMENT PILOT PROJECTS

Type of Assistance: Grants ranging from $700,000 to $25,000,000.

Applicant Eligibility: State and local governments.

Objective: The program is designed as a national experiment to test the impact on high school return, retention, and completion of a part-time school year and full-time summer job guarantee for all 16- to 19-year-old economically disadvantaged youth residing in a designated area who are in secondary school, or who are willing to return to school or enroll in a course leading to a certificate of high school equivalency; and to ascertain the longer-term impacts of the entitlement experience on the earnings of program participants subsequent to their completing or otherwise leaving high school.

Contact: Employment and Training Administration, Department of Labor, 601 D Street, N.W., Washington, DC 20213, 202-376-2649.

17.243 SPECIAL PROGRAMS AND ACTIVITIES FOR THE DISADVANTAGED

Type of Assistance: Grants ranging from $70,000 to $16,000,000.
Applicant Eligibility: Nonprofit organizations, state and local governments.
Objective: To provide, foster, and promote training and other employment-related services to groups with particular disadvantages in the labor market; to promote and foster new or improved linkages between the network of federal, state and local employment and training agencies and components of the private sector; and to carry out other special federal responsibilities under the Comprehensive Employment and Training Act.

Contact: Administrator, Office of National Programs, Employment and Training Administration, Department of Labor, 601 D Street, N.W., Washington, DC 20213, 202-376-6093.

EMPLOYMENT STANDARDS ADMINISTRATION

17.302 LONGSHOREMEN'S AND HARBOR WORKERS' COMPENSATION

Type of Assistance: Direct payments up to 66⅔ percent of average weekly wage.
Applicant Eligibility: Individuals.
Objective: To provide compensation for disability or death resulting from injury, including occupational disease, to longshoremen, harbor workers, and certain other employees engaged in maritime employment on navigable waters of the United States and the adjoining pier and dock areas; employees engaged in activities on the Outer Continental Shelf; employees of nonappropriated fund instrumentalities; employees of private employers engaged in work outside of the United States under contracts with the United States Government; and others as specified, including survivors of the above.

Contact: Office of Workers' Compensation Programs, Division of Longshoremen's and Harbor Workers' Compensation, Department of Labor, Washington, DC 20210, 202-523-8721.

17.307 COAL MINE WORKERS' COMPENSATION
Type of Assistance: Direct payments up to $508 monthly.
Applicant Eligibility: Individuals.
Objective: To provide benefits to coal miners who have become totally disabled due to coal workers' pneumoconiosis (CWP), and to widows and other surviving dependents of miners who have died of this disease or who were totally disabled from the disease at the time of death.
Contact: Division of Coal Mine Workers' Compensation, Office of Workers' Compensation Programs, Employment Standards Administration, Department of Labor, Washington, DC 20210, 202-523-6692.

BUREAU OF
INTERNATIONAL LABOR AFFAIRS

17.400 TRADE ADJUSTMENT ASSISTANCE—WORKERS
Type of Assistance: Specialized services and direct payments up to $250 per week.
Applicant Eligibility: Individuals.
Objective: To provide adjustment assistance to workers adversely affected by increase of imports of articles similar to or directly competitive with articles produced by such workers' firm.
Contact: Director, Office of Trade Adjustment Assistance, Bureau of International Labor Affairs, Department of Labor, Washington, DC 20210, 202-523-6225.

OCCUPATIONAL SAFETY
AND HEALTH ADMINISTRATION

17.500 OCCUPATIONAL SAFETY AND HEALTH
Type of Assistance: Dissemination of technical information, investigation of complaints, and grants (dollar amount not available).
Applicant Eligibility: Individuals, nonprofit organizations, and state governments.
Objective: To assure safe and healthful working conditions.
Contact: Assistant Secretary, Occupational Safety and Health Administration, Department of Labor, 200 Constitution Avenue, N.W., Washington, DC 20210, 202-523-6091.

MINE SAFETY AND HEALTH ADMINISTRATION

17.600   MINE HEALTH AND SAFETY GRANTS

Type of Assistance: Grants ranging from $24,426 to $1,229,297.
Applicant Eligibility: State governments.
Objective: To assist states in developing and enforcing effective mine health and safety laws and regulations, to improve state workmen's compensation and occupational disease laws and programs, and to promote federal-state coordination and cooperation in improving health and safety conditions.
Contact: State Grants Program Office, Mine Safety and Health Administration, Department of Labor, Ballston Towers No. 3, Arlington, VA 22203, 703-235-8264.

U.S. DEPARTMENT OF STATE

OFFICE OF THE LEGAL ADVISER

19.200 CLAIMS AGAINST FOREIGN GOVERNMENTS
Type of Assistance: Specialized services.
Applicant Eligibility: Individuals.
Objective: To obtain settlements of all legally valid claims of nationals of the United States against foreign governments. A claim may result from any one of a number of situations in which a national of the United States may be injured by a foreign government in violation of international law. It can, for example, be based upon a taking of property without payment of prompt, adequate, and effective compensation; other acts or omissions of governmental organs incompatible with international obligations; acts of individuals, insurgents, and mobs under circumstances establishing a lack of due diligence on the part of government officials; etc.
Contact: Assistant Legal Adviser for International Claims, Office of the Legal Adviser, Department of State, Washington, DC 20520, 202-632-1365.

19.201 PROTECTION OF SHIPS FROM FOREIGN SEIZURE
Type of Assistance: Insurance (dollar amount not available).
Applicant Eligibility: Individuals.
Objective: To reimburse a financial loss to owners of vessels registered in the United States for fines paid to secure the release of vessels seized for operation in waters which are not recognized as territorial waters by the United States.
Contact: Assistant Legal Adviser for International Claims, Office of the Legal Adviser, Department of State, Washington, DC 20520, 202-632-1365.

U.S. DEPARTMENT OF TRANSPORTATION

FEDERAL AVIATION ADMINISTRATION

20.105 LOAN GUARANTEES FOR PURCHASE OF AIRCRAFT AND SPARE PARTS

Type of Assistance: Guaranteed/insured loans ranging from $1,500,000 to $89,500,000.
Applicant Eligibility: Individuals.
Objective: To guarantee loans under certain conditions for the purchase of aircraft and spare parts.
Contact: Federal Aviation Administration, Office of Aviation Policy, Department of Transportation, APO3, 800 Independence Avenue, S.W., Washington, DC 20591, 202-426-3711.

FEDERAL HIGHWAY ADMINISTRATION

20.205 HIGHWAY RESEARCH, PLANNING, AND CONSTRUCTION

Type of Assistance: Grants ranging from $16,708,000 to $528,132,000.
Applicant Eligibility: State governments.
Objective: To assist state highway agencies in constructing and rehabilitating the Interstate highway system and building or improving primary, secondary, and urban systems roads and streets; to provide aid for their repair following disasters; to foster safe highway design; and to replace or rehabilitate unsafe bridges. Also provides for the improvement of some highways in Guam, the Virgin Islands, American Samoa, and the Northern Mariana Islands.
Contact: Federal Highway Administrator, Federal Highway Administration, Department of Transportation, Washington, DC 20590, 202-426-0650.

20.214 HIGHWAY BEAUTIFICATION—CONTROL OF OUTDOOR ADVERTISING AND CONTROL OF JUNKYARDS

Type of Assistance: Grants ranging from $6,750 to $1,125,950.
Applicant Eligibility: State governments.
Objective: To beautify highways and their vicinities.

Contact: Federal Highway Administrator, Federal Highway Administration, Department of Transportation, Washington, DC 20590, 202-426-0650.

20.216 HIGHWAY EDUCATIONAL GRANTS

Type of Assistance: Training and grants ranging from $250 to $6,000.
Applicant Eligibility: State and local governments.
Objective: To assist state and local agencies and the Federal Highway Administration (FHWA) in developing the expertise needed for implementation of their highway programs. The programs are intended to address identified training needs of state and local agencies and FHWA-identified national emphasis areas, which currently include highway safety, energy conservation, and civil rights.
Contact: Director, National Highway Institute, Federal Highway Administration, HHI-3, Washington, DC 20590, 202-426-3100.

FEDERAL RAILROAD ADMINISTRATION

20.303 GRANTS-IN-AID FOR RAILROAD SAFETY— STATE PARTICIPATION

Type of Assistance: Grants up to $22,000 per state inspector.
Applicant Eligibility: State governments.
Objective: To promote safety in all areas of railroad operations; to reduce railroad-related accidents; to reduce deaths and injuries to persons, and to reduce damage to property caused by accidents involving any carrier of hazardous materials by providing for state participation in the enforcement and promotion of safety practices.
Contact: Associate Administrator for Safety, Federal Railroad Administration, 400 7th Street, S.W., Washington, DC 20590, 202-426-0895.

20.308 LOCAL RAIL SERVICE ASSISTANCE

Type of Assistance: Grants ranging from $100,000 to $3,000,000.
Applicant Eligibility: State governments.
Objective: To maintain efficient local rail freight services. Grants may be used by states to assist in the continuation of local rail freight service on lines eligible to be abandoned by finding of the Interstate Commerce Commission pursuant to Section 803 of the Rail Revitalization and Regulatory Reform Act; grants may also be used for rehabilitation and improvement on lines certified by the railroad as having carried three million gross ton miles per mile or less during the prior year, state rail planning, and substitute service projects.
Contact: Office of State Assistance Programs, Federal Railroad Administration, Rm. 5404, RFA-30, 400 7th Street, S.W., Washington, DC 20590, 202-426-1677.

20.309   RAILROAD REHABILITATION AND IMPROVEMENT— GUARANTEE OF OBLIGATIONS

Type of Assistance: Guaranteed/insured loans ranging from $5,000,000 to $35,000,000.

Applicant Eligibility: Individuals, nonprofit organizations, state and local governments.

Objective: To provide financial assistance for the acquisition or rehabilitation and improvement of railroad facilities or equipment. Equipment and facilities include locomotives, freight cars, track, roadbed and related structures, communication and power transmission systems, signals, yard and terminal facilities and shop or repair facilities.

Contact: Office of National Freight Assistance Programs, Federal Railroad Administration, 400 7th Street, S.W., Washington, DC 20590, 202-426-9657.

20.310   RAILROAD REHABILITATION AND IMPROVEMENT— REDEEMABLE PREFERENCE SHARES

Type of Assistance: Direct loans ranging from $5,000,000 to $100,000,000.

Applicant Eligibility: Individuals.

Objective: To provide railroads with financial assistance for the rehabilitation and improvement of equipment and facilities or such other purposes approved by the Secretary of Transportation.

Contact: Office of National Freight Assistance Programs, Federal Railroad Administration, 400 7th Street, S.W., Washington, DC 20590, 202-426-9657.

URBAN MASS TRANSPORTATION ADMINISTRATION

20.500   URBAN MASS TRANSPORTATION CAPITAL IMPROVEMENT GRANTS

Type of Assistance: Grants ranging from $1,216 to $800,000,000.

Applicant Eligibility: Individuals, nonprofit organizations, state and local governments.

Objective: To assist in financing the acquisition, construction, reconstruction, and improvement of facilities and equipment for use, by operation, lease, or otherwise, in mass transportation service in urban areas, and in coordinating service with highway and other transportation in such areas.

Contact: Office of Transit Assistance, Office of Grants Assistance, Urban Mass Transportation Administration, 400 7th Street, S.W., Washington, DC 20590, 202-472-6976.

20.501 URBAN MASS TRANSPORTATION CAPITAL IMPROVEMENT LOANS

Type of Assistance: Direct loans (dollar amount not available).
Applicant Eligibility: Individuals, nonprofit organizations, state and local governments.
Objective: To finance the acquisition, construction, reconstruction, and improvement of facilities and equipment for use, by operation, lease, or otherwise, in mass transportation service in urban areas.
Contact: Office of Transit Assistance, Office of Grants Assistance, Urban Mass Transportation Administration, 400 7th Street, S.W., Washington, DC 20590, 202-426-6976.

20.502 URBAN MASS TRANSPORTATION GRANTS FOR UNIVERSITY RESEARCH AND TRAINING

Type of Assistance: Grants up to $100,000.
Applicant Eligibility: Individuals, nonprofit organizations, state and local governments.
Objective: To sponsor research studies and training in the problems of transportation in urban areas.
Contact: Office of Policy Research, Office of Policy, Budget, and Program Development, Urban Mass Transportation Administration, Department of Transportation, 400 7th Street, S.W., Washington, DC 20590, 202-426-0080.

20.503 URBAN MASS TRANSPORTATION MANAGERIAL TRAINING GRANTS

Type of Assistance: Grants ranging from $1,091 to $12,000.
Applicant Eligibility: Individuals.
Objective: To provide fellowships for training of managerial, technical, and professional personnel employed in the urban mass transportation field.
Contact: Director, Office of Transportation Management, Urban Mass Transportation Administration, Department of Transportation, 400 7th Street, S.W., Washington, DC 20590, 202-426-9274.

20.504 MASS TRANSPORTATION TECHNOLOGY

Type of Assistance: Grants (dollar amount not available).
Applicant Eligibility: Individuals, nonprofit organizations, state and local governments.
Objective: To obtain, in conventional bus and rail transit design, equipment manufacture, or construction, either substantial reductions in life-cycle costs without sacrificing performance, safety, or service capability, or substantial improvements in performance, safety, or service capability, in a cost-effective manner; to support selected high-risk, high-technology projects promising significant potential increases in productivity through the introduction of automation into transit operations where these initiatives are beyond the fi-

nancial or other capabilities of the private sector; and to support national priorities, such as central city revitalization, accessibility for the elderly and handicapped, energy conservation, and environmental protection.
Contact: Associate Administrator, Office of Technology Development and Deployment, Urban Mass Transportation Administration, Department of Transportation, 400 7th Street, S.W., Washington, DC 20590, 202-426-4052.

20.505   URBAN MASS TRANSPORTATION TECHNICAL STUDIES GRANTS

Type of Assistance: Grants ranging from $10,000 to $4,500,000.
Applicant Eligibility: State and local governments.
Objective: To assist in planning, engineering, and designing of urban mass transportation projects, and other technical studies in a program for a unified or officially coordinated urban transportation system.
Contact: Director, Office of Planning Assistance (UPM-10), Office of Planning, Management, and Demonstration, Urban Mass Transportation Administration, Department of Transportation, 400 7th Street, S.W., Washington, DC 20590, 202-426-2360.

20.506   URBAN MASS TRANSPORTATION DEMONSTRATION GRANTS

Type of Assistance: Grants (dollar amount not available).
Applicant Eligibility: Nonprofit organizations, state and local governments.
Objective: To demonstrate new, innovative techniques and methods in an operational environment that will reduce urban transportation problems and improve mass transportation service.
Contact: Director, Office of Service and Methods Demonstrations, Urban Mass Transportation Administration, Department of Transportation, 400 7th Street, S.W., Washington, DC 20590, 202-426-4995.

20.507   URBAN MASS TRANSPORTATION CAPITAL AND OPERATING ASSISTANCE FORMULA GRANTS

Type of Assistance: Grants (dollar amount not available).
Applicant Eligibility: Nonprofit organizations, state and local governments.
Objective: To assist in financing the acquisition, construction, and improvement of facilities and equipment for use by operation or lease or otherwise in mass transportation service, and the payment of operating expenses to improve or to continue such service by operation, lease, contract, or otherwise.
Contact: Office of Transit Assistance, Urban Mass Transportation Administration, Department of Transportation, 400 7th Street, S.W., Washington, DC 20590, 202-472-6976.

20.509 PUBLIC TRANSPORTATION FOR NONURBANIZED AREAS

Type of Assistance: Grants (dollar amount not available).
Applicant Eligibility: Nonprofit organizations, state and local governments.
Objective: To improve or continue public transportation service in rural and small urban areas by providing financial assistance for the acquisition, construction, and improvement of facilities and equipment and the payment of operating expenses by operating contract, lease, or otherwise.
Contact: Federal Highway Administration, Rural and Small Urban Areas Public Transportation Branch, Department of Transportation, 400 7th Street, S.W., Washington, DC 20590, 202-426-0153.

20.510 URBAN MASS TRANSPORTATION PLANNING METHODS RESEARCH AND DEVELOPMENT

Type of Assistance: Dissemination of technical information and grants (dollar amount not available).
Applicant Eligibility: Nonprofit organizations, state and local governments.
Objective: To develop and demonstrate improved transportation planning methods, both computerized and manual.
Contact: Office of Planning, Management and Demonstrations, Urban Mass Transportation Administration, Department of Transportation, 400 7th Street, S.W., Washington, DC 20590, 202-426-4031.

NATIONAL HIGHWAY TRAFFIC SAFETY ADMINISTRATION

20.600 STATE AND COMMUNITY HIGHWAY SAFETY

Type of Assistance: Grants ranging from $973,000 to $15,844,000.
Applicant Eligibility: State governments.
Objective: To provide a coordinated national highway safety program to reduce traffic accidents, deaths, injuries, and property damage.
Contact: Acting Director, Office of State Program Assistance, Traffic Safety Programs, National Highway Traffic Safety Administration, Washington, DC 20590, 202-426-0068.

U.S. DEPARTMENT OF THE TREASURY

INTERNAL REVENUE SERVICE

21.006 TAX COUNSELING FOR THE ELDERLY
Type of Assistance: Direct payments ranging from $1,762 to $744,585.
Applicant Eligibility: Nonprofit organizations.
Objective: To authorize the Internal Revenue Service to enter into agreement with private or public nonprofit agencies or organizations to establish a network of trained volunteers to provide free income tax information and return preparation assistance to elderly taxpayers.
Contact: Tax Counseling for the Elderly, Taxpayer Service Division, TX:T:1, Internal Revenue Service, 1111 Constitution Avenue, N.W., Washington, DC 20224, 202-566-4904.

OFFICE OF REVENUE SHARING

21.300 STATE AND LOCAL GOVERNMENT FISCAL ASSISTANCE—GENERAL REVENUE SHARING
Type of Assistance: Grants up to $289,402,174.
Applicant Eligibility: State and local governments.
Objective: To provide financial assistance to state and local governments. Revenue sharing funds may be used by a recipient government for any purpose which is a legal use of its own source revenues, pursuant to authorization of the governing body following two public hearings held specifically to permit the public to discuss possible uses of funds and a proposed budget of revenue sharing funds.
Contact: Intergovernmental Relations Division, Office of Revenue Sharing, Department of the Treasury, 2401 E Street, N.W., Washington, DC 20226, 202-634-5200.

APPALACHIAN REGIONAL COMMISSION

23.001 APPALACHIAN REGIONAL DEVELOPMENT
Type of Assistance: See individual Appalachian program descriptions for details.
Applicant Eligibility: Nonprofit organizations, state and local governments.
Objective: To stimulate substantial public investments in public facilities that will start the region on its way toward accelerated social and economic development; to help establish a set of institutions in Appalachia capable of permanently directing the long-term development of the region; and on a joint federal-state-local basis to develop comprehensive plans and programs to help accomplish the overall objectives of Appalachian development, including meeting the special demands created by the nation's energy needs and policies. This plan applies to designated counties in Alabama, Georgia, Maryland, Mississippi, New York, North Carolina, Ohio, Pennsylvania, South Carolina, Tennessee, and Virginia, and all counties in West Virginia.
Contact: Executive Director, Appalachian Regional Commission, 1666 Connecticut Avenue, N.W., Washington, DC 20235, 202-673-7874.

23.002 APPALACHIAN SUPPLEMENTS TO FEDERAL GRANTS-IN-AID (COMMUNITY DEVELOPMENT)
Type of Assistance: Grants ranging from $2,395 to $6,000,000.
Applicant Eligibility: Nonprofit organizations and state governments.
Objective: To meet the basic needs of local areas and assist in providing community development opportunities by funding such development facilities as water and sewer systems, sewage treatment plants, recreation centers, industrial sites and others. Grants may supplement other federal grants, or when sufficient federal funds are unavailable, funds may be provided entirely by this program.
Contact: Executive Director, Appalachian Regional Commission, 1666 Connecticut Avenue, N.W., Washington, DC 20235, 202-673-7874.

23.003 APPALACHIAN DEVELOPMENT HIGHWAY SYSTEM
Type of Assistance: Grants (dollar amount not available).
Applicant Eligibility: State governments.
Objective: To provide a highway system which, in conjunction with other federally aided highways, will open up areas with development potential within the Appalachian region where commerce and communications have been inhibited by lack of adequate access.
Contact: Executive Director, Appalachian Regional Commission, 1666 Connecticut Avenue, N.W., Washington, DC 20235, 202-673-7874.

23.004 APPALACHIAN HEALTH PROGRAMS
Type of Assistance: Grants ranging from $2,596 to $1,250,000.
Applicant Eligibility: Nonprofit organizations, state and local governments.
Objective: To provide a flexible approach to the development of health demonstration projects through community planning on a multicounty basis and implementation of that planning through service.
Contact: Executive Director, Appalachian Regional Commission, 1666 Connecticut Avenue, N.W., Washington, DC 20235, 202-673-7874.

23.005 APPALACHIAN HOUSING PROJECT PLANNING LOAN, TECHNICAL ASSISTANCE GRANT AND SITE DEVELOPMENT AND OFF-SITE IMPROVEMENT GRANT
Type of Assistance: Grants ranging from $155,000 to $1,692,681.
Applicant Eligibility: Nonprofit organizations, state and local governments.
Objective: To stimulate low- and moderate-income housing construction and rehabilitation, and to assist in developing site and off-site improvements for low- and moderate-income housing in the Appalachian region.
Contact: Executive Director, Appalachian Regional Commission, 1666 Connecticut Avenue, N.W., Washington, DC 20235, 202-673-7874.

23.008 APPALACHIAN LOCAL ACCESS ROADS
Type of Assistance: Grants ranging from $35,000 to $2,000,000.
Applicant Eligibility: Nonprofit organizations, state and local governments.
Objective: To provide access to industrial, commercial, educational, recreational, residential, and related transportation facilities which directly or indirectly relate to the improvement of the areas determined by the states to have significant development potential, and to meet the objectives stated under the program entitled Appalachian Regional Development.
Contact: Executive Director, Appalachian Regional Commission, 1666 Connecticut Avenue, N.W., Washington, DC 20235, 202-673-7874.

23.009 APPALACHIAN LOCAL DEVELOPMENT DISTRICT ASSISTANCE
Type of Assistance: Grants ranging from $6,045 to $705,369.
Applicant Eligibility: Local governments.
Objective: To provide planning and development resources in multicounty areas; to help develop the technical competence essential to sound development assistance; and to meet the objectives stated under the program entitled Appalachian Regional Development.
Contact: Executive Director, Appalachian Regional Commission, 1666 Connecticut Avenue, N.W., Washington, DC 20235, 202-673-7874.

23.010   APPALACHIAN MINE AREA RESTORATION

Type of Assistance: Grants ranging from $26,250 to $1,910,625.
Applicant Eligibility: Nonprofit organizations, state and local government.
Objective: To further the economic development of the region by rehabilitating areas presently damaged by deleterious mining practices and by controlling or abating mine drainage pollution.
Contact: Executive Director, Appalachian Regional Commission, 1666 Connecticut Avenue, N.W., Washington, DC 20235, 202-673-7874.

23.011   APPALACHIAN STATE RESEARCH, TECHNICAL ASSISTANCE, AND DEMONSTRATION PROJECTS

Type of Assistance: Grants ranging from $2,000 to $550,000.
Applicant Eligibility: State and local governments.
Objective: To expand the knowledge of the region to the fullest extent possible by means of state-sponsored research, including investigations, studies, technical assistance, and demonstration projects.
Contact: Executive Director, Appalachian Regional Commission, 1666 Connecticut Avenue, N.W., Washington, DC 20235, 202-673-7874.

23.012   APPALACHIAN VOCATIONAL AND OTHER EDUCATION FACILITIES AND OPERATIONS

Type of Assistance: Grants ranging from $1,420 to $1,300,000.
Applicant Eligibility: Nonprofit organizations, state and local governments.
Objective: To provide the people of the region with the basic facilities, equipment, and operating funds for training and education necessary to obtain employment at their best capability for available job opportunities.
Contact: Executive Director, Appalachian Regional Commission, 1666 Connecticut Avenue, N.W., Washington, DC 20235, 202-673-7874.

23.013   APPALACHIAN CHILD DEVELOPMENT

Type of Assistance: Grants ranging from $5,312 to $1,433,461.
Applicant Eligibility: Nonprofit organizations, state and local governments.
Objective: To create a state and substate capability for planning child development programs and a program to provide child development services in underserved areas throughout the region and to test innovative projects and programs for replicability.
Contact: Executive Director, Appalachian Regional Commission, 1666 Connecticut Avenue, N.W., Washington, DC 20235, 202-673-7874.

23.017   APPALACHIAN SPECIAL TRANSPORTATION-RELATED PLANNING, RESEARCH, AND DEMONSTRATION PROGRAM

Type of Assistance: Grants ranging from $3,360 to $100,000.
Applicant Eligibility: Nonprofit organizations, state and local governments.
Objective: To encourage the preparation of action-oriented plans and pro-

grams that reinforce and enhance transportation (particularly highway) investments.

Contact: Executive Director, Appalachian Regional Commission, 1666 Connecticut Avenue, N.W., Washington, DC 20235, 202-673-7874.

CIVIL AERONAUTICS BOARD

26.001 AIR CARRIER PAYMENTS
Type of Assistance: Direct payments ranging from $308,000 to $19,504,173.
Applicant Eligibility: Individuals.
Objective: To fix rates of subsidy compensation for development of air transportation to the extent and quality required for the commerce of the United States, the postal service, and the national defense. Payments are made to eligible certificated air carriers who have demonstrated a statutory need therefor. Subsidy is provided to cover the carrier's operating loss incurred under honest, economical, and efficient management and to provide it an opportunity to earn a fair return (after taxes) on investment used in air transportation services.
Contact: Director, Bureau of Domestic Aviation, B-60, Civil Aeronautics Board, 1825 Connecticut Avenue, N.W., Washington, DC 20428, 202-673-5319.

26.003 PAYMENTS FOR ESSENTIAL AIR SERVICES
Type of Assistance: Direct payments (dollar amount not available).
Applicant Eligibility: Individuals.
Objective: To provide essential air transportation to eligible communities by subsidizing air service. Payments are made to air carriers that are providing essential air services which would not be provided but for subsidy.
Contact: Director, Bureau of Domestic Aviation, B-60, Civil Aeronautics Board, 1825 Connecticut Avenue, N.W., Washington, DC 20428, 202-673-5319.

OFFICE OF PERSONNEL MANAGEMENT

27.012 INTERGOVERNMENTAL PERSONNEL GRANTS
Type of Assistance: Grants ranging from $1,200 to $1,000,000.
Applicant Eligibility: State and local governments.
Objective: To assist state and local governments and Indian tribal governments in strengthening their productivity and central management capabilities through programs to improve personnel systems; and to train professional, administrative, and technical employees and officials.
Contact: Deputy Assistant Director for Grants Administration, Office of Intergovernmental Personnel Programs, Office of Personnel Management, P.O. Box 14184, Washington, DC 20044, 202-632-6274.

EQUAL EMPLOYMENT OPPORTUNITY COMMISSION

30.002 EMPLOYMENT DISCRIMINATION—STATE AND LOCAL ANTIDISCRIMINATION AGENCY CONTRACTS

Type of Assistance: Grants ranging from $35,000 to $1,299,900.

Applicant Eligibility: State and local governments.

Objective: To assist the Equal Employment Opportunity Commission in the enforcement of Title VII of the Civil Rights Act of 1964, as amended, by attempting settlement and investigating and resolving charges of employment discrimination based on race, color, religion, sex, or national origin.

Contact: State and Local Division, Office of Field Services, Equal Employment Opportunity Commission, Room 4233, 2401 E Street, N.W., Washington, DC 20506, 202-634-6040.

30.005 EMPLOYMENT DISCRIMINATION—PRIVATE BAR PROJECT AND DEMONSTRATION CONTRACTS

Type of Assistance: Grants and direct payments (dollar amount not available).

Applicant Eligibility: Individuals.

Objective: To assist aggrieved individuals who have obtained notices of right to sue in contacting members of the private bar; to provide loans to aggrieved parties and their attorneys to pay the litigation costs involved in Title VII cases; to establish and revitalize the attorneys' referral mechanism; to provide technical assistance to the private bar; and to coordinate the strategies of the private bar with those of the Commission.

Contact: Support Programs, Office of General Council, Equal Employment Opportunity Commission, 2401 E Street, N.W., Washington, DC 20506, 703-634-6690.

30.009 EMPLOYMENT DISCRIMINATION PROJECT CONTRACTS—INDIAN TRIBES

Type of Assistance: Grants (dollar amount not available).

Applicant Eligibility: Local governments.

Objective: To insure the protection of employment rights of Indians working on reservations.

Contact: Office of Special Projects and Programs, Equal Employment Opportunity Commission, 2401 E Street, N.W., Washington, DC 20506, 703-634-6040.

FEDERAL TRADE COMMISSION

36.002   PUBLIC RULEMAKING PARTICIPATION

Type of Assistance: Direct payments ranging from $120 to $26,591.
Applicant Eligibility: Individuals.
Objective: To provide funds for the representation of certain interests in trade regulation rulemaking proceedings when the expense of participation would otherwise make such representation impossible.
Contact: Assistant for Public Participation, Office of the General Counsel, Federal Trade Commission, 6th and Pennsylvania Avenue, N.W., Washington, DC 20580, 202-523-3796.

FOREIGN CLAIMS SETTLEMENT COMMISSION OF THE UNITED STATES

37.005   CLAIMS OF PRISONERS OF WAR IN VIETNAM

Type of Assistance: Direct payments ranging from $5 to $13,000.

Applicant Eligibility: Individuals.

Objective: To provide compensation to members of the Armed Forces of the United States who were held as prisoners of war for any period of time during the Vietnam conflict by any force hostile to the United States.

Contact: Office of the General Counsel, Foreign Claims Settlement Commission of the United States, 1111 20th Street, N.W., Washington, DC 20579, 202-653-6166.

37.009   SECOND CHINA CLAIMS PROGRAM

Type of Assistance: Direct payments (dollar amount not available).

Applicant Eligibility: Individuals.

Objective: To provide for determination of the validity and amounts of outstanding claims against the People's Republic of China which arose out of the nationalization, expropriation, or other taking of property interests of nationals of the United States between November 6, 1966 and May 11, 1979 in China.

Contact: Office of the General Counsel, Foreign Claims Settlement Commission of the United States, 1111 20th Street, N.W., Washington, DC 20579, 202-653-6166.

GENERAL SERVICES ADMINISTRATION

39.002 DISPOSAL OF FEDERAL SURPLUS REAL PROPERTY
Type of Assistance: Sale, exchange, or donation of property and goods.
Applicant Eligibility: Individuals, nonprofit organizations, state and local governments.
Objective: To dispose of surplus real property. Surplus real property may be conveyed for public park or recreation use and public health or educational purposes at discounts up to 100 percent; public airport purposes; wildlife conservation; replacement housing; historic monument purposes without monetary consideration; and for general public purposes without restrictions at a price equal to the estimated fair market value of the property.
Contact: Office of Real Property, Federal Property Resource Service, General Services Administration, Washington, DC 20406, 703-557-1619.

39.003 DONATION OF FEDERAL SURPLUS PERSONAL PROPERTY
Type of Assistance: Sale, exchange, or donation of property and goods.
Applicant Eligibility: Nonprofit organizations, state and local governments.
Objective: To transfer surplus property to the states for distribution to state and local public agencies for public purposes or to certain nonprofit educational and public activities; to public airports; and to educational activities of special interest to the armed services. Surplus items are used by state and local public agencies for carrying out or promoting one or more public purposes, for residents of a given political area, such as conservation, parks and recreation, education, public health, public safety, and economic development; by certain nonprofit, tax-exempt educational or public health institutions or organizations; or by public airports for airport development, operation, or maintenance.
Contact: Director, Donation Division, Office of Personal Property, Federal Property Resources Service, General Services Administration, Washington, DC 20406, 703-557-3852.

39.006 NATIONAL HISTORICAL PUBLICATIONS AND RECORDS GRANTS
Type of Assistance: Grants ranging from $5,000 to $90,000.
Applicant Eligibility: Nonprofit organizations, state and local governments.
Objective: To carry out the National Historical Documents Program, which will help preserve important historical documents.
Contact: National Historical Publications and Records Commission, General Services Administration, Washington, DC 20408, 202-724-1083.

39.007 SALE OF FEDERAL SURPLUS PERSONAL PROPERTY

Type of Assistance: Sale, exchange, or donation of property and goods.

Applicant Eligibility: Individuals, nonprofit organizations, state and local governments.

Objective: To sell property no longer needed by the government in an economical and efficient manner and obtain the maximum net return from sales. General Services Administration conducts the sale of personal property for most of the civil agencies; the Department of Defense handles the sale of its own surplus property.

Contact: Director, Sales Division, Office of Personal Property, Federal Property Resources Service, General Services Administration, Washington, DC 20406, 703-557-3699.

NATIONAL CREDIT UNION ADMINISTRATION

44.001   CREDIT UNION CHARTER, EXAMINATION, SUPERVISION, AND INSURANCE

Type of Assistance: Specialized services and insurance (dollar amount not available).

Applicant Eligibility: Nonprofit organizations.

Objective: To offer to groups that have a common bond the opportunity to establish and operate their own credit unions.

Contact: National Credit Union Administration, Office of Examinations and Insurance, 1776 G Street, N.W., Washington, DC 20456, 202-357-1060.

NATIONAL FOUNDATION ON THE ARTS AND THE HUMANITIES

NATIONAL ENDOWMENT FOR THE ARTS

45.001 PROMOTION OF THE ARTS—DESIGN ARTS
Type of Assistance: Grants up to $20,000.
Applicant Eligibility: Individuals, nonprofit organizations, state and local governments.
Objective: To provide grants for projects including research, professional education, and public awareness in architecture, landscape architecture, and urban, interior, fashion, industrial, and environmental design. The program attempts to encourage creativity and to make the public aware of the benefits of good design.
Contact: Director, Design Arts Program, National Endowment for the Arts, 2401 E Street, N.W., Washington, DC 20506, 202-634-4276.

45.002 PROMOTION OF THE ARTS—DANCE
Type of Assistance: Grants ranging from $1,000 to $251,400.
Applicant Eligibility: Individuals, nonprofit organizations, state and local governments.
Objective: To assist dancers, choreographers, and dance organizations, and to make the highest-quality dance widely available.
Contact: Director, Dance Program, National Endowment for the Arts, 2401 E Street, N.W., Washington, DC 20506, 202-634-6383.

45.003 PROMOTION OF THE ARTS—ARTISTS-IN-EDUCATION
Type of Assistance: Grants ranging from $2,000 to $80,000.
Applicant Eligibility: Nonprofit organizations, state and local governments.
Objective: To provide grants for special innovative projects in arts education.
Contact: Director, Artists-in-Education Program, National Endowment for the Arts, 2401 E Street, N.W., Washington, DC 20506, 202-634-6028.

45.004 PROMOTION OF THE ARTS—LITERATURE
Type of Assistance: Grants ranging from $500 to $470,000.
Applicant Eligibility: Individuals, nonprofit organizations, state and local governments.

Objective: To provide fellowships for creative writers, and to support organizations devoted to development of the literary arts in America.
Contact: Director, Literature Program, National Endowment for the Arts, 2401 E Street, N.W., Washington, DC 20506, 202-634-6044.

45.005 PROMOTION OF THE ARTS—MUSIC

Type of Assistance: Grants ranging from $500 to $600,000.
Applicant Eligibility: Individuals, nonprofit organizations, state and local governments.
Objective: To support excellence in music performance and creativity and to develop informed audiences for music throughout the country.
Contact: Director, Music Program, National Endowment for the Arts, 2401 E Street, N.W., Washington, DC 20506, 202-634-6390.

45.006 PROMOTION OF THE ARTS—MEDIA ARTS: FILM/RADIO/TELEVISION

Type of Assistance: Grants ranging from $2,000 to $500,000.
Applicant Eligibility: Individuals, nonprofit organizations, state and local governments.
Objective: To provide grants in support of projects designed to assist individuals and groups to produce films, radio, and video of high aesthetic quality, and to exhibit and disseminate media arts. The Endowment also assists the American Film Institute, which carries out a number of assistance programs for film.
Contact: Director, Media Arts Program, National Endowment for the Arts, 2401 E Street, N.W., Washington, DC 20506, 202-634-6300.

45.007 PROMOTION OF THE ARTS—STATE PROGRAM

Type of Assistance: Grants ranging from $2,000 to $500,000.
Applicant Eligibility: State and local governments.
Objective: To assist state and regional public arts agencies in the development of programs for the encouragement of the arts and artists.
Contact: Directors, State Program, National Endowment for the Arts, 2401 E Street, N.W., Washington, DC 20506, 202-634-6055.

45.008 PROMOTION OF THE ARTS—THEATER

Type of Assistance: Grants ranging from $1,000 to $200,000.
Applicant Eligibility: Nonprofit organizations, state and local governments.
Objective: To provide grants to aid professional theater companies and organizations.
Contact: Director, Theater Program, National Endowment for the Arts, 2401 E Street, N.W., Washington, DC 20506, 202-634-6387.

45.009 PROMOTION OF THE ARTS—VISUAL ARTS
Type of Assistance: Grants ranging from $500 to $50,000.
Applicant Eligibility: Individuals, nonprofit organizations, state and local governments.
Objective: To provide grants to assist painters, sculptors, craftsmen, photographers, and printmakers; to support institutions devoted to the development of the visual arts in America.
Contact: Director, Visual Arts Program, National Endowment for the Arts, 2401 E Street, N.W., Washington, DC 20506, 202-634-1566.

45.010 PROMOTION OF THE ARTS—EXPANSION ARTS
Type of Assistance: Grants ranging from $1,000 to $70,000.
Applicant Eligibility: Nonprofit organizations, state and local governments.
Objective: To provide grants to professionally directed, community-based arts organizations involved with urban, suburban, and rural communities. Particular attention is given to those organizations that serve citizens—including ethnic minorities—whose cultural needs are not met by the major arts institutions.
Contact: Director, Expansion Arts Program, National Endowment for the Arts, 2401 E Street, N.W., Washington, DC 20506, 202-634-6010.

45.011 PROMOTION OF THE ARTS—INTER-ARTS
Type of Assistance: Grants ranging from $1,080 to $100,000.
Applicant Eligibility: Nonprofit organizations, state and local governments.
Objective: To provide grants for a limited number of special projects which do not fit other Endowment program guidelines, or projects which involve two or more art forms or program areas.
Contact: Director, Office of Inter-Arts, National Endowment for the Arts, 2401 E Street, N.W., Washington, DC 20506, 202-634-6020.

45.012 PROMOTION OF THE ARTS—MUSEUMS
Type of Assistance: Grants ranging from $370 to $500,000.
Applicant Eligibility: Individuals, nonprofit organizations, state and local governments.
Objective: To provide grants in support of American museums' essential activities. Grants may be used for mounting special exhibitions, utilization of collections, visiting specialists, conservation, training museum professions, renovation (climate control, security, storage), museum education, purchase of works by living American artists, and cataloguing.
Contact: Director, Museum Program, National Endowment for the Arts, 2401 E Street, N.W., Washington, DC 20506, 202-634-6164.

45.013 PROMOTION OF THE ARTS—CHALLENGE GRANTS
Type of Assistance: Grants ranging from $30,000 to $1,500,000.
Applicant Eligibility: Nonprofit organizations, state and local governments.

Objective: To enable cultural organizations and institutions to increase the levels of continuing support and to increase the range of contributors to the programs of such organizations or institutions; to provide administrative and management improvements for cultural organizations and institutions, particularly in the field of long-range financial planning; to enable cultural organizations and institutions to increase audience participation, and appreciation of programs sponsored by such organizations and institutions; to stimulate greater cooperation among cultural organizations and institutions especially designed to better serve the communities in which such organizations or institutions are located; and to foster greater citizen involvement in planning the cultural development of a community.

Contact: Challenge Grants Program, National Endowment for the Arts, 2401 E Street, N.W., Washington, DC 20506, 202-632-4783.

45.014   PROMOTION OF THE ARTS—FOLK ARTS

Type of Assistance: Grants ranging from $1,500 to $40,000.

Applicant Eligibility: Nonprofit organizations, state and local governments.

Objective: To provide grants to assist, foster, and make publicly available the diverse traditional American folk arts throughout the country, and to encourage projects involving those community- or family-based arts that have endured through several generations and that carry with them a sense of community aesthetic.

Contact: Director, Folk Arts Program, National Endowment for the Arts, 2401 E Street, N.W., Washington, DC 20506, 202-634-4282.

45.015   PROMOTION OF THE ARTS—OPERA AND MUSICAL THEATER

Type of Assistance: Grants ranging from $2,000 to $700,000.

Applicant Eligibility: Nonprofit organizations, state and local governments.

Objective: To support excellence in the performance and creation of professional opera and musical theater throughout the nation. Funds may be used to assist professional producing organizations of high artistic and managerial quality, and national service organizations.

Contact: Director, Opera/Musical Theater Program, National Endowment for the Arts, 2401 E Street, N.W., Washington, DC 20506, 202-634-7144.

45.020   PROMOTION OF THE ARTS—NATIONAL ENDOWMENT FELLOWSHIP PROGRAM

Type of Assistance: Grants up to $3,300 stipend plus round-trip travel.

Applicant Eligibility: Individuals, nonprofit organizations, state and local governments.

Objective: To provide a limited number of 13-week fellowships for professionals and students in arts administration and related fields. The internship is located at Endowment headquarters in Washington, DC. The program is designed to acquaint the participants with the policies, procedures, and operations of the Endowment and to give them an overview of arts activities in this country.

Contact: National Endowment Fellowship Program, National Endowment for the Arts, 2401 E Street, N.W., Washington, DC 20506, 202-634-6586.

NATIONAL ENDOWMENT FOR THE HUMANITIES

45.104   PROMOTION OF THE HUMANITIES—MEDIA HUMANITIES PROJECTS

Type of Assistance: Grants ranging from $4,000 to $1,500,000.

Applicant Eligibility: Nonprofit organizations, state and local governments.

Objective: To encourage and support radio and television production that advances public understanding and use of the humanities, including such fields as history, jurisprudence, literature, anthropology, philosophy, and archeology; is of the highest professional caliber both in terms of scholarship in the humanities and in terms of technical production; and is suitable for national or regional television broadcast and distribution, or for national, regional, or local radio broadcast.

Contact: Media Humanities Projects, Division of Public Programs, National Endowment for the Humanities, MS 403, Washington, DC 20506, 202-724-0318.

45.109   PROMOTION OF THE HUMANITIES—FELLOWSHIPS AND STIPENDS FOR THE PROFESSIONS

Type of Assistance: Grants up to $2,000 per month.

Applicant Eligibility: Individuals.

Objective: To advance public understanding and use of the humanities as a resource by giving professional leaders the opportunity to stand back from their work and explore a wide range of issues of national concern under the direction of scholars in the humanities, and to give teachers in law schools and medical and other health-care schools the opportunity to sharpen their understanding of the humanistic foundations of their fields and to improve their ability to convey this to their students and other scholars.

Contact: Program Officer for Fellowships for the Professions, Division of Fellowships, National Endowment for the Humanities, MS 101, Washington, DC 20506, 202-724-0376.

45.111   PROMOTION OF THE HUMANITIES—HIGHER EDUCATION/REGIONAL AND NATIONAL GRANTS

Type of Assistance: Grants ranging from $5,000 to $250,000.

Applicant Eligibility: Individuals, nonprofit organizations, state and local governments.

Objective: To promote the development and testing of imaginative approaches to education in the humanities by supporting projects that can be completed within a specified period of time. Most projects are planned and implemented by small groups of faculty, last one or two years, and are concerned with the design of model humanities programs intended for widespread use, the development of curriculum materials, and increased collaboration among educational and other cultural institutions. Projects also encourage excellence in teaching and promote serious attention to the central issues in the humanities by bringing groups of college faculty into residence at institutes for periods ranging from four to eight weeks or, in exceptional circumstances, longer for joint curriculum planning.

Contact: Assistant Director, Higher Education Projects, Education Programs, National Endowment for the Humanities, MS 202, Washington, DC 20506, 202-724-0311.

45.113 PROMOTION OF THE HUMANITIES— PROGRAM DEVELOPMENT

Type of Assistance: Grants ranging from $10,000 to $200,000.

Applicant Eligibility: Individuals, nonprofit organizations, state and local governments.

Objective: To encourage and support exemplary projects that demonstrate new ways of relating the humanities to new audiences. Projects must draw upon resources and scholars in the fields of the humanities. Priorities include projects undertaken by national organizations which bring humanities programming to members and affiliates, and projects using previously untested techniques for involving the public in programs examining the cultural, philosophical, and historical dimensions of contemporary society.

Contact: Program Development, Division of Special Programs, National Endowment for the Humanities, MS 401, Washington, DC 20506, 202-724-0398.

45.115 PROMOTION OF THE HUMANITIES—YOUTH GRANTS

Type of Assistance: Grants up to $15,000.

Applicant Eligibility: Individuals, nonprofit organizations, state and local governments.

Objective: To support humanities projects initiated and conducted by young persons. Grants are awarded for research, education, film, and community projects in one or more of the fields included in the humanities: history, philosophy, language, linguistics, literature, archaeology, jurisprudence, art history and criticism, and the humanistic social sciences. (Youth grants are not awarded to anyone over the age of 30.)

Contact: Director, Office of Youth Programs, MS 103, National Endowment for the Humanities, Washington, DC 20506, 202-724-0396.

45.116 PROMOTION OF THE HUMANITIES—SUMMER SEMINARS FOR COLLEGE TEACHERS

Type of Assistance: Grants ranging from $45,000 to $56,000.
Applicant Eligibility: Individuals.
Objective: To provide opportunities for teachers at undergraduate private and state colleges and junior and community colleges to work during the summer in their areas of interest under the direction of distinguished scholars at institutions with first-rate libraries.
Contact: Program Officer for Summer Seminars, Division of Fellowships, National Endowment for the Humanities, MS 101, Washington, DC 20506, 202-724-0376.

45.121 PROMOTION OF THE HUMANITIES— SUMMER STIPENDS

Type of Assistance: Grants for $2,500.
Applicant Eligibility: Individuals.
Objective: To provide time for uninterrupted study and research to scholars, teachers, writers, and other interpreters of the humanities, who have produced or demonstrated promise of producing significant contributions to humanistic knowledge.
Contact: Program Officer for Summer Stipends, Division of Fellowships, National Endowment for the Humanities, MS 101, Washington, DC 20506, 202-724-0376.

45.122 PROMOTION OF THE HUMANITIES—FELLOWSHIPS AT CENTERS FOR ADVANCED STUDY

Type of Assistance: Grants ranging from $15,400 to $150,000.
Applicant Eligibility: Individuals and nonprofit organizations.
Objective: To provide fellowships for study and research in the humanities to independent centers for advanced study in order to increase the opportunities for the uninterrupted and extended interchange of ideas which these centers make possible.
Contact: Humanist Administrator, Division of Fellowships, National Endowment for the Humanities, Washington, DC 20506, 202-724-0236.

45.123 PROMOTION OF THE HUMANITIES—CONSULTANT GRANT PROGRAM

Type of Assistance: Grants ranging from $500 to $10,000.
Applicant Eligibility: Individuals, nonprofit organizations, state and local governments.
Objective: The Consultant Grants Program is designed to assist college faculty and administrators in the planning of improvements in humanities curricula in context by furnishing expert consultants and supporting consequent costs.

Contact: Division of Education Programs, National Endowment for the Humanities, Washington, DC 20506, 202-724-1978.

45.124   PROMOTION OF THE HUMANITIES— RESEARCH RESOURCES

Type of Assistance: Grants ranging from $1,500 to $150,000.
Applicant Eligibility: Individuals, nonprofit organizations, state and local governments.
Objective: To fund, wholly or partially, projects that will improve and facilitate scholarly access to significant resources in order to contribute to greater knowledge and understanding of the humanities.
Contact: Director, Research Resources Programs, Division of Research Programs, National Endowment for the Humanities, MS 350, Washington, DC 20506, 202-724-0341.

45.125   PROMOTION OF THE HUMANITIES— MUSEUMS AND HISTORICAL ORGANIZATIONS HUMANITIES PROJECTS

Type of Assistance: Grants up to $50,000.
Applicant Eligibility: Individuals, state and local governments.
Objective: To assist museums and historical organizations to implement effective and imaginative programs which convey and interpret knowledge of America's and other nations' cultural legacies to the general public.
Contact: Humanities Projects and Museums and Historical Organizations Humanities Projects, Division of Public Programs, National Endowment for the Humanities, Washington, DC 20506, 202-724-0327.

45.127   PROMOTION OF THE HUMANITIES—ELEMENTARY AND SECONDARY EDUCATION PROGRAM

Type of Assistance: Grants ranging from $1,000 to $500,000.
Applicant Eligibility: Individuals, nonprofit organizations, state and local governments.
Objective: To promote the development and testing of imaginative approaches to precollegiate education in the humanities by supporting demonstration projects that can be completed within a specified period of time. Most projects are planned and implemented by groups of school and/or university faculty, last one to three years, and are concerned with the design of model courses or programs, teacher training institutes, or the development of curricular materials, including an emphasis on teacher training. Projects often involve increased collaboration between schools, higher education institutions, and cultural institutions. The division particularly seeks projects that show promise of serving as models for other institutions.
Contact: Assistant Director, Division of Education Programs, National Endowment for the Humanities, MS 202, Washington, DC 20506, 202-724-0373.

45.128 PROMOTION OF THE HUMANITIES—PLANNING AND ASSESSMENT STUDIES PROGRAM

Type of Assistance: Grants ranging from $3,000 to $100,000.

Applicant Eligibility: Individuals, nonprofit organizations, state and local governments.

Objective: To aid projects that address national humanistic concerns and that analyze the resources and needs in specific areas of the humanities, develop new sources of information that foster a more critical assessment of the humanities, and design, test, and implement tools for evaluation and policy analysis.

Contact: Director, Evaluation and Assessment Studies, Office of Planning and Policy Assessment, National Endowment for the Humanities, MS 303, Washington, DC 20506, 202-724-0369.

45.129 PROMOTION OF THE HUMANITIES— STATE PROGRAMS

Type of Assistance: Grants ranging from $309,000 to $390,000.

Applicant Eligibility: Nonprofit organizations and state governments.

Objective: To promote local humanities programming through renewable program grants to humanities councils within each of the states for the purpose of regranting funds to local organizations, institutions, and groups.

Contact: Director, Division of State Programs, National Endowment for the Humanities, MS 404, Washington, DC 20506, 202-724-0286.

45.130 PROMOTION OF THE HUMANITIES—CHALLENGE GRANT PROGRAM

Type of Assistance: Direct payments ranging from $2,000 to $1,500,000.

Applicant Eligibility: Nonprofit organizations, state and local governments.

Objective: To provide financial assistance to institutions that store, research, or disseminate the humanities; to broaden the base of financial support by "challenging" institutions to raise three private dollars for every federal grant dollar; to help secure financial stability in order to maintain existing services and resources.

Contact: Challenge Grant Program, National Endowment for the Humanities, MS 800, Washington, DC 20506, 202-724-0267.

45.132 PROMOTION OF THE HUMANITIES—RESEARCH MATERIALS: PUBLICATIONS

Type of Assistance: Grants ranging from $2,000 to $10,000.

Applicant Eligibility: Individuals and nonprofit organizations.

Objective: To ensure through grants to publishing entities the dissemination of works of scholarly distinction that without support could not be published.

Contact: Assistant Director, Division of Research Programs for Research Materials, National Endowment for the Humanities, MS 350, Washington, DC 20506, 202-724-1672.

45.133 PROMOTION OF THE HUMANITIES—SCIENCE, TECHNOLOGY AND HUMAN VALUES

Type of Assistance: Grants ranging from $15,000 to $300,000.
Applicant Eligibility: Individuals, nonprofit organizations, state and local governments.
Objective: To support a very limited number of projects that will serve as central references in the field of science values, or as models of scientist-humanist collaboration.
Contact: Coordinator, Program of Science, Technology and Human Values, National Endowment for the Humanities, MS 104, Washington, DC 20506, 202-724-0354.

45.134 PROMOTION OF THE HUMANITIES— RESEARCH CONFERENCES

Type of Assistance: Grants ranging from $5,200 to $10,000.
Applicant Eligibility: Individuals, nonprofit organizations, state and local governments.
Objective: To support conferences, symposia, and workshops that enable scholars to discuss and advance the current state of research on a particular topic or to consider means of improving conditions for research.
Contact: Program Officer, Research Conferences Program, Division of Research Programs, National Endowment for the Humanities, MS 350, Washington, DC 20506, 202-724-0226/0227.

45.135 PROMOTION OF THE HUMANITIES— YOUTH PROJECTS

Type of Assistance: Grants up to $5,000.
Applicant Eligibility: Individuals, nonprofit organizations, state and local governments.
Objective: To support humanities projects that provide educational opportunities beyond those of in-school programs for large groups of young people under the direction of experienced professionals in the humanities and professionals in youth work. These may be sponsored by educational, cultural, scholarly, civic, media, or youth organizations.
Contact: Director, Office of Youth Programs, National Endowment for the Humanities, MS 103, Washington, DC 20506, 202-724-0396.

45.137 PROMOTION OF THE HUMANITIES— DIVISION OF PUBLIC PROGRAMS, LIBRARIES HUMANITIES PROJECTS

Type of Assistance: Grants ranging from $5,000 to $400,000.
Applicant Eligibility: Nonprofit organizations, state and local governments.
Objective: To encourage public interest in libraries' humanities resources and stimulate their use through thematic programs, exhibits, media, publications, and other library activities.

Contact: Assistant Director for Libraries, Humanities Projects, Division of Public Programs, National Endowment for the Humanities, MS 406, Washington, DC 20506, 202-724-0760.

45.138 PROMOTION OF THE HUMANITIES—EDUCATION PILOT GRANTS

Type of Assistance: Grants ranging from $22,000 to $50,000.

Applicant Eligibility: Individuals, nonprofit organizations, state and local governments.

Objective: Pilot Grants are designed to support programs that will strengthen the humanities curriculum and thus effect general institutional changes. Such programs will be pervasive and long-range, rather than specific and of limited duration. It is primarily this factor that distinguishes such grants from those made in the project category.

Contact: Program Officer, Pilot Grants, MS 202, Division of Education Programs, National Endowment for the Humanities, Washington, DC 20506, 202-724-0393.

45.139 PROMOTION OF THE HUMANITIES—EDUCATION IMPLEMENTATION GRANTS

Type of Assistance: Grants ranging from $75,000 to $300,000.

Applicant Eligibility: Individuals, nonprofit organizations, state and local governments.

Objective: Implementation Grants are designed to assist in the full-scale development of programs that will strengthen the teaching of the humanities at individual institutions. Such programs will be pervasive and long-range, rather than specific and of limited duration.

Contact: Program Officer for Implementation Grants, MS 202, Division of Education Programs, National Endowment for the Humanities, Washington, DC 20506, 202-724-0393.

45.140 PROMOTION OF THE HUMANITIES— BASIC RESEARCH

Type of Assistance: Grants ranging from $5,000 to $300,000.

Applicant Eligibility: Individuals, nonprofit organizations, state and local governments.

Objective: To advance basic research that is interpretative in all fields of the humanities. Collaborative, interdisciplinary scholarship involving the efforts of several individuals at the professional, assistant, and clerical levels is encouraged as well as the use of innovative methodologies. Foreign and domestic archaeology projects are supported in the program.

Contact: Basic Research Program, Division of Research Programs, National Endowment for the Humanities, MS 350, Washington, DC 20506, 202-724-0276.

45.141 PROMOTION OF THE HUMANITIES—STATE, LOCAL, AND REGIONAL STUDIES

Type of Assistance: Grants ranging from $5,000 to $100,000.

Applicant Eligibility: Individuals, nonprofit organization, state and local governments.

Objective: To encourage the production of original narrative work relating to the history and customs of regions and communities in the United States drawing upon various disciplines in the humanities such as economics, history, politics, languages and literature, folklore, archaeology, and art history; and to encourage cooperation among scholars and citizens in developing and using the resources of the humanities.

Contact: Regional and Local History Program, Division of Research Programs, National Endowment for the Humanities, MS 350, Washington, DC 20506, 202-724-0276.

45.142 PROMOTION OF THE HUMANITIES—FELLOWSHIPS FOR INDEPENDENT STUDY AND RESEARCH

Type of Assistance: Grants up to $22,000.

Applicant Eligibility: Individuals.

Objective: To provide time for uninterrupted study and research to scholars, teachers, and other interpreters of the humanities who can make significant contributions to thought and knowledge in the humanities. The fellowships free applicants from the day-to-day responsibilities of teaching and other work for extended periods of uninterrupted, full-time study and research so that fellows may enlarge their contributions and continue to develop their abilities as scholars and interpreters of the humanities.

Contact: Program Officer for Fellowships for Independent Study and Research, Division of Fellowships, National Endowment for the Humanities, MS 101, Washington, DC 20502, 202-724-0333.

45.143 PROMOTION OF THE HUMANITIES—FELLOWSHIPS FOR COLLEGE TEACHERS

Type of Assistance: Grants up to $22,000.

Applicant Eligibility: Individuals.

Objective: To provide opportunities for college teachers to pursue full-time independent study and research that will enhance their abilities as teachers and interpreters of the humanities.

Contact: Division of Fellowships, National Endowment for the Humanities, MS 101, Washington, DC 20506, 202-724-0333.

45.144 PROMOTION OF THE HUMANITIES—RESIDENTIAL FELLOWSHIPS FOR COLLEGE TEACHERS

Type of Assistance: Grants up to $20,000.

Applicant Eligibility: Individuals.

Objective: To provide to undergraduate and two-year college teachers who

are concerned primarily with increasing their understanding of their fields, opportunities to work with distinguished scholars at universities with libraries and facilities suitable for advanced study and research.
Contact: Division of Fellowships, National Endowment for the Humanities, MS 101, Washington, DC 20506, 202-724-0333.

45.145 PROMOTION OF THE HUMANITIES—RESEARCH MATERIALS: TOOLS AND REFERENCE WORKS

Type of Assistance: Grants ranging from $2,500 to $300,000.
Applicant Eligibility: Individuals, nonprofit organizations, state and local governments.
Objective: To fund, wholly or partially, projects that create reference works and resources important for scholarly research as cultural documents.
Contact: Assistant Director, Division of Research Programs for Research Materials, National Endowment for the Humanities, MS 350, Washington, DC 20506, 202-724-1672.

45.146 PROMOTION OF THE HUMANITIES—RESEARCH MATERIALS: EDITIONS

Type of Assistance: Grants ranging from $2,500 to $200,000.
Applicant Eligibility: Individuals, nonprofit organizations, state and local governments.
Objective: To fund, wholly or partially, projects that create editions of materials important for scholarly research in the humanities and as cultural documents.
Contact: Assistant Director, Division of Research Programs for Research Materials, National Endowment for the Humanities, MS 350, Washington, DC 20506, 202-724-1672.

45.147 PROMOTION OF THE HUMANITIES—RESEARCH MATERIALS: TRANSLATIONS

Type of Assistance: Grants ranging from $2,500 to $300,000.
Applicant Eligibility: Individuals, nonprofit organizations, state and local governments.
Objective: To support the translation into English of texts and documents that will make an important contribution to research in the humanities and to greater public awareness of the traditions and achievements of other cultures.
Contact: Assistant Director, Division of Research Programs for Research Materials, National Endowment for the Humanities, MS 350, Washington, DC 20506, 202-724-1672.

45.148   PROMOTION OF THE HUMANITIES— INTERCULTURAL RESEARCH

Type of Assistance: Grants ranging from $50,000 to $200,000.
Applicant Eligibility: Nonprofit organizations.
Objective: To increase understanding of the traditions, culture, and values of foreign countries as a base for the study of contemporary international affairs, and to foster this nation's standing in international scholarship by providing support to American scholars to pursue research abroad in all fields of the humanities.
Contact: Assistant Director for Intercultural Research, MS 350, National Endowment for the Humanities, Washington, DC 20506, 202-724-0226.

45.149   PROMOTION OF THE HUMANITIES— RESEARCH RESOURCES, CONSERVATION AND PRESERVATION GRANTS

Type of Assistance: Grants ranging from $7,500 to $150,000.
Applicant Eligibility: Individuals and nonprofit organizations.
Objective: To fund projects that will promote the conservation and preservation of library and archival collections relative to the humanities in the United States.
Contact: Associate Director, Division of Research Programs for Research Resources, MS 350, National Endowment for the Humanities, Washington, DC 20506, 202-724-0341.

FEDERAL COUNCIL ON THE ARTS AND THE HUMANITIES

45.201   ARTS AND ARTIFACTS INDEMNITY

Type of Assistance: Insurance ranging from $500,000 to $50,000,000.
Applicant Eligibility: Individuals, nonprofit organizations, state and local governments.
Objective: To provide for indemnification against loss or damage for eligible art works, artifacts, and objects when borrowed from abroad on exhibition in the U.S.; and from the U.S. for exhibition abroad when there is an exchange exhibition from a foreign country.
Contact: Director, Museums Program, National Endowment for the Arts, Washington, DC 20506, 202-634-6164.

NATIONAL SCIENCE FOUNDATION

47.009   SCIENTIFIC PERSONNEL IMPROVEMENT

Type of Assistance: Grants ranging from $4,300 to $55,000.

Applicant Eligibility: Individuals.

Objective: To help create a more effective supply of scientific manpower by providing a few highly skilled graduate students with resources to pursue their training at the institutions of their choice; encouraging training for research and teaching at all levels; encouraging research participation and short courses for science faculty; providing research experience to a number of talented high school and college students showing early promise in science; and stimulating more participation in science by women, and by minorities and the handicapped.

Contact: Division of Scientific Personnel Improvement, National Science Foundation, 1800 G Street, N.W., Washington, DC 20550, 202-282-7754.

47.036   INTERGOVERNMENTAL PROGRAM

Type of Assistance: Grants ranging from $10,000 to $250,000.

Applicant Eligibility: Individuals, nonprofit organizations, state and local governments.

Objective: To facilitate the integration of scientific and technical resources into the policy formulation, management support, and program operation activities in state and local governments.

Contact: Director, Intergovernmental Program, Division of Intergovernmental Science and Public Technology, National Science Foundation, 1800 G Street, N.W., Washington, DC 20550, 202-357-7552.

47.041   ENGINEERING AND APPLIED SCIENCE

Type of Assistance: Grants ranging from $1,000 to $800,000.

Applicant Eligibility: Individuals, nonprofit organizations, state and local governments.

Objective: To strengthen the engineering and applied science research base of the U.S. and enhance the links between research and applications in meeting national goals. Areas of research include Applied Social and Behavioral Sciences; Applied Physical, Mathematical, and Biological Sciences; Intergovernmental Programs; Small Business Innovation Programs, Industrial Programs, and Appropriate Technology; Problem-Focused Research (programs currently include Earthquake Hazards Mitigation, Alternative Biological Sources of Materials, Science and Technology to Aid the Handicapped, and Human Nutrition); Integrated Basic Research and Prob-

lem Analysis; Electrical, Computer, and Systems Engineering; Chemical and Process Engineering; and Civil and Mechanical Engineering.
Contact: Programs and Resources Officer, Directorate for Engineering and Applied Science, National Science Foundation, 1800 G Street, N.W., Washington, DC 20550, 202-357-9854.

47.048 SCIENCE EDUCATION DEVELOPMENT AND RESEARCH AND RESOURCES IMPROVEMENT

Type of Assistance: Grants ranging from $1,000 to $250,000.
Applicant Eligibility: Individuals, nonprofit organizations, state and local governments.
Objective: To improve capabilities of academic institutions for education and research training by improving science instruction at the elementary and secondary school levels; developing curricula and modes of instruction that will improve the teaching capabilities of undergraduate students who expect to become precollege science teachers; providing support for science education improvement to four-year colleges, two-year colleges, and undergraduate components of universities—including institutions whose enrollment is predominantly black, Native American, or Spanish-speaking; strengthening programs of training and research for young scientists at the graduate and postgraduate levels; and stimulating the incorporation of new knowledge and instructional strategies into college and university courses through local restructuring of science offerings, and the use of instructional scientific equipment.
Contact: Division Director, Science Education Development and Research, National Science Foundation, 1800 G Street, N.W., Washington, DC 20550, 202-282-7900.

47.049 MATHEMATICAL AND PHYSICAL SCIENCES

Type of Assistance: Grants ranging from $10,000 to $4,200,000.
Applicant Eligibility: Individuals, nonprofit organizations, state and local governments.
Objective: To promote the progress of science and thereby insure the continued scientific strength of the nation; and to increase the store of scientific knowledge and enhance understanding of major problems confronting the nation. Most of the research supported is basic in character. The program includes support of research project grants in the following disciplines: physics, chemistry, mathematical sciences, materials research, and computer research. Support is also provided for research workshops, symposia, and conferences, and for the purchase of scientific equipment. In addition, awards are made to encourage innovative engineering research by scientists recently awarded their Ph.D. degrees.
Contact: Assistant Director, Mathematical and Physical Sciences, National Science Foundation, 1800 G Street, N.W., Washington, DC 20550, 202-632-7342.

47.050   ASTRONOMICAL, ATMOSPHERIC, EARTH, AND OCEAN SCIENCES

Type of Assistance: Grants ranging from $2,000 to $985,000.

Applicant Eligibility: Individuals, nonprofit organizations, state and local governments.

Objective: To strengthen and enhance the national scientific enterprise through the expansion of fundamental knowledge and increased understanding of the earth's natural environment and of the universe. Activities include encouragement and support of basic research in the astronomical, atmospheric, earth, and ocean sciences, and in the biological and physical disciplines in the Antarctic and Arctic. Major objectives include new knowledge of astronomy and atmospheric sciences over the entire spectrum of physical phenomena; a better understanding of the physical and chemical makeup of the earth and its geological history; increased insight into the world's oceans, their composition, structure, behavior, and tectonics; and new knowledge of natural phenomena and processes in the Antarctic and Arctic regions.

Contact: National Science Foundation, 1800 G Street, N.W., Washington, DC 20550, 202-632-5717.

47.051   BIOLOGICAL, BEHAVIORAL, AND SOCIAL SCIENCES

Type of Assistance: Grants ranging from $800 to $2,000,000.

Applicant Eligibility: Individuals, nonprofit organizations, state and local governments.

Objective: To promote the progress of science and thereby insure the continued scientific strength of the nation, and to increase the store of scientific knowledge and enhance understanding of major problems confronting the nation. Most of the research supported is basic in character. The program includes support of research project grants in the following disciplines: physiology, cellular and molecular biology, behavioral and neural sciences, environmental biology, and social and economic science. Support is also provided for research workshops, symposia, and conferences, and for the purchase of scientific equipment. In addition, awards are made to improve the quality of doctoral dissertations in behavioral, social, and environmental sciences.

Contact: Assistant Director, Biological, Behavioral, and Social Sciences, National Science Foundation, 1800 G Street, N.W., Washington, DC 20550, 202-632-7867.

47.053   SCIENTIFIC, TECHNOLOGICAL, AND INTERNATIONAL AFFAIRS

Type of Assistance: Grants ranging from $1,000 to $2,500,000.

Applicant Eligibility: Individuals, nonprofit organizations, state and local governments.

Objective: To address a broad range of scientific and technological issues of concern to policy makers and research and development managers in the public and private sector. Programs are designed to monitor and analyze the nation's science and technology enterprise and to improve national and international exchange of scientific information.

Contact: Assistant Director, Directorate for Scientific, Technological, and International Affairs, National Science Foundation, 1800 G Street, N.W., Washington, DC 20550, 202-254-3020.

47.054   INDUSTRY/UNIVERSITY COOPERATIVE RESEARCH

Type of Assistance: Grants ranging from $80,000 to $160,000.

Applicant Eligibility: Individuals, nonprofit organizations, state and local governments.

Objective: To encourage more effective communication and cooperation between researchers in universities and researchers in industry in order to strengthen the ties between these two segments of the nation's scientific and technological efforts. Grants are made for support of cooperative research projects involving both universities and industrial firms.

Contact: Director, Industrial Science and Technological Innovation, National Science Foundation, 1800 G Street, N.W., Washington, DC 20550, 202-357-7527.

47.055   TWO-YEAR AND FOUR-YEAR COLLEGE RESEARCH INSTRUMENTATION

Type of Assistance: Grants up to $25,000.

Applicant Eligibility: Nonprofit organizations, state and local governments.

Objective: To provide research equipment costing not more than $25,000 to U.S. colleges and universities having substantial undergraduate programs in sciences, mathematics, and/or engineering, but granting fewer than 20 Ph.D. degrees annually in those disciplines.

Contact: Director, Office of Planning and Resources Management, National Science Foundation, 1800 G Street, N.W., Washington, DC 20550, 202-632-5876.

47.056   RESEARCH INITIATIONS IN MINORITY INSTITUTIONS

Type of Assistance: Grants ranging from $20,000 to $100,000.

Applicant Eligibility: Nonprofit organizations, state and local governments.

Objective: To help predominantly minority colleges and universities develop greater research capability on their campuses and encourage participating faculty to compete for research funds from all appropriate sources.

Contact: Director, Office of Planning and Resources Management, National Science Foundation, 1800 G Street, N.W., Washington, DC 20550, 202-632-4378.

COMMUNITY SERVICES ADMINISTRATION

49.002 COMMUNITY ACTION

Type of Assistance: Grants ranging from $10,000 to $35,000,000.

Applicant Eligibility: Nonprofit organizations, state and local governments.

Objective: The Community Action Agency (CAA) is the prime mechanism for implementing Community Action Programs. The objectives of the CAA are to mobilize and channel the resources of private and public organizations and institutions into antipoverty action; to increase the capabilities as well as opportunities for participation of the poor in the planning, conduct, and evaluation of programs affecting their lives; to stimulate new and more effective approaches to the solution of poverty problems; and to strengthen communications, achieve mutual understanding; and strengthen the planning and coordination of antipoverty programs in the community.

Contact: Director for Community Action, Community Services Administration, 1200 19th Street, N.W., Washington, DC 20506, 202-254-6110.

49.005 COMMUNITY FOOD AND NUTRITION

Type of Assistance: Grants ranging from $5,000 to $300,000.

Applicant Eligibility: Nonprofit organizations, state and local governments.

Objective: To help communities counteract the conditions of hunger and malnutrition among the poor.

Contact: Community Food and Nutrition Program, Office of Community Action, Community Services Administration, 1200 19th Street, N.W., Washington, DC 20506, 202-632-6694.

49.010 OLDER PERSONS OPPORTUNITIES AND SERVICES

Type of Assistance: Grants ranging from $500 to $2,362,000.

Applicant Eligibility: Nonprofit organizations, state and local governments.

Objective: This program is designed to identify and meet the needs of poor persons above the age of 60 in projects that serve or employ older persons as the predominant or exclusive beneficiary or employee group.

Contact: Older Americans Programs, Office of Community Action, Community Services Adminstration, Rm. 330, 1200 19th Street, N.W., Washington, DC 20506, 202-632-5196.

49.011 COMMUNITY ECONOMIC DEVELOPMENT

Type of Assistance: Grants ranging from $150,000 to $7,000,000.

Applicant Eligibility: Nonprofit organizations.

Objective: To promote special programs of assistance to private, locally initiated community development corporations (CDCs) that are directed toward making a measurable impact in arresting tendencies toward dependency, chronic unemployment, and community deterioration in urban and rural areas having concentrations or substantial numbers of low-income persons; and invest to start, expand, or locate enterprises in or near the area served so as to provide employment and community ownership opportunities for the residents of such areas.

Contact: Administrative Services Division, Office of Economic Development, Community Services Administration, 1200 19th Street, N.W., Washington, DC 20506, 202-254-6180.

49.013   STATE ECONOMIC OPPORTUNITY OFFICES

Type of Assistance: Grants ranging from $40,000 to $600,000.

Applicant Eligibility: State governments.

Objective: To advise and assist the governors and grantees on antipoverty matters; to coordinate state antipoverty activities; to provide assistance to states and local agencies in connection with Title II programs of the Community Services Act of 1974; to mobilize state resources; and to provide technical assistance to CSA grantees.

Contact: Director for Community Action, Community Services Administration, 1200 19th Street, N.W., Washington, DC 20506, 202-254-6110.

49.014   EMERGENCY ENERGY CONSERVATION SERVICES

Type of Assistance: Grants (dollar amount not available).

Applicant Eligibility: Nonprofit organizations and state governments.

Objective: To enable low-income individuals and families, including elderly and near poor, to lessen the impact of the high cost of energy and to reduce individual and family energy consumption.

Contact: Office of Community Action, Community Services Administration, 1200 19th Street, N.W., Washington, DC 20506, 202-632-6503.

49.015   SUMMER YOUTH RECREATION

Type of Assistance: Grants ranging from $2,000 to $1,600,000.

Applicant Eligibility: Nonprofit organizations.

Objective: To provide recreational opportunities for low-income children between the ages of eight and thirteen during the summer months.

Contact: Office of Program Development, Office of Community Action, Community Services Administration, 1200 19th Street, N.W., Washington, DC 20506, 202-254-5276.

49.016   NATIONAL YOUTH SPORTS PROGRAM

Type of Assistance: Grants ranging from $25,000 to $55,000.

Applicant Eligibility: Educational institutions.

Objective: To provide economically disadvantaged youth aged 10–18 from urban and rural areas valuable experiences through physical fitness, supervised sports skills training and athletic competition, counseling in career and educational opportunities, drug and alcohol abuse education, instruction in nutrition and good health practices, study practices, job responsibilities and a range of related cultural and educational activities.

Contact: Office of Program Development, Office of Community Action, Community Services Administration, 1200 19th Street, N.W., Washington, DC 20506, 202-254-5276.

49.017 RURAL DEVELOPMENT LOAN FUND

Type of Assistance: Loans and loan guarantees ranging from $500,000 to $5,000,000.

Applicant Eligibility: Nonprofit organizations.

Objective: To arrest tendencies toward dependency, chronic unemployment, and community deterioration in rural areas through the provision of loans and loan guarantees to eligible borrowers at the lowest reasonable cost which will provide new employment and ownership opportunities for low-income persons through group ventures.

Contact: Planning, Design and Evaluation Division, Office of Economic Development, Community Services Administration, 1200 19th Street, N.W., Washington, DC 20506, 202-254-5320.

49.018 HOUSING AND COMMUNITY DEVELOPMENT

Type of Assistance: Grants ranging from $25,000 to $750,000.

Applicant Eligibility: State and local governments, and nonprofit organizations.

Objective: To actively and aggressively seek new ways to correct the inequitable distribution of housing in the United States so that even the poorest in our society may have a decent home and a suitable living environment.

Contact: Housing Programs, Office of Community Services Administration, 1200 19th Street, N.W., Washington, DC 20506, 202-254-6390.

RAILROAD RETIREMENT BOARD

57.001   SOCIAL INSURANCE FOR RAILROAD WORKERS
Type of Assistance: Direct payments up to $995 monthly.
Applicant Eligibility: Local governments.
Objective: To protect against loss of income for railroad workers and their families resulting from retirement, death, disability, unemployment, or sickness of the wage earner.
Contact: Information Service, Railroad Retirement Board, 844 Rush Street, Chicago, IL 60611, 312-751-4777.

57.002   BENEFITS FOR MILWAUKEE RAILROAD WORKERS
Type of Assistance: Direct payments (dollar amount not available).
Applicant Eligibility: Employees of the Milwaukee Railroad on September 30, 1979, who were separated or furloughed due to a restructuring transaction.
Objective: To provide assistance to employees adversely affected by the restructuring of the Milwaukee Railroad.
Contact: Director, Bureau of Unemployment and Sickness Insurance, Railroad Retirement Board, 844 Rush Street, Chicago, IL 60611, 312-751-4800.

SMALL BUSINESS ADMINISTRATION

59.001   DISPLACED BUSINESS LOANS

Type of Assistance: Direct loans and guaranteed/insured loans ranging from $5,000 to $904,000.
Applicant Eligibility: Individuals.
Objective: To assist small businesses to continue in business, purchase a business, or establish a new business if substantial economic injury has been suffered as a result of displacement by, or location in or near a program or project involving federal government funds or a program or project by a state or local government or public service entity having authority to exercise the right of eminent domain on such program or project.
Contact: Director, Office of Disaster Operations, Small Business Administration, 1441 L Street, N.W., Washington, DC 20416, 202-653-6376.

59.002   ECONOMIC INJURY DISASTER LOANS

Type of Assistance: Direct loans and guaranteed/insured loans ranging from $250,000 to $1,083,200.
Applicant Eligibility: Individuals.
Objective: To assist business concerns suffering economic injury as a result of certain Presidential, SBA, and Department of Agriculture disaster designations.
Contact: Director, Office of Disaster Operations, Small Business Administration, 1441 L Street, N.W., Washington, DC 20416, 202-653-6376.

59.003   ECONOMIC OPPORTUNITY LOANS
FOR SMALL BUSINESSES

Type of Assistance: Direct loans and guaranteed/insured loans ranging from $1,000 to $315,600.
Applicant Eligibility: Individuals.
Objective: To provide loans up to $100,000 with maximum maturity of 15 years, to small businesses owned by low-income or socially or economically disadvantaged persons.
Contact: Director, Office of Financing, Small Business Administration, 1441 L Street, N.W., Washington, DC 20416, 202-653-6570.

59.007   MANAGEMENT AND TECHNICAL ASSISTANCE FOR
DISADVANTAGED BUSINESSMEN

Type of Assistance: Grants ranging from $15,000 to $306,250.
Applicant Eligibility: Individuals and nonprofit organizations.
Objective: To provide management and technical assistance through public

or private organizations to existing or potential businessmen who are economically or socially disadvantaged; or who are located in areas of high concentration of unemployment; or who are participants in activities authorized by sections 7 (i) and 8a of the Small Business Act.
Contact: Assistant Administrator for Management Assistance, Small Business Administration, 1441 L Street, N.W., Washington, DC 20416, 202-653-6894.

59.008 PHYSICAL DISASTER LOANS
Type of Assistance: Direct loans and guaranteed/insured loans up to $500,000.
Applicant Eligibility: Individuals.
Objective: To provide loans to restore, as nearly as possible, the living conditions of victims of physical-type disasters to predisaster condition.
Contact: Director, Office of Disaster Loans, Small Business Administration, 1441 L Street, N.W., Washington, DC 20416, 202-653-6376.

59.010 PRODUCT DISASTER LOANS
Type of Assistance: Direct loans and guaranteed/insured loans ranging from $3,700 to $268,800.
Applicant Eligibility: Individuals.
Objective: To assist small business concerns that have suffered economic injury as a result of inability to market a product for human consumption because of a finding of toxicity in the product.
Contact: Director, Office of Disaster Loans, Small Business Administration, 1441 L Street, N.W., Washington, DC 20416, 202-653-6376.

59.011 SMALL BUSINESS INVESTMENT COMPANIES
Type of Assistance: Direct loans and guaranteed/insured loans ranging from $50,000 to $35,000,000.
Applicant Eligibility: Individuals.
Objective: To make equity and venture capital available to the small business community with maximum use of private sector participation, and a minimum of government interference in the free market; to provide advisory services and counseling.
Contact: Associate Administrator for Finance and Investment, Small Business Development-Management, Small Business Administration, 1441 L Street, N.W., Washington, DC 20416, 202-653-6848.

59.012 SMALL BUSINESS LOANS
Type of Assistance: Direct loans and guaranteed/insured loans ranging from $1,000 to $500,000.
Applicant Eligibility: Individuals.
Objective: To aid small businesses that are unable to obtain financing in the private credit marketplace, including agricultural enterprises. Funds may be

used to construct, expand, or convert facilities; to purchase building equipment or materials; or for working capital.

Contact: Director, Office of Financing, Small Business Administration, 1441 L Street, N.W., Washington, DC 20416, 202-653-6570.

59.013 STATE AND LOCAL DEVELOPMENT COMPANY LOANS

Type of Assistance: Direct loans and guaranteed/insured loans ranging from $13,000 to $500,000.

Applicant Eligibility: Nonprofit organizations, state and local governments.

Objective: To make federal funds available to state and local development companies to provide long-term financing to small business concerns located in their areas. Both state and local development companies are corporations chartered for the purpose of promoting economic growth within specific areas.

Contact: Office of Financing, Small Business Administration, 1441 L Street, N.W., 8th Floor, Washington, DC 20416, 202-653-6574.

59.014 MINE SAFETY AND HEALTH LOANS

Type of Assistance: Direct loans and guaranteed/insured loans (dollar amount not available).

Applicant Eligibility: Individuals.

Objective: To assist small coal mine operators in complying with federal safety and health standards.

Contact: Director, Office of Disaster Loans, Small Business Administration, 1441 L Street, N.W., Washington, DC 20416, 202-653-6376.

59.016 BOND GUARANTEES FOR SURETY COMPANIES

Type of Assistance: Guaranteed/insured loans ranging from $2,000 to $1,000,000.

Applicant Eligibility: Individuals.

Objective: To encourage the commercial surety market to make surety bonds more available to small contractors unable for various reasons to obtain a bond without a guarantee.

Contact: Chief, Surety Bond Guarantee Division, Small Business Administration, Suite 301, 1815 N. Lynn Street, Arlington, VA 22209, 703-235-2900.

59.017 CONSUMER PROTECTION LOANS

Type of Assistance: Direct loans and guaranteed/insured loans ranging from $70,635 to $165,000.

Applicant Eligibility: Individuals.

Objective: To assist small business concerns that have suffered substantial economic injury caused by compliance with standards established under the Egg Products Inspection Act of 1970, the Wholesome Poultry and Poultry

Products Act of 1968, or the Wholesome Meat Act of 1967, or any other regulation or order of a duly authorized federal, state, regional, or local agency issued in conformity with such federal law designed to protect the consumer.

Contact: Director, Office of Disaster Loans, Small Business Administration, 1441 L Street, N.W., Washington, DC 20416, 202-653-6879.

59.018 OCCUPATIONAL SAFETY AND HEALTH LOANS

Type of Assistance: Direct loans and guaranteed/insured loans ranging from $2,000 to $1,200,000.

Applicant Eligibility: Individuals.

Objective: To assist small business concerns that are likely to suffer substantial economic injury caused by compliance with standards established by the Occupational Safety and Health Act of 1970 without this special assistance.

Contact: Director, Office of Disaster Loans, Small Business Administration, 1441 L Street, N.W., Washington, DC 20416, 202-653-6376.

59.020 BASE CLOSING ECONOMIC INJURY LOANS

Type of Assistance: Direct loans and guaranteed/insured loans ranging from $6,000 to $500,000.

Applicant Eligibility: Individuals.

Objective: To assist small business concerns subject to economic injury as the result of closing by the federal government of a major military installation under the Department of Defense, or as the result of a severe reduction in the scope and size of operation of such an installation.

Contact: Director, Office of Disaster Loans, Small Business Administration, 1441 L Street, N.W., Washington, DC 20416, 202-653-6376.

59.021 HANDICAPPED ASSISTANCE LOANS

Type of Assistance: Direct loans and guaranteed/insured loans ranging from $500 to $350,000.

Applicant Eligibility: Individuals.

Objective: To provide loans and loan guarantees for nonprofit sheltered workshops and other similar organizations to enable them to produce and provide marketable goods and services; and to assist in the establishment, acquisition, or operation of a small business owned by handicapped individuals.

Contact: Director, Business Loans, Small Business Administration, 1441 L Street, N.W., Washington, DC 20416, 202-653-6570.

59.022 EMERGENCY ENERGY SHORTAGE ECONOMIC INJURY LOANS

Type of Assistance: Direct loans and guaranteed/insured loans ranging from $1,000 to $500,000.

Applicant Eligibility: Individuals.

Objective: To assist small business concerns seriously and adversely affected by a shortage of fuel, electrical energy, energy-producing resources, or by a shortage of raw or processed materials resulting from such shortages.
Contact: Director, Office of Disaster Loans, Small Business Administration, 1441 L Street, N.W., Washington, DC 20416 202-653-6376.

59.023 STRATEGIC ARMS ECONOMIC INJURY LOANS
Type of Assistance: Direct loans and guaranteed/insured loans (dollar amount not available).
Applicant Eligibility: Individuals.
Objective: To assist small businesses subject to economic injury as a result of international strategic arms limitation treaties.
Contact: Director, Office of Disaster Loans, Small Business Administration, 1441 L Street, N.W., Washington, DC 20416, 202-653-6376.

59.024 WATER POLLUTION CONTROL LOANS
Type of Assistance: Direct loans and guaranteed/insured loans ranging from $5,687 to $470,000.
Applicant Eligibility: Individuals.
Objective: To assist small business concerns that are likely to suffer substantial economic injury caused by adding to or altering their equipment, facilities, or methods of operation to comply with standards established by the Federal Water Pollution Control Act.
Contact: Director, Office of Disaster Loans, Small Business Administration, 1441 L Street, N.W., Washington, DC 20416, 202-653-6879.

59.025 AIR POLLUTION CONTROL LOANS
Type of Assistance: Direct loans and guaranteed/insured loans ranging from $35,000 $2,585,600.
Applicant Eligibility: Individuals.
Objective: To assist small business concerns subject to economic injury as the result of meeting requirements of the Clean Air Act of 1970, or laws and regulations issued pursuant thereto.
Contact: Director, Office of Disaster Loans, Small Business Administration, 1441 L Street, N.W., Washington, DC 20416, 202-653-6376.

59.027 ECONOMIC DISLOCATION LOANS
Type of Assistance: Direct loans and guaranteed/insured loans ranging from $3,900 to $100,000.
Applicant Eligibility: Individuals.
Objective: To assist those otherwise financially sound businesses in the impacted regions or business sectors that will either become insolvent or be unable to return quickly to their former level of operations. Economic dislocation includes extraordinary, severe, and temporary natural conditions or other economic dislocation as defined by SBA.

Contact: Director, Office of Disaster Loans, Small Business Administration, 1441 L Street, N.W., Washington, DC 20416, 202-653-6376.

59.028 REGULATORY LOANS

Type of Assistance: Direct loans and guaranteed/insured loans (dollar amount not available).

Applicant Eligibility: Individuals.

Objective: To assist any small business concern in effecting addition to or alterations in its plant, facilities, or methods of operation to meet requirements imposed on such concern pursuant to any federal law, any state law enacted in conformity therewith, or any regulation or order of a duly authorized federal, state, regional, or local agency issued in conformity with such federal law if substantial economic injury has been suffered as a result of such order.

Contact: Director, Office of Disaster Loans, Small Business Administration, 1441 L Street, N.W., Washington, DC 20416, 202-653-6376.

59.029 DISASTER ASSISTANCE TO NONAGRICULTURAL BUSINESSES (MAJOR SOURCE OF EMPLOYMENT)

Type of Assistance: Direct loans and guaranteed/insured loans (no dollar limit).

Applicant Eligibility: Individuals.

Objective: To enable a nonagricultural business that is a major source of employment in a major disaster area and which is no longer in substantial operation as a result of such disaster to resume operations in order to assist in restoring the economic viability of the disaster area.

Contact: Office of Disaster Loans, Small Business Administration, 1441 L Street, N.W., Washington, DC 20416, 202-653-6376.

59.030 SMALL BUSINESS ENERGY LOANS

Type of Assistance: Direct loans and guaranteed/insured loans (dollar amount not available).

Applicant Eligibility: Individuals.

Objective: To assist small business concerns to finance plant construction, expansion, conversion, or start-up, and the acquisition of equipment facilities, machinery, supplies, or materials to enable such concerns to manufacture, design, market, install, or service specific energy measures.

Contact: Business Loans, Small Business Administration, 1441 L Street, N.W., Washington, DC 20416, 202-653-6570.

59.031 SMALL BUSINESS POLLUTION CONTROL FINANCING GUARANTEE

Type of Assistance: Guaranteed/insured loans up to $5,000,000.

Applicant Eligibility: Individuals.

Objective: To help small businesses meet pollution control requirements and remain competitive.

Contact: Chief, Pollution Control Financing Division, Office of Special Guarantees, Small Business Administration, 1815 N. Lynn Street, Arlington, VA 22209 703-235-2902.

59.032   OFFICE OF WOMEN'S BUSINESS ENTERPRISE
Type of Assistance: Grants ranging from $5,000 to $150,000.
Applicant Eligibility: No restrictions.
Objective: To develop effective business management skills of potentially successful women entrepreneurs in significant numbers, and improve the business environment for women-owned businesses.
Contact: Planning, Evaluation and Research, Office of Women's Business Enterprise, Small Business Administration, 1441 L Street, N.W., Washington, DC 20416, 202-653-8000.

59.034   SMALL BUSINESS ECONOMIC RESEARCH
Type of Assistance: Grants ranging from $5,000 to $500,000.
Applicant Eligibility: No restrictions.
Objective: To encourage economic research which deals with the effects of government programs, policies, and regulation on small business, the contribution of small business to the economic and social welfare of the United States, and the development of theories or methodologies useful in studying small business problems.
Contact: Grants Management Officer, Small Business Administration, 1441 L Street, N.W., Washington, DC 20416, 202-653-7744.

SMITHSONIAN INSTITUTION

60.001 SMITHSONIAN INSTITUTION PROGRAMS IN BASIC RESEARCH IN COLLABORATION WITH SMITHSONIAN INSTITUTION STAFF

Type of Assistance: Grants up to $14,000 a year.
Applicant Eligibility: Individuals.
Objective: To make available to qualified investigators at various levels of educational accomplishment, the facilities, collections, and professional staff of the Smithsonian.
Contact: Director, Office of Fellowships and Grants, Smithsonian Institution, Rm. 3300, 955 L'Enfant Plaza, Washington, DC 20560, 202-287-3271.

60.007 MUSEUMS—ASSISTANCE AND ADVICE

Type of Assistance: Grants ranging from $500 to $66,500.
Applicant Eligibility: Individuals, nonprofit organizations, state and local governments.
Objective: To support the study of museum problems, to encourage training of museum personnel, and to assist research in museum techniques, with emphasis on museum conservation.
Contact: Program Coordinator, National Museum Act, Office of Museum Programs, Smithsonian Institution, Washington, DC 20560, 202-357-2257.

60.016 SMITHSONIAN SPECIAL FOREIGN CURRENCY GRANTS FOR MUSEUM PROGRAMS, SCIENTIFIC AND CULTURAL RESEARCH, AND RELATED EDUCATIONAL ACTIVITIES

Type of Assistance: Grants and direct payments ranging from $10,000 to $50,000.
Applicant Eligibility: Individuals, nonprofit organizations, state and local governments.
Objective: To support the research activities of American institutions of higher learning through grants in countries where the U.S. Treasury has determined that the United States holds currencies in excess to its needs. Grants in the form of a contract between the Smithsonian and the grantee American institution of higher learning are awarded for basic research in subjects of Smithsonian competence: anthropology, archaeology, and related disciplines; systematic and environmental biology; astrophysics and earth sciences; and museum programs.
Contact: Grants Specialist, Smithsonian Foreign Currency Program, Office

of Fellowships and Grants, Smithsonian Institution, Washington, DC 20560, 202-287-3271.

60.020 WOODROW WILSON INTERNATIONAL CENTER FOR SCHOLARS—FELLOWSHIPS AND GUEST SCHOLAR PROGRAMS

Type of Assistance: Grants (dollar amount not available).

Applicant Eligibility: Individuals.

Objective: The theme of the fellowship program is designed to accentuate aspects of Wilson's ideals and concerns for which he is perhaps best known—his search for international peace and his imaginative new approaches in meeting the pressing issues of his day—translated into current terms.

Contact: Director, Woodrow Wilson International Center for Scholars, Smithsonian Institution, Washington, DC 20560, 202-357-2763.

VETERANS ADMINISTRATION

DEPARTMENT OF MEDICINE AND SURGERY

64.002   VETERANS COMMUNITY NURSING HOME CARE
Type of Assistance: Direct payments (dollar amount not available).
Applicant Eligibility: Nonprofit organizations.
Objective: To provide service-connected veterans with nursing home care and to aid the nonservice-connected veteran in making the transition from a hospital to a community care facility by providing up to six months of nursing care at VA expense.
Contact: Assistant Chief Medical Director for Extended Care (181), Department of Medicine and Surgery, Veterans Administration, Central Office, 810 Vermont Avenue, N.W., Washington, DC 20420, 202-389-3692.

64.004   EXCHANGE OF MEDICAL INFORMATION
Type of Assistance: Grants ranging from $14,639 to $751,785.
Applicant Eligibility: Nonprofit organizations.
Objective: To strengthen VA hospitals not affiliated with medical schools or remotely located from medical teaching centers to foster the cooperation and consultation among all members of the medical profession, within or outside the Veterans Administration.
Contact: Special Assistant to ACMD for Academic Affairs (14c), Veterans Administration, Central Office, 810 Vermont Avenue, N.W., Washington, DC 20420, 202-389-3811.

64.005   GRANTS TO STATES FOR CONSTRUCTION OF STATE HOME FACILITIES
Type of Assistance: Grants ranging from $8,000 to $5,000,000.
Applicant Eligibility: State governments.
Objective: To assist states to construct state home facilities for furnishing domiciliary or nursing home care to veterans, and to expand, remodel, or alter existing buildings for furnishing domiciliary, nursing home, or hospital care to veterans to state homes.
Contact: Assistant Chief Medical Director for Extended Care (182), Veterans Administration, Central Office, 810 Vermont Avenue, N.W., Washington, DC 20420, 202-389-3679.

64.006 REHABILITATIVE RESEARCH

Type of Assistance: Direct payments ranging from $6,000 to $280,000.
Applicant Eligibility: Nonprofit organizations, state and local governments.
Objective: To develop new and improved prosthetic devices, sensory aids, mobility aids, automotive adaptive equipment, and related appliances for the primary benefit of disabled veterans. Through comprehensive educational and informational programs, the results of such research are made available for the benefit of the disabled throughout the world.
Contact: Director, Rehabilitation Engineering Research and Development Service (153), Veterans Administration, Central Office, 810 Vermont Avenue, N.W., Washington, DC 20420, 202-389-2616.

64.014 VETERANS STATE DOMICILIARY CARE

Type of Assistance: Grants ranging from $34,117 to $1,106,600.
Applicant Eligibility: State governments.
Objective: To provide financial assistance to states furnishing domiciliary care to veterans in state veterans homes that meet the standards prescribed by the VA Administrator.
Contact: Assistant Chief Medical Director for Extended Care (182), Veterans Administration, Central Office, 810 Vermont Avenue, N.W., Washington, DC 20420, 202-389-3679.

64.015 VETERANS STATE NURSING HOME CARE

Type of Assistance: Grants ranging from $61,635 to $1,757,658.
Applicant Eligibility: State governments.
Objective: To provide financial assistance to states furnishing nursing home care to veterans in the state veterans homes that meet the standards prescribed by the VA Administrator.
Contact: Assistant Chief Medical Director for Extended Care (182), Veterans Administration, Central Office, 810 Vermont Avenue, N.W., Washington, DC 20420, 202-389-3679.

64.016 VETERANS STATE HOSPITAL CARE

Type of Assistance: Grants ranging from $14,272 to $1,686,096.
Applicant Eligibility: State governments.
Objective: To provide financial assistance to states furnishing hospital care to veterans in state veterans homes that meet the standards prescribed by the VA Administrator.
Contact: Assistant Chief Medical Director for Extended Care (182), Veterans Administration, Central Office, 810 Vermont Avenue, N.W., Washington, DC 20420, 202-389-2679.

DEPARTMENT OF VETERANS BENEFITS

64.100 AUTOMOBILES AND ADAPTIVE EQUIPMENT FOR CERTAIN DISABLED VETERANS AND MEMBERS OF THE ARMED FORCES

Type of Assistance: Direct payments up to $3,800.

Applicant Eligibility: Individuals.

Objective: To provide financial assistance to certain disabled veterans toward the purchase price of an automobile or other conveyance, not to exceed $3,800, and an additional amount for adaptive equipment deemed necessary to insure the eligible person will be able to operate or make use of the automobile or other conveyance.

Contact: Veterans Administration, Central Office, 810 Vermont Avenue, N.W., Washington, DC 20420, 202-389-2356.

64.101 BURIAL ALLOWANCE FOR VETERANS

Type of Assistance: Direct payments up to $1,100.

Applicant Eligibility: Individuals.

Objective: To provide a monetary allowance not to exceed $300 toward the funeral and burial expenses plus $150 for plot or interment expenses if not buried in a national cemetery. If death is service-connected, $1,100 or the amount authorized to be paid in the case of a federal employee whose death occurs as a result of an injury sustained in the performance of duty, is payable for funeral and burial expenses. In addition to the statutory burial allowance, the cost of transporting the remains from place of death to site of burial is paid by VA if death occurs in a VA facility.

Contact: Veterans Administration, Central Office, 810 Vermont Avenue, N.W., Washington, DC 20420, 202-389-2356.

64.102 COMPENSATION FOR SERVICE-CONNECTED DEATHS FOR VETERANS' DEPENDENTS

Type of Assistance: Direct payments up to $121 monthly.

Applicant Eligibility: Individuals.

Objective: To compensate surviving widows, widowers, children, and dependent parents for the death of any veteran who died before January 1, 1957 because of a service-connected disability.

Contact: Veterans Administration, Central Office, 810 Vermont Avenue, N.W., Washington, DC 20420, 202-389-2356.

64.103 LIFE INSURANCE FOR VETERANS

Type of Assistance: Direct loans and insurance (dollar amount not available).

Applicant Eligibility: Individuals.

Objective: To provide life insurance protection for veterans of World War I, World War II, the Korean conflict, and service-disabled veterans of the Vietnam conflict, and to provide mortgage protection life insurance under a group policy for those disabled veterans who are given a VA grant to secure specially adapted housing.

Contact: Veterans Administration Center, P.O. Box 8079, Philadelphia, PA 19101, 215-438-5225.

64.104 PENSION FOR NONSERVICE-CONNECTED DISABILITY FOR VETERANS

Type of Assistance: Direct payments up to $536 monthly for a veteran with three dependents plus $55 for each additional child.

Applicant Eligibility: Individuals.

Objective: To assist wartime veterans in need whose nonservice-connected disabilities are permanent and total and prevent them from following a substantially gainful occupation.

Contact: Veterans Administration, Central Office, 810 Vermont Avenue, N.W., Washington, DC 20420, 202-389-2356.

64.105 PENSION TO VETERANS' SURVIVING SPOUSES AND CHILDREN

Type of Assistance: Direct payments up to $285-plus monthly for a widow or widower with one child plus $55 for each additional child.

Applicant Eligibility: Individuals.

Objective: To provide a partial means of support for needy widows or widowers, and children of deceased wartime veterans whose deaths were not due to service.

Contact: Veterans Administration, Central Office, 810 Vermont Avenue, N.W., Washington, DC 20420, 202-389-2356.

64.106 SPECIALLY ADAPTED HOUSING FOR DISABLED VETERANS

Type of Assistance: Direct payments up to $30,000.

Applicant Eligibility: Individuals.

Objective: To assist certain totally disabled veterans in acquiring suitable housing units, with special fixtures and facilities made necessary by the nature of the veterans' disabilities.

Contact: Veterans Administration, Central Office, 810 Vermont Avenue, N.W., Washington, DC 20420, 202-389-2356.

64.109 VETERANS COMPENSATION FOR SERVICE-CONNECTED DISABILITY

Type of Assistance: Direct payments up to $2,536 a month.
Applicant Eligibility: Individuals.
Objective: To compensate veterans for disabilities due to military service according to the average impairment in earning capacity such disability would cause in civilian occupations.
Contact: Veterans Administration, Central Office, 810 Vermont Avenue, N.W., Washington, DC 20420, 202-389-2356.

64.110 VETERANS DEPENDENCY AND INDEMNITY COMPENSATION FOR SERVICE-CONNECTED DEATH

Type of Assistance: Direct payments up to $993 monthly.
Applicant Eligibility: Individuals.
Objective: To compensate surviving widows or widowers, children, and parents for the death of any veteran who died on or after January 1, 1957 because of a service-connected disability.
Contact: Veterans Administration, Central Office, 810 Vermont Avenue, N.W., Washington, DC 20420, 202-389-2356.

64.111 VETERANS EDUCATIONAL ASSISTANCE

Type of Assistance: Direct payments up to $422 monthly.
Applicant Eligibility: Individuals.
Objective: To make service in the Armed Forces more attractive by extending benefits of a higher education to qualified young persons who might not otherwise be able to afford such an education; and to restore lost educational opportunities to those whose education was interrupted by active duty after January 31, 1955 and before January 1, 1977.
Contact: Veterans Administration, Central Office, 810 Vermont Avenue, N.W., Washington, DC 20420, 202-389-2356.

64.113 VETERANS HOUSING— DIRECT LOANS AND ADVANCES

Type of Assistance: Direct loans up to $33,000.
Applicant Eligibility: Individuals.
Objective: To provide direct housing credit assistance to veterans, service personnel, and certain unmarried widows and widowers of veterans and spouses of service personnel living in rural areas and small cities and towns (not near large metropolitan areas) where private capital is not generally available for VA guaranteed or insured loans.
Contact: Veterans Administration, Central Office, 810 Vermont Avenue, N.W., Washington, DC 20420, 202-389-2356.

64.114 VETERANS HOUSING—
GUARANTEED AND INSURED LOANS

Type of Assistance: Guaranteed/insured loans ranging from $30,000 to $58,000.

Applicant Eligibility: Individuals.

Objective: To assist veterans, certain service personnel, and certain unmarried widows or widowers of veterans in obtaining credit for the purchase, construction, or improvement of homes on more liberal terms than are generally available to nonveterans.

Contact: Veterans Administration, Central Office, 810 Vermont Avenue, N.W., Washington, DC 20420, 202-389-2356.

64.116 VOCATIONAL REHABILITATION
FOR DISABLED VETERANS

Type of Assistance: Direct payments and direct loans up to $351-plus monthly.

Applicant Eligibility: Individuals.

Objective: To train veterans for the purpose of restoring employability to the extent consistent with the degree of a service-connected disability.

Contact: Veterans Administration, Central Office, 810 Vermont Avenue, N.W., Washington, DC 20420, 202-389-2356.

64.117 DEPENDENTS EDUCATIONAL ASSISTANCE

Type of Assistance: Direct payments and direct loans up to $311 monthly.

Applicant Eligibility: Individuals.

Objective: To provide partial support to those seeking to advance their education who are qualifying spouses, surviving spouses, or children of deceased or disabled veterans, or of service personnel who have been listed for a total of more than 90 days as missing in action or as prisoners of war.

Contact: Veterans Administration, Central Office, 810 Vermont Avenue, N.W., Washington, DC 20420, 202-389-2356.

64.118 VETERANS HOUSING—DIRECT LOANS FOR
DISABLED VETERANS

Type of Assistance: Direct loans up to $33,000.

Applicant Eligibility: Individuals.

Objective: To provide certain totally disabled veterans with direct housing credit and to supplement grants authorized to assist the veterans in acquiring suitable housing units with special features or movable facilities made necessary by the nature of their disabilities.

Contact: Veterans Administration, Central Office, 810 Vermont Avenue, N.W., Washington, DC 20420, 202-389-2356.

64.119 VETERANS HOUSING—MOBILE HOME LOANS

Type of Assistance: Guaranteed/insured loans ranging from $12,500 to $21,354.

Applicant Eligibility: Individuals.

Objective: To assist veterans, service persons, and certain unmarried widows or widowers of veterans in obtaining credit for the purchase of a mobile home on more liberal terms than are available to nonveterans.

Contact: Veterans Administration, Central Office, 810 Vermont Avenue, N.W., Washington, DC 20420, 202-389-2356.

64.120 POST-VIETNAM ERA VETERANS EDUCATIONAL ASSISTANCE PROGRAM

Type of Assistance: Direct payments and direct loans up to $8,100.

Applicant Eligibility: Individuals.

Objective: To provide educational assistance to persons first entering the Armed Forces after December 31, 1976; to assist young persons in obtaining an education they might otherwise not be able to afford; and to promote and assist the all-volunteer military program of the United States by attracting qualified persons to serve in the Armed Forces.

Contact: Veterans Administration, Central Office, 810 Vermont Avenue, N.W., Washington, DC 20420, 202-389-2356.

WATER RESOURCES COUNCIL

65.001 WATER RESOURCES PLANNING
Type of Assistance: Grants ranging from $54,480 to $295,500.
Applicant Eligibility: State governments.
Objective: To provide grants for increased participation by the states in water and related land resources planning.
Contact: State Programs Division, Water Resources Council, 2120 L Street, N.W., Washington, DC 20037, 202-254-6446.

ENVIRONMENTAL PROTECTION AGENCY

OFFICE OF AIR, NOISE, AND RADIATION

66.001 AIR POLLUTION CONTROL PROGRAM GRANTS

Type of Assistance: Grants ranging from $7,025 to $6,449,000.
Applicant Eligibility: State and local governments.
Objective: To assist state, municipal, intermunicipal, and interstate agencies in planning, developing, establishing, improving, and maintaining adequate programs for prevention and control of air pollution or implementation of national primary and secondary air quality standards.
Contact: Control Programs Development Division, Office of Air Quality Planning and Standards, Office of Air, Noise, and Radiation, Environmental Protection Agency, Research Triangle Park, NC 27711, 919-688-8146.

66.003 AIR POLLUTION CONTROL MANPOWER TRAINING GRANTS

Type of Assistance: Grants ranging from $6,000 to $80,000.
Applicant Eligibility: Nonprofit organizations, state and local governments.
Objective: To develop career-oriented personnel qualified to work in pollution abatement and control. Grants are awarded to assist in planning, implementing, and improving environmental training programs; to increase the number of adequately trained pollution control and abatement personnel; to upgrade the level of training among state and local environmental control personnel; and to bring new people into the environmental control field.
Contact: Control Programs Development Division, Office of Air Quality Planning and Standards, Office of Air, Noise, and Radiation, Environmental Protection Agency, Research Triangle Park, NC 27711, 919-541-2401.

66.031 QUIET COMMUNITIES—STATES AND LOCAL CAPACITY BUILDING ASSISTANCE

Type of Assistance: Grants ranging from $10,000 to $50,000.
Applicant Eligibility: State and local governments.
Objective: To promote the development of effective state and local noise control programs, by identifying noise problems and establishing or augmenting a noise control capability in such jurisdictions.
Contact: Director, State and Local Programs Division, Office of Noise Abatement and Control, Environmental Protection Agency, Washington, DC 20460, 703-557-7695.

OFFICE OF WATER AND WASTE MANAGEMENT

66.418 CONSTRUCTION GRANTS FOR WASTEWATER TREATMENT WORKS

Type of Assistance: Grants ranging from $675 to $290,800,000.
Applicant Eligibility: State and local governments.
Objective: To assist and serve as an incentive in construction of municipal sewage treatment works, which are required to meet state and federal water quality standards.
Contact: Director, Municipal Construction Division, WH-547, Office of Water Program Operations, Environmental Protection Agency, Washington, DC 20460, 202-426-8986.

66.419 WATER POLLUTION CONTROL—STATE AND INTERSTATE PROGRAM GRANTS

Type of Assistance: Grants ranging from $8,000 to $2,870,000.
Applicant Eligibility: State and local governments.
Objective: To assist state and interstate agencies in establishing and maintaining adequate measures for prevention and control of water pollution.
Contact: Director, Water Program Operations, Office of Water Planning and Standards, Office of Water and Waste Management, Environmental Protection Agency, Washington, DC 20460, 202-755-6928.

66.420 WATER POLLUTION CONTROL—STATE AND LOCAL MANPOWER PROGRAM DEVELOPMENT

Type of Assistance: Grants ranging from $10,000 to $100,000.
Applicant Eligibility: Individuals, state and local governments.
Objective: To design and carry out innovative and imaginative training programs that respond to the highest publicly owned treatment works (POTW)-related training needs. Operator training projects to be part of a development plan for a continuing training activity and support the development of state self-sufficiency.
Contact: Director, National Training and Operational Technology Center, Municipal Operations and Training Division, Office of Water Program Operations, Cincinnati, OH 45268, 513-684-7515.

66.426 WATER POLLUTION CONTROL—STATE AND AREAWIDE WATER QUALITY MANAGEMENT PLANNING AGENCY

Type of Assistance: Grants ranging from $3,000 to $4,200,000.
Applicant Eligibility: State and local governments.
Objective: To encourage and facilitate the development of water quality management plans by areawide agencies in designated areas and by the state in nondesignated planning areas.
Contact: Director, Water Program Operations, Office of Water Planning

and Standards, Office of Water and Waste Management, Environmental Protection Agency, Washington, DC 20460, 202-755-6928.

66.430 WATER POLLUTION CONTROL FELLOWSHIPS

Type of Assistance: Grants ranging from $250 to $6,000.
Applicant Eligibility: Individuals.
Objective: To provide technical and professional training for state and local water pollution control agency personnel; and to encourage and promote the specialized training of individuals as practitioners in water pollution abatement and control.
Contact: Liaison Office, Office of Water Program Operations, Environmental Protection Agency, Washington, DC 20460, 202-426-3971.

66.432 STATE PUBLIC WATER SYSTEM SUPERVISION PROGRAM GRANTS

Type of Assistance: Grants ranging from $98,200 to $1,970,900.
Applicant Eligibility: State governments.
Objective: To foster development of state program plans and programs to assist in implementing the Safe Drinking Water Act.
Contact: Office of Drinking Water, Office of Water and Waste Management, Environmental Protection Agency, Washington, DC 20460, 202-472-4152.

66.433 STATE UNDERGROUND WATER SOURCE PROTECTION PROGRAM GRANTS

Type of Assistance: Grants (dollar amount not available).
Applicant Eligibility: State governments.
Objective: To foster development and implementation of underground injection control programs under the Safe Drinking Water Act.
Contact: Ground Water Protection Branch, Office of Water and Waste Management, Environmental Protection Agency, Washington, DC 20460, 202-426-3934.

66.435 WATER POLLUTION CONTROL—LAKE RESTORATION COOPERATIVE AGREEMENTS

Type of Assistance: Grants ranging from $11,710 to $3,500,000.
Applicant Eligibility: State and local governments.
Objective: To establish the trophic status of a state's publicly owned freshwater lakes and support and promote the coordination and acceleration of demonstration and evaluation projects relating to the causes, effects, extent, prevention, reduction, and elimination of water pollution in publicly owned freshwater lakes.
Contact: Criteria and Standards Division, Office of Water Relations and Standards, Office of Water and Waste Management, Environmental Protection Agency, Washington, DC 20460, 202-755-0100.

66.438 CONSTRUCTION MANAGEMENT ASSISTANCE GRANTS

Type of Assistance: Grants ranging from $3,927,000 to $16,118,000.

Applicant Eligibility: State governments.

Objective: To assist and serve as an incentive in the process of delegating to the states a maximum amount of authority for conducting day-to-day matters related to the management of the construction grant program. An overriding goal is to eliminate unnecessary duplicative reviews and functions.

Contact: Chief, Program Policy Branch, Municipal Construction Division, WH-547, Office of Water Programs Operations, Environmental Protection Agency, Washington, DC 20460, 202-426-8820.

66.451 SOLID AND HAZARDOUS WASTE MANAGEMENT PROGRAM SUPPORT GRANTS

Type of Assistance: Grants ranging from $71,500 to $1,318,200.

Applicant Eligibility: State and local governments.

Objective: To assist state, interstate, regional, county, municipal, and inter-municipal agencies, authorities, and organizations in the development and implementation of state and local programs and to support rural and special communities in programs and projects leading to the solution of solid waste management problems and the control of solid waste management systems.

Contact: Office of Solid Waste, WH-564, Environmental Protection Agency, Washington, DC 20460, 202-755-9113.

66.452 SOLID WASTE MANAGEMENT DEMONSTRATION GRANTS

Type of Assistance: Grants (dollar amount not available).

Applicant Eligibility: Individuals, nonprofit organizations, state and local governments.

Objective: To promote the demonstration and application of solid waste management and resource recovery technologies and systems which preserve and enhance the quality of the environment and conserve resources, and to conduct solid waste management and resource recovery studies, investigations and surveys.

Contact: Office of Solid Waste, WH-562, Environmental Protection Agency, Washington, DC 20460, 202-755-9160.

66.453 SOLID WASTE MANAGEMENT TRAINING GRANTS

Type of Assistance: Grants ranging from $8,000 to $1,000,000.

Applicant Eligibility: Individuals, nonprofit organizations, state and local governments.

Objective: To assist grantees in developing, expanding, or carrying out a program for training persons in the management, supervision, design, operation, or maintenance of solid waste management systems, technologies, and facilities; for training instructors and supervisory personnel in the field of solid waste management; and for the conduct of technical and public information and education programs.

Contact: Office of Solid Waste, WH-562, Environmental Protection Agency, Washington, DC 20460, 202-755-9160.

OFFICE OF RESEARCH AND DEVELOPMENT

66.500 ENVIRONMENTAL PROTECTION—CONSOLIDATED RESEARCH GRANTS

Type of Assistance: Grants ranging from $10,000 to $504,283.

Applicant Eligibility: Individuals, nonprofit organizations, state and local governments.

Objective: To support research to determine the environmental effects and hence the control requirements associated with energy; to identify, develop, and demonstrate necessary pollution control techniques; and to evaluate the economic and social consequences of alternative strategies for pollution control of energy systems. Also to support research to explore and develop strategies and mechanisms for those in the economic, social, governmental, and environmental systems to use in environmental managements.

Contact: Office of Research and Development, RD-675, Environmental Protection Agency, Washington, DC 20460, 202-426-2355.

66.501 AIR POLLUTION CONTROL RESEARCH GRANTS

Type of Assistance: Grants ranging from $5,900 to $440,000.

Applicant Eligibility: Individuals, nonprofit organizations, state and local governments.

Objective: To support and promote research and development projects relating to the causes, effects, extent, prevention, and control of air pollution.

Contact: Office of Research Program Management, RD-675, Office of Research and Development, Environmental Protection Agency, Washington, DC 20460, 202-426-2355.

66.502 PESTICIDES CONTROL RESEARCH GRANTS

Type of Assistance: Grants ranging from $20,000 to $3,000,000.

Applicant Eligibility: Individuals, nonprofit organizations, state and local governments.

Objective: To support and promote the coordination of research projects relating to human and ecological effects from pesticides, pesticide degradation products, and alternatives to pesticides.

Contact: Office of Research Program Management, RD-675, Office of Research and Development, Environmental Protection Agency, Washington, DC 20460, 202-426-2355.

66.504 SOLID WASTE DISPOSAL RESEARCH GRANTS

Type of Assistance: Grants ranging from $9,977 to $216,881.

Applicant Eligibility: Individuals, nonprofit organizations, state and local governments.

Objective: To support and promote the coordination of research and development in the area of collection, storage, utilization, salvage, or final disposal of solid waste.

Contact: Office of Research Program Management, RD-675, Office of Research and Development, Environmental Protection Agency, Washington, DC 20460, 202-426-2355.

66.505 WATER POLLUTION CONTROL—RESEARCH, DEVELOPMENT, AND DEMONSTRATION GRANTS

Type of Assistance: Grants ranging from $5,000 to $7,000,000.

Applicant Eligibility: Individuals, nonprofit organizations, state and local governments.

Objective: To support and promote the coordination and acceleration of research, development, and demonstration projects relating to the causes, effects, extent, prevention, reduction, and elimination of water pollution.

Contact: Office of Research Program Management, RD-675, Office of Research and Development, Environmental Protection Agency, Washington, DC 20460, 202-426-2355.

66.506 SAFE DRINKING WATER RESEARCH AND DEMONSTRATION GRANTS

Type of Assistance: Grants ranging from $15,000 to $778,590.

Applicant Eligibility: Individuals, nonprofit organizations, state and local governments.

Objective: To conduct research relating to the causes, diagnosis, treatment, control, and prevention of physical and mental diseases and other impairments resulting directly or indirectly from contaminants in water, and to the provision of a dependably safe supply of drinking water; to develop and demonstrate any project that will show a new or improved method, approach, or technology for providing a dependably safe supply of drinking water to the public or will investigate and demonstrate health implications involved in the reclamation, recycling, and reuse of waste waters for drinking, and/or the preparation of safe and acceptable drinking water.

Contact: Office of Research Program Management, RD-675, Office of Research and Development, Environmental Protection Agency, Washington DC 20460, 202-426-2355.

66.507 TOXIC SUBSTANCES RESEARCH GRANTS

Type of Assistance: Grants ranging from $25,280 to $210,000.

Applicant Eligibility: Individuals, nonprofit organizations, state and local governments.

Objective: To support and promote the coordination of research projects relating to the effects, extent, prevention, and control of toxic chemical substances or mixtures.

Contact: Office of Research Program Management, RD-675, Office of Research and Development, Environmental Protection Agency, Washington, DC 20460, 202-426-2355.

OFFICE OF PLANNING AND MANAGEMENT

66.600   ENVIRONMENTAL PROTECTION CONSOLIDATED GRANTS—PROGRAM SUPPORT

Type of Assistance: Grants (dollar amount not available).

Applicant Eligibility: State governments.

Objective: To enable states to coordinate and manage environmental approaches to their pollution control activities. Consolidated grants are alternate grant delivery mechanisms. These mechanisms provide for consolidation into one grant instrument, those grants awarded separately to states for management of environmental protection activities including but not limited to air pollution control, water pollution control, and solid waste management.

Contact: Grants Administration Division, PM 216, Environmental Protection Agency, Washington, DC 20460, 202-755-2896.

66.602   ENVIRONMENTAL PROTECTION CONSOLIDATED GRANTS—SPECIAL PURPOSE

Type of Assistance: Grants ranging from $39,000 to $740,000.

Applicant Eligibility: State governments.

Objective: To provide an alternate grant mechanism that will consolidate into one grant instrument grants awarded separately for specific and definite environmental protection activities.

Contact: Grants Administration Division, PM 216, Environmental Protection Agency, Washington, DC 20460, 202-755-2896.

66.603   LOAN GUARANTEES FOR CONSTRUCTION OF TREATMENT WORKS

Type of Assistance: Guaranteed/insured loans (dollar amount not available).

Applicant Eligibility: State and local governments.

Objective: To assist and serve as an incentive in construction of municipal sewage treatment works which are required to meet state and federal water quality standards; and ensure that inability to borrow necessary funds from other sources on reasonable terms does not prevent the construction of any waste water treatment works for which a grant has been or will be awarded.

Contact: Grants Administration Division, PM 216, Environmental Protection Agency, Washington, DC 20460 202-755-0850.

OFFICE OF ENFORCEMENT

66.700 PESTICIDES ENFORCEMENT PROGRAM GRANTS
Type of Assistance: Grants ranging from $10,000 to $1,258,052.
Applicant Eligibility: State governments.
Objective: To assist states in developing and maintaining comprehensive pesticide enforcement programs; sponsoring cooperative surveillance, monitoring, and analytical procedures; avoiding the duplication of effort; and encouraging regulatory activities within the states.
Contact: Director, Pesticides and Toxic Substances Enforcement Division, EN-342, Environmental Protection Agency, Washington, DC 20460, 202-755-0970.

OFFICE OF TOXIC SUBSTANCES

66.800 STATE TOXIC SUBSTANCES CONTROL PROJECTS
Type of Assistance: Grants ranging from $100,000 to $500,000.
Applicant Eligibility: State governments.
Objective: To establish and operate programs to prevent or eliminate unreasonable risks associated with chemical substances and with respect to which EPA is unable or unlikely to take action under the Toxic Substances Control Act.
Contact: Office of Program Integration and Information, Office of Toxic Substances, Environmental Protection Agency, Washington, DC 20460, 202-426-1800.

OVERSEAS PRIVATE INVESTMENT CORPORATION

70.002 FOREIGN INVESTMENT GUARANTEES

Type of Assistance: Guaranteed/insured loans (dollar amount not available).

Applicant Eligibility: Individuals.

Objective: To guarantee loans and other investments made by eligible U.S. investors in developing friendly countries and areas.

Contact: Information Officer, Overseas Private Investment Corporation, Washington, DC 20527, 202-653-2800.

70.003 FOREIGN INVESTMENT INSURANCE

Type of Assistance: Insurance ranging from $4,000 to $100,000,000.

Applicant Eligibility: Individuals.

Objective: To insure investments of eligible U.S. investors in developing friendly countries and areas, against the risks of inconvertibility, expropriation, and war, revolution and insurrection.

Contact: Information Officer, Overseas Private Investment Corporation, Washington, DC 20527, 202-653-2800.

70.004 PRE-INVESTMENT ASSISTANCE

Type of Assistance: Direct payments ranging from $10,000 to $300,000.

Applicant Eligibility: Individuals.

Objective: To initiate and support through financial participation, the identification, assessment, surveying, and promotion of private investment opportunities.

Contact: Information Officer, Overseas Private Investment Corporation, Washington, DC 20527, 202-653-2800.

70.005 DIRECT INVESTMENT LOANS

Type of Assistance: Direct loans ranging from $325,000 to $2,500,000.

Applicant Eligibility: Individuals.

Objective: To make loans for projects in developing countries sponsored by or significantly involving U.S. small businesses or cooperatives.

Contact: Information Officer, Overseas Private Investment Corporation, Washington, DC 20527, 202-653-2800.

ACTION

72.001 THE FOSTER GRANDPARENT PROGRAM
Type of Assistance: Grants ranging from $89,000 to $1,060,000.
Applicant Eligibility: Nonprofit organizations, state and local governments.
Objective: To provide part-time volunteer service opportunities for low-income persons 60 years of age and over and to render supportive person-to-person services in health, education, welfare, and related settings to children having special or exceptional needs, through development of community-oriented, cost-shared projects.
Contact: Chief, Foster Grandparent Program, ACTION, 806 Connecticut Avenue, N.W., M-1006, Washington, DC 20525, 202-254-7310.

72.002 RETIRED SENIOR VOLUNTEER PROGRAM
Type of Assistance: Grants ranging from $10,000 to $450,000.
Applicant Eligibility: Nonprofit organizations, state and local governments.
Objective: To establish a recognized role in the community and a meaningful life in retirement by developing a wide variety of community volunteer service opportunities for persons 60 years of age or over through development of community-oriented, cost-shared projects.
Contact: Director, Older Americans Volunteer Program, ACTION, 806 Connecticut Avenue, N.W., M-1006, Washington, DC 20525, 202-254-7310.

72.003 VOLUNTEERS IN SERVICE TO AMERICA
Type of Assistance: Grants (dollar amount not available).
Applicant Eligibility: Nonprofit organizations, state and local governments.
Objective: To supplement efforts of community organizations to eliminate poverty and poverty-related human, social, and environmental problems by enabling persons from all walks of life and all age groups to perform meaningful and constructive service as volunteers in situations where the application of human talent and dedication may help the poor to overcome the handicaps of poverty and poverty-related problems and secure opportunities for self-advancement.
Contact: Director of VISTA, Office of Domestic Operations, ACTION, 806 Connecticut Avenue, N.W., Washington, DC 20525, 202-254-5195.

72.008 THE SENIOR COMPANION PROGRAM
Type of Assistance: Grants ranging from $145,000 to $262,000.
Applicant Eligibility: State and local governments.
Objective: To provide volunteer opportunities for low-income older people

that enhance their ability to remain active and provide critically needed community services; to play a critical role in providing long-term care by assisting adults, primarily older persons with mental, emotional, and physical impairments, to achieve and maintain their fullest potential to be healthy and to manage their lives independently through development of community-oriented, cost-shared projects.

Contact: Chief, Senior Companion Program, ACTION, Rm. 1106, 806 Connecticut Avenue, N.W., Washington, DC 20525, 202-254-7310.

72.010   MINI-GRANT PROGRAM

Type of Assistance: Grants ranging from $800 to $5,000.

Applicant Eligibility: State and local governments.

Objective: To provide small amounts of money (not to exceed $5,000 per grant) to local, public, and private nonprofit organizations for the purpose of mobilizing relatively large numbers of part-time, uncompensated volunteers to work on human, social, and environmental needs, particularly those related to poverty.

Contact: Director, Office of Voluntary Citizen Participation, ACTION, Suite 907, 806 Connecticut Avenue, N.W., Washington, DC 20525, 202-254-7262.

72.011   STATE OFFICE OF VOLUNTARY CITIZEN PARTICIPATION

Type of Assistance: Grants up to $100,000.

Applicant Eligibility: State governments.

Objective: To provide grants to states to establish and/or strengthen offices of volunteer services to improve opportunities for volunteer efforts concerned with human, social, and environmental needs, particularly those related to poverty.

Contact: Director, Office of Voluntary Citizen Participation, ACTION, Suite 907, 806 Connecticut Avenue, N.W., Washington, DC 20525, 202-254-7262.

72.012   SPECIAL VOLUNTEER PROGRAMS

Type of Assistance: Grants ranging from $15,000 to $200,000.

Applicant Eligibility: Nonprofit organizations, state and local governments.

Objective: To strengthen and supplement efforts to meet a broad range of human, social, and environmental needs, particularly those related to poverty, by encouraging and enabling persons from all walks of life and from all age groups to perform constructive volunteer service; to test or demonstrate new or improved volunteer delivery systems or methods; to encourage wider volunteer participation, particularly on a short-term basis; and to identify segments of the poverty community that could benefit from volunteer efforts.

Contact: Policy Development Division, Office of Policy and Planning, AC-

TION, Rm. 606, 806 Connecticut Avenue, N.W., Washington, DC 20525, 202-254-8420.

72.013   SUPPORT SERVICES ASSISTANCE

Type of Assistance: Grants averaging $35,000.

Applicant Eligibility: State and local governments, and nonprofit organizations.

Objective: To increase the capability of small voluntary organizations to respond to the training, technical assistance, and management needs of volunteers and organizations undertaking voluntary efforts; to stimulate capacity-building of grass roots organizations with volunteer components; and to develop and exchange materials and information related to volunteering.

Contact: Office of Voluntary Citizen Participation, Suite 907, ACTION, 806 Connecticut Avenue, N.W., Washington, DC 20525, 800-424-8867. (In Washington, DC, 202-254-8079.)

NUCLEAR REGULATORY COMMISSION

77.003 ENHANCE TECHNOLOGY TRANSFER AND DISSEMINATION OF NUCLEAR ENERGY PROCESS AND SAFETY INFORMATION

Type of Assistance: Grants ranging from $15,000 to $20,000.
Applicant Eligibility: Public and private nonprofit organizations, state and local governments.
Objective: To stimulate research to provide a technological base for the safety assessment of system and subsystem technologies used in nuclear power applications; to increase public understanding of nuclear safety; to enlarge the fund of theoretical and practical knowledge and technical information; and to enhance the protection of the public health and safety.
Contact: Office of Nuclear Regulatory Research, Nuclear Regulatory Commission, Washington, DC 20555, 301-427-4344.

77.004 ENHANCE TECHNOLOGY ADVANCEMENT OF NUCLEAR ENERGY SAFETY

Type of Assistance: Grants ranging from $100,000 to $200,000.
Applicant Eligibility: Public and private nonprofit organizations, state and local governments.
Objective: To support research necessary to provide a technology base to assess the safety of nuclear power operation, plant siting, and waste disposal; and to develop qualified professionals in the disciplines required for reactor safety evaluations and operations.
Contact: Office of Nuclear Regulatory Research, Nuclear Regulatory Commission, Washington, DC 20555, 301-427-4344.

U.S. DEPARTMENT OF ENERGY

81.004 UNIVERSITY-LABORATORY COOPERATIVE PROGRAM
Type of Assistance: Grants (dollar amount not available).
Applicant Eligibility: Individuals and nonprofit organizations.
Objective: To provide college and university science and engineering faculty and students with energy-related training and experience in areas of energy research at DOE facilities.
Contact: Director, University and Industry Division, Office of Energy Research, Department of Energy, Washington, DC 20585, 202-252-6833.

81.007 TEACHER DEVELOPMENT PROJECTS IN ENERGY
Type of Assistance: Grants up to $31,000.
Applicant Eligibility: Nonprofit organizations.
Objective: To train or to update the training of college and university faculty, high school, junior high, and elementary teachers in energy resource alternatives, conservation, environmental effects, and social/political aspects of energy development.
Contact: Education Division, Office of Consumer Affairs, Department of Energy, Washington, DC 20585, 202-252-1634.

81.036 ENERGY-RELATED INVENTIONS
Type of Assistance: Use of property, facilities and equipment, dissemination of technical information, and grants averaging $67,000.
Applicant Eligibility: Individuals and nonprofit organizations.
Objective: To encourage innovation in developing nonnuclear energy technology by providing assistance to individual inventors and small business research and development companies in the development of promising energy-related inventions.
Contact: NBS Office of Energy-Related Inventions, National Bureau of Standards, Washington, DC 20234, 301-921-3694.

81.040 GRANTS FOR OFFICES OF CONSUMER SERVICES
Type of Assistance: Grants ranging from $40,000 to $244,000.
Applicant Eligibility: State governments.
Objective: To assist in the establishment of state utility consumer offices to represent consumer interests in electric proceedings before utility regulatory commissions.
Contact: Office of Utility Systems, Economic Regulatory Administration, Department of Energy, Rm. 4306, 2000 M Street, N.W., Washington, DC 20461, 202-653-3917.

81.041   STATE ENERGY CONSERVATION
Type of Assistance: Grants ranging from $163,000 to $2,380,200.
Applicant Eligibility: State governments.
Objective: To promote the conservation of energy and reduce the rate of growth of energy demand by authorizing DOE to establish procedures and guidelines for the development and implementation of specific state energy conservation programs and to provide federal financial and technical assistance to states in support of such programs.
Contact: Conservation and Renewable Energy, Office of State and Local Assistance Programs, Department of Energy, Forrestal Building, 1000 Independence Avenue, S.W., Washington, DC 20585, 202-252-2360.

81.042   WEATHERIZATION ASSISTANCE FOR
LOW-INCOME PERSONS
Type of Assistance: Grants ranging from $433,900 to $18,442,000.
Applicant Eligibility: State and local governments.
Objective: To insulate the dwellings of low-income persons, particularly the elderly and handicapped, in order to conserve needed energy and to aid those persons least able to afford higher utility costs.
Contact: Weatherization Assistance Program, Conservation and Energy, Department of Energy, Forrestal Building, 1000 Independence Avenue, S.W., Washington, DC 20585, 202-252-2204.

81.043   SUPPLEMENTAL STATE ENERGY CONSERVATION
Type of Assistance: Grants ranging from $44,000 to $783,500.
Applicant Eligibility: State governments.
Objective: To promote further the conservation of energy and reduce the rate of growth of energy demand by authorizing DOE to establish procedures and guidelines for the development and implementation of supplemental state energy conservation plans and to provide federal financial and technical assistance to the states in support of such programs.
Contact: Conservation and Renewable Energy, Office of State and Local Assistance Programs, Department of Energy, Forrestal Building, 1000 Independence Avenue, S.W., Washington, DC 20585, 202-252-2360.

81.047   PRE-FRESHMAN EDUCATION FOR MINORITIES AND
WOMEN IN ENGINEERING
Type of Assistance: Grants up to $25,000.
Applicant Eligibility: Nonprofit organizations.
Objective: To promote equitable participation of all Americans in energy-related careers, specifically to increase the educational opportunities available to qualified and qualifiable minority group members and women in the field of engineering.
Contact: Division of University and Industry Programs, Department of En-

ergy, Forrestal Building, 1000 Independence Avenue, S.W., MS35-032, Washington, DC 20585, 202-252-1634.

81.049 BASIC ENERGY SCIENCES, HIGH ENERGY/NUCLEAR PHYSICS, FUSION ENERGY, AND PROGRAM ANALYSIS

Type of Assistance: Grants ranging from $10,000 to $1,000,000.
Applicant Eligibility: Individuals.
Objective: To provide financial support for fundamental research in the basic sciences and advanced technology concepts and assessments in fields related to energy.
Contact: Construction Management, Department of Energy, Germantown ER-65, Washington, DC 20585, 301-353-5544.

81.050 ENERGY EXTENSION SERVICE

Type of Assistance: Grants averaging $486,000.
Applicant Eligibility: State governments.
Objective: To encourage individuals and small establishments to reduce energy consumption and convert to alternative energy sources; and assist in building a credible, nonduplicative, state-planned and -operated energy outreach program responsive to local needs.
Contact: Director, Energy Extension Service, Department of Energy, 1725 Lincoln Road, N.E., Washington, DC 20005, 202-576-7112.

81.051 APPROPRIATE ENERGY TECHNOLOGY

Type of Assistance: Grants ranging from $250 to $50,000.
Applicant Eligibility: Individuals, nonprofit organizations and local governments.
Objective: To encourage research and development of energy-related smallscale technologies.
Contact: Inventions and Small-Scale Technologies, Department of Energy, Washington, DC 20585, 202-252-9104.

81.052 ENERGY CONSERVATION FOR INSTITUTIONAL BUILDINGS

Type of Assistance: Grants ranging from $150,000 to $1,000,000.
Applicant Eligibility: Nonprofit organizations, state and local governments.
Objective: To provide grants to states and to public and private nonprofit schools, hospitals, units of local government, and public care institutions to identify and implement energy conservation maintenance and operating procedures, and, for schools and hospitals only, to acquire energy conservation measures to reduce consumption.
Contact: Institutional Buildings Conservation Programs, Office of State and Local Programs, CS, Department of Energy, MS CE-26, Washington, DC 20585, 202-252-2330.

81.055 SMALL HYDROELECTRIC POWER PROJECT FEASIBILITY STUDIES

Type of Assistance: Direct loans ranging from $30,000 to $50,000.

Applicant Eligibility: Individuals, nonprofit organizations, state and local governments.

Objective: To encourage accelerated renovation and development of existing small hydroelectric dam sites by lending up to 90 percent of the cost of a feasibility study.

Contact: Hydroelectric Resource Development, Department of Energy, Rm. 1422, 12th and Pennsylvania Avenue, N.W., Washington, DC 20461, 202-633-8828.

81.056 COAL LOAN GUARANTEES

Type of Assistance: Guaranteed/insured loans up to $30 million.

Applicant Eligibility: Individuals.

Objective: To encourage and assist small and medium-sized coal producers to increase production of underground low-sulfur coal and to enhance competition in the coal industry.

Contact: Acting Director, Office of Coal Loan Programs, Department of Energy, Rm. 3515, 1200 Pennsylvania Avenue, N.W., Washington, DC 20461, 202-633-8200.

81.057 UNIVERSITY COAL RESEARCH

Type of Assistance: Grants (dollar amount not available).

Applicant Eligibility: Nonprofit organizations, state and local governments.

Objective: To improve scientific and technical understanding of the fundamental processes involved in the conversion and utilization of coal; to furnish technical support for the ongoing and developing coal conversion process; to produce clean fuels in an environmentally acceptable manner; and to develop new approaches to the design of future coal conversion and utilization technologies.

Contact: Office of Advanced Research and Technology, Office of Fossil Energy, Department of Energy, Washington, DC 20585, 301-353-2784.

81.058 GEOTHERMAL LOAN GUARANTEES

Type of Assistance: Guaranteed/insured loans up to $200 million.

Applicant Eligibility: Individuals, nonprofit organizations, state and local governments.

Objective: To accelerate the commercial development and utilization of geothermal energy by minimizing a lender's risk to assure the flow of credit for geothermal projects; enhancing competition; encouraging new entrants into the geothermal marketplace; developing normal borrower-lender relationships; and demonstrating the commercial viability of several projects.

Contact: Program Manager, Geothermal Loan Guaranty Program, Department of Energy, Rm. 7112, 1200 Pennsylvania Avenue, N.W., Washington, DC 20461, 202-633-8760.

81.060 ELECTRIC AND HYBRID VEHICLE LOAN GUARANTEES

Type of Assistance: Guaranteed/insured loans up to $3 million.
Applicant Eligibility: Individuals and nonprofit organizations.
Objective: To accelerate the development of electric and hybrid vehicles for introduction into the nation's transportation fleet by encouraging and assisting qualified borrowers; minimizing a lender's financial risk to encourage the flow of credit; and developing normal borrower-lender relationships.
Contact: Chief, Demonstration and Incentives Branch, Electric and Hybrid Vehicles Division, Office of Transportation Programs, Department of Energy, Washington, DC 20585, 202-252-8034.

81.061 OIL SHALE STATE GRANTS

Type of Assistance: Grants ranging from $8,000 to $350,000.
Applicant Eligibility: State and local governments.
Objective: To develop planning and management expertise at the state and local level to deal with the impacts associated with oil shale development.
Contact: Office of Oil Shale Resource Applications, Department of Energy, MS 3344, 1200 Pennsylvania Avenue, N.W., Washington, DC 20461, 202-633-8644.

81.063 OFFICE OF MINORITY ECONOMIC IMPACT LOANS

Type of Assistance: Loans ranging from $1,000 to $25,000.
Applicant Eligibility: Minority business enterprises.
Objective: To provide direct loans to minority business enterprises to assist them in defraying bid and proposal costs they would incur in participating in Department of Energy research, development, demonstration, and contact activities.
Contact: Office of Minority Economic Impact, M1-1, Department of Energy, Rm. 5B-100, Forrestal Building, 1000 Independence Avenue, S.W., Washington, DC 20585, 202-252-8383.

81.065 RESEARCH AND DEVELOPMENT NUCLEAR ENERGY PROGRAMS

Type of Assistance: Grants and direct payments (dollar amount not available).
Applicant Eligibility: Individuals, profit and nonprofit organizations, and state and local governments.
Objective: To increase the potential for increased near-term commercial deployment of light water reactors; to assess advanced fission options for their nonproliferation, economic, technical, and institutional merits; to provide a

nuclear space option for the country; to demonstrate the beneficial use of radioisotopes in terrestrial applications; and to assure that existing and future nuclear waste, including spent fuel, is isolated from the biosphere and poses no significant threat to public health and safety.

Contact: Nuclear Reactor Programs, Code NE520, Department of Energy, Washington, DC 20545, 301-353-4509.

81.066   AMERICAN INDIAN ENERGY PRODUCTION AND EFFICIENCY

Type of Assistance: Grants ranging from $22,000 to $70,000.
Applicant Eligibility: American Indian Tribes or Alaskan Native Villages.
Objective: To stimulate energy production and efficiency among American Indians.
Contact: Department of Energy, Rm. 7-E054, Forrestal Building, 1000 Independence Avenue, S.W., Washington, DC 20585, 202-252-5595.

81.068   BIOMASS LOAN GUARANTEES

Type of Assistance: Guaranteed loans (dollar amount not available).
Applicant Eligibility: No restrictions.
Objective: To accelerate the commercialization of biomass energy systems for production and conversion of biomass to useable energy forms to reduce the dependence of the United States on imported petroleum and natural gas.
Contact: Biomass Energy Systems Division, Department of Energy, 600 E Street, N.W., Washington, DC 20585, 202-376-1615.

81.069   GASOLINE RATIONING—STATE PREIMPLEMENTATION ACTIVITIES

Type of Assistance: Grants ranging from $100,000 to $400,000.
Applicant Eligibility: State governments.
Objective: To provide financial assistance to the states in preimplementation procedures for the state ration plan and to develop final state rationing plans for the operation of ration reserves.
Contact: Gasoline Rationing Preimplementation Project Office, Department of Energy, Rm. 4070, Vanguard Building, 1111 20th Street, N.W., Washington, DC 20461, 202-653-4133.

81.070   ENERGY AUDITOR TRAINING AND CERTIFICATION GRANTS

Type of Assistance: Grants up to $50,000.
Applicant Eligibility: State governments.
Objective: To encourage states to train and certify individuals to conduct energy audits of residential and commercial buildings.
Contact: Buildings and Community Systems, Department of Energy, RMGH068, 1000 Independence Avenue, S.W., Washington, DC 20585, 202-252-9161.

81.071 EMERGENCY ENERGY CONSERVATION ACT PLANS

Type of Assistance: Grants up to $29,000.

Applicant Eligibility: State governments.

Objective: To enable states to prepare management plans, thereby extending the emergency planning capability within the states.

Contact: Office of Emergency Programs, Conservation and Solar Energy, Department of Energy, 1000 Independence Avenue, S.W., Washington, DC 20585, 202-252-4966.

INTERNATIONAL COMMUNICATION AGENCY

82.001 EDUCATIONAL EXCHANGE—GRADUATE STUDENTS
Type of Assistance: Grants ranging from $1,000 to $15,000.
Applicant Eligibility: Individuals.
Objective: To improve and strengthen the international relations of the United States by promoting better mutual understanding among the peoples of the world through educational exchanges.
Contact: Institute of International Education, 809 United Nations Plaza, New York, NY 10017, 212-883-8200.

82.002 EDUCATIONAL EXCHANGE— UNIVERSITY LECTURERS (PROFESSORS) AND RESEARCH SCHOLARS
Type of Assistance: Grants ranging from $2,000 to $30,000.
Applicant Eligibility: Individuals.
Objective: To improve and strengthen the international relations of the United States by promoting better mutual understanding among the peoples of the world through educational exchanges.
Contact: Council for International Exchange of Scholars, 11 Dupont Circle, Suite 300, Washington, DC 20036, 202-833-4950.

82.003 PRIVATE SECTOR PROGRAMS
Type of Assistance: Grants ranging from $2,500 to $478,000.
Applicant Eligibility: Nonprofit organizations.
Objective: To support the enhancement of Americans' competence in world affairs through greater understanding of other societies—their peoples, values, cultures and aspirations.
Contact: Office of Private Sector Programs, Associate Directorate for Educational and Cultural Affairs, International Communication Agency, 1776 Pennsylvania Avenue, N.W., Washington, DC 20547, 202-724-9702.

FEDERAL EMERGENCY MANAGEMENT AGENCY

UNITED STATES FIRE ADMINISTRATION

83.001   ACADEMY PLANNING ASSISTANCE
Type of Assistance: Grants ranging from $11,000 to $50,000.
Applicant Eligibility: State governments.
Objective: To assist states in the development of training and education in the fire prevention and control area.
Contact: Field Programs Division, National Fire Academy, National Emergency Training Center, Federal Emergency Management Agency, 16825 S. Seton Avenue, Emmitsburg, MD 21727, 301-447-6771.

83.002   STATE FIRE INCIDENT REPORTING ASSISTANCE
Type of Assistance: Grants up to $70,000.
Applicant Eligibility: State governments.
Objective: To assist states in the establishment and operation of a statewide fire incident and casualty reporting system.
Contact: Associate Administrator, National Fire Data Center, U.S. Fire Administration, Federal Emergency Management Agency, Washington, DC 20472, 202-634-7561.

83.003   PUBLIC EDUCATION ASSISTANCE PROGRAM
Type of Assistance: Grants up to $15,000.
Applicant Eligibility: State governments.
Objective: To develop or improve states' capacity to provide communities with leadership, information and materials, technical assistance and training in planning, implementing, and evaluating public fire education programs that will reduce state and local fire losses.
Contact: Project Manager, Office of Planning and Education, U.S. Fire Administration, Federal Emergency Management Agency, Washington, DC 20472, 202-634-7553.

83.006   STUDENT STIPEND PROGRAM
Type of Assistance: Direct payments up to $285.
Applicant Eligibility: A student who is a member of a fire department and has been accepted to a course.
Objective: To provide stipends to students attending National Fire Academy Courses.
Contact: Student Services Section, National Fire Academy, 16825 S. Seton

Avenue, Emmitsburg, MD 21727, 800-638-9600. (In Maryland 301-447-6771; in Washington, DC 202-428-3591.)

83.007 REIMBURSEMENT FOR FIREFIGHTING ON FEDERAL PROPERTY

Type of Assistance: Direct payments up to $500,000.
Applicant Eligibility: Fire departments.
Objective: To provide each fire service which engages in firefighting operations on federal property reimbursement for their direct expenses and direct losses incurred in firefighting.
Contact: Administrator, Fire Administration, Federal Energy Management Agency, Washington, DC 20412, 202-634-7654.

FEDERAL INSURANCE ADMINISTRATION

83.100 FLOOD INSURANCE

Type of Assistance: Insurance ranging from $1 to $100,000.
Applicant Eligibility: State and local governments.
Objective: To enable persons to purchase insurance against losses from physical damage to or loss of real or personal property caused by floods, mudslides, or flood-caused erosion in the United States, and to promote wise flood plain management practices in the nation's flood-prone and mudslide-prone areas.
Contact: Administrator, Federal Insurance Administration, Federal Emergency Management Agency, Washington, DC 20472, 202-755-7894.

83.101 URBAN PROPERTY INSURANCE

Type of Assistance: Insurance ranging from $60 to $900,000.
Applicant Eligibility: State and local governments.
Objective: To assure availability of essential insurance coverage for urban property, particularly that located in areas possibly subject to riots or civil disturbance, by providing reinsurance to insurers against catastrophic losses from riot or civil disorder.
Contact: Administrator, Federal Insurance Administration, Federal Emergency Management Agency, Washington, DC 20410, 202-755-5581.

83.102 CRIME INSURANCE

Type of Assistance: Insurance up to $15,000.
Applicant Eligibility: Individuals.
Objective: To enable businessmen and residents of homes and apartments to

purchase burglary and robbery insurance in states where there is a critical problem of crime insurance availability at affordable rates, which problem is not being resolved by appropriate state action.

Contact: Federal Emergency Management Agency, Federal Insurance Administration, 1725 I Street, N.W., Washington, DC 20472, 202-755-6555.

83.103 STATE ASSISTANCE— NATIONAL FLOOD INSURANCE PROGRAM

Type of Assistance: Grants ranging from $50,000 to $200,000.

Applicant Eligibility: State governments.

Objective: To facilitate each state's achievement of a level of expertise in the National Flood Insurance Program (NFIP) and in flood-hazard mitigation, which will enable the state to provide assistance to its constituent communities in discharging local responsibilities under the NFIP.

Contact: Office of Natural Hazard Reductions and Evaluations, Federal Insurance Administration, Federal Emergency Management Agency, Washington, DC 20472, 202-755-5581.

OFFICE OF PLANS AND PREPAREDNESS

83.200 CIVIL DEFENSE—STATE AND LOCAL MANAGEMENT

Type of Assistance: Grants ranging from $343 to $3,287,576.

Applicant Eligibility: State governments.

Objective: To develop effective civil defense organizations in the states and their political subdivisions in order to plan for and coordinate emergency activities in the event of attack or other than enemy-caused disaster.

Contact: State and Local Programs, Population Protection Office, Federal Emergency Management Agency, 1725 I Street, N.W., Washington, DC 20472, 202-566-0550.

83.201 CIVIL DEFENSE— STATE AND LOCAL MAINTENANCE AND SERVICES

Type of Assistance: Grants ranging from $500 to $75,302.

Applicant Eligibility: State and local governments.

Objective: To maintain the civil defense readiness of state and local governments by furnishing matching funds for annual recurring and maintenance costs for state and local civil defense direction, control, alerting, and warning systems, and for emergency public information services and supplies required to conduct a viable civil defense program.

Contact: Chief, Director and Control Branch, State and Local Operation Systems Division, State and Local Programs and Support, Federal Emergency Management Agency, Washington, DC 20472, 202-566-0760.

83.203   STATE DISASTER PREPAREDNESS GRANTS

Type of Assistance: Grants ranging from $12,500 to $25,000.
Applicant Eligibility: State governments.
Objective: To assist states in developing and improving the state and local plans, programs, and capabilities for disaster preparedness and prevention.
Contact: Federal Emergency Management Agency, Washington, DC 20472, 202-566-0930.

83.204   EARTHQUAKE AND HURRICANE LOSS STUDY AND CONTINGENCY PLANNING GRANTS

Type of Assistance: Grants ranging from $100,000 to $150,000.
Applicant Eligibility: State and local governments.
Objective: To prepare plans for all levels of government for preparedness capabilities for severe earthquakes or hurricanes in certain high-density, high-risk areas.
Contact: Federal Emergency Management Agency, Washington, DC 20472, 202-566-0981.

83.206   CIVIL DEFENSE—RADIOLOGICAL INSTRUMENTS MAINTENANCE AND CALIBRATION

Type of Assistance: Grants ranging from $15,541 to $142,168.
Applicant Eligibility: State and local governments.
Objective: To assist in developing a capability in every locality for the detection and measurement of hazardous levels of radiation; to maintain all civil defense radiological instruments in a calibrated and operationally ready condition; to assist in the development and maintenance of radiological emergency plans.
Contact: Chief, Radiological Defense and Technological Hazards Branch, Office of Plans and Preparedness, Federal Emergency Management Agency, Washington, DC 20472, 202-566-1975.

OFFICE OF DISASTER RESPONSE AND RECOVERY

83.300   DISASTER ASSISTANCE

Type of Assistance: Grants ranging from $21 to $39,202,722.
Applicant Eligibility: Individuals, state and local governments.
Objective: To provide assistance to states, local governments, selected private nonprofit facilities, and individuals in alleviating suffering and hardship resulting from emergencies or major disasters declared by the President.
Contact: Disaster Response and Recovery, Federal Emergency Management Agency, Washington, DC 20472, 202-634-7800.

OFFICE OF TRAINING AND EDUCATION

83.400 EMERGENCY MANAGEMENT INSTITUTE

Type of Assistance: Grants ranging from $34 to $355.

Applicant Eligibility: Individuals.

Objective: To assist in defraying the expenses of professional training for state and local emergency management defense personnel and training for instructors who conduct courses under contract.

Contact: Training and Education, Federal Emergency Management Agency, Washington, DC 20472, 202-653-7727.

U.S. DEPARTMENT OF EDUCATION

EDUCATION-1

84.001 ACADEMIC FACILITIES RECONSTRUCTION AND RENOVATION FOR REMOVAL OF ARCHITECTURAL BARRIERS

Type of Assistance: Grants ranging from $2,500 to $100,000.
Applicant Eligibility: Colleges and universities.
Objective: To provide for the reconstruction and renovation for removal of architectural barriers.
Contact: Office of Postsecondary Education, Academic Facilities Branch, Department of Education, 400 Maryland Avenue, S.W., Washington, DC 20202, 202-245-3253.

84.002 ADULT EDUCATION— STATE-ADMINISTERED PROGRAM

Type of Assistance: Grants ranging from $73,172 to $8,334,833.
Applicant Eligibility: State governments.
Objective: To expand educational opportunities for adults and to encourage the establishment of programs of adult education that will enable all adults to acquire basic skills necessary to function in society; enable adults who so desire to continue their education to at least the level of completion of secondary school; and make available the means to secure training that will enable adults to become more employable, productive, and responsible citizens.
Contact: Division of Adult Education, Bureau of Occupational and Adult Education, Department of Education, Washington, D.C. 20202, 202-245-2278.

84.003 BILINGUAL EDUCATION

Type of Assistance: Grants ranging from $25,000 to $2,000,000.
Applicant Eligibility: Nonprofit organizations, state and local governments.
Objective: To develop and carry out elementary and secondary school programs, including activities at the preschool level, to meet the educational needs of children of limited proficiency in English; to demonstrate effective ways of providing such children instruction designed to enable them, while using their native language, to achieve competence in English; and to develop the human and material resources required for such programs.

Contact: Director, Office of Bilingual Education, Department of Education, 400 Maryland Avenue, S.W., Washington, DC 20202, 202-245-2600.

84.004 CIVIL RIGHTS TECHNICAL ASSISTANCE AND TRAINING

Type of Assistance: Grants ranging from $14,000 to $400,000.
Applicant Eligibility: Nonprofit organizations, state and local governments.
Objective: To provide direct and indirect technical assistance and training services to school districts to cope with educational problems occasioned by desegregation by race, sex, and national origin.
Contact: Director, Division of Technical Assistance, Bureau of Elementary and Secondary Education, Department of Education, 400 Maryland Avenue, S.W., Washington, DC 20202, 202-245-8840.

84.005 COLLEGE LIBRARY RESOURCES

Type of Assistance: Grants averaging $3,963.
Applicant Eligibility: Nonprofit organizations, state and local governments.
Objective: To assist and encourage institutions of higher education and other eligible institutions in the acquisition of library materials.
Contact: Library Education and Postsecondary Resources Branch, Division of Library Programs, Office of Libraries and Learning Resources, Bureau of Elementary and Secondary Education, Department of Education, 400 Maryland Avenue, S.W., Washington, DC 20202, 202-245-9530.

84.006 TEACHER CENTERS

Type of Assistance: Grants ranging from $5,000 to $250,000.
Applicant Eligibility: Nonprofit organizations, state and local governments.
Objective: To meet better the needs of elementary and secondary school students by assisting local educational agencies and institutions of higher education in operating teacher centers designed to provide improved in-service training for teachers and to develop improved curricula for the schools.
Contact: Teacher Centers Program, Division of Educational Systems Development, Bureau of Higher and Continuing Education, Department of Education, 400 Maryland Avenue, Washington, DC 20202, 202-472-5940.

84.007 SUPPLEMENTAL EDUCATIONAL OPPORTUNITY GRANTS

Type of Assistance: Direct payments ranging from $235 to $4,409,060.
Applicant Eligibility: Nonprofit organizations, state and local governments.
Objective: To enable students with exceptional financial need to pursue higher education by providing grant assistance for educational expenses.
Contact: Chief, Policy Section, Campus-Based Branch, Division of Policy and Program Development, Bureau of Student Financial Assistance, Department of Education, 400 Maryland Avenue, S.W., Washington, DC 20202, 202-245-9720.

84.009 PROGRAM FOR EDUCATION OF HANDICAPPED CHILDREN IN STATE-OPERATED OR -SUPPORTED SCHOOLS

Type of Assistance: Grants ranging from $238,742 to $17,810,136.
Applicant Eligibility: State and local governments.
Objective: To extend and improve comprehensive educational programs for handicapped children enrolled in state-operated or state-supported schools.
Contact: Division of Assistance to States, Bureau of Education for the Handicapped, Department of Education, 400 Maryland Avenue, S.W., Washington, DC 20202, 202-472-2638.

84.010 EDUCATIONALLY DEPRIVED CHILDREN—LOCAL EDUCATIONAL AGENCIES

Type of Assistance: Grants ranging from $636,102 to $276,154,892.
Applicant Eligiblity: State governments.
Objective: To expand and improve educational programs to meet the needs of educationally disadvantaged children in low-income areas, whether enrolled in public or private elementary and secondary schools.
Contact: Director, Division of Education for the Disadvantaged, Bureau of Elementary and Secondary Education, Department of Education, 7th and D Streets, S.W., Washington, DC 20202, 202-245-2638.

84.011 MIGRANT EDUCATION PROGRAM—STATE FORMULA GRANT PROGRAM

Type of Assistance: Grants ranging from $36,902 to $55,534,124.
Applicant Eligibility: State governments.
Objective: To expand and improve programs to meet the special educational needs of children of migratory agricultural workers or of migratory fishers.
Contact: Director, Division of Migrant Education, Office of Compensatory Educational Programs, Bureau of Elementary and Secondary Education, Department of Education, 400 Maryland Avenue, S.W., Washington, DC 20202, 202-245-2222.

84.012 EDUCATIONALLY DEPRIVED CHILDREN— STATE ADMINISTRATION

Type of Assistance: Grants ranging from $50,000 to $4,473,058.
Applicant Eligibility: State governments.
Objective: To improve and expand educational programs for disadvantaged children through financial assistance to state education agencies.
Contact: Director, Division of Education for the Disadvantaged, Bureau of Elementary and Secondary Education, Department of Education, 7th and D Streets, S.W., Washington, DC 20202, 202-245-2638.

84.013 EDUCATIONALLY DEPRIVED CHILDREN IN STATE-ADMINISTERED INSTITUTIONS SERVING NEGLECTED OR DELINQUENT CHILDREN

Type of Assistance: Grants ranging from $2,062 to $2,771,434.
Applicant Eligibility: State governments.
Objective: To expand and improve educational programs to meet the special needs of institutionalized children for whom the state has an educational responsibility.
Contact: Director, Division of Education for the Disadvantaged, Bureau of Elementary and Secondary Education, Department of Education, 7th and D Streets, S.W., Washington, DC 20202, 202-245-2638.

84.014 FOLLOW THROUGH

Type of Assistance: Grants ranging from $6,300 to $1,783,000.
Applicant Eligibility: Nonprofit organizations, state and local governments.
Objective: To sustain and augment in primary grades the gains that children from low-income families make in Head Start and other quality preschool programs. Follow Through provides special programs of instruction as well as health, nutrition, and other related services, which will aid in the continued development of children to their full potential. Active participation of parents is stressed.
Contact: Follow Through Division, Bureau of Elementary and Secondary Education, Department of Education, ROB-3, 7th and D Streets, S.W., Washington, DC 20202, 202-245-2638.

84.015 NATIONAL RESOURCE CENTERS AND FELLOWSHIPS IN INTERNATIONAL STUDIES

Type of Assistance: Grants ranging from $37,000 to $174,500, and fellowships at $5,850 per year.
Applicant Eligibility: Nonprofit organizations, state and local governments.
Objective: To promote instruction in those modern foreign languages and area and international studies critical to national needs by supporting the establishment and operation of such programs at colleges and universities; to meet the critical needs of American education for experts in foreign languages, area studies, and world affairs by supporting fellowships for advanced study at institutions for higher education.
Contact: International Studies Branch, Division of International Education, Department of Education, ROB-3, 7th and D Streets, S.W., Washington, DC 20202, 202-245-9425.

84.016 INTERNATIONAL STUDIES PROGRAMS

Type of Assistance: Grants ranging from $24,000 to $50,000.
Applicant Eligiblity: Nonprofit organizations, state and local governments.
Objective: To strengthen the international and global focus in the curricula

of institutions of higher education by establishing international and global studies programs at the graduate or undergraduate levels.
Contact: International Studies Branch, Division of International Education, Department of Education, ROB-3, 7th and D Streets, S.W., Washington, DC 20202, 202-245-2794.

84.017 INTERNATIONAL RESEARCH AND STUDIES

Type of Assistance: Grants ranging from $2,500 to $100,000.
Applicant Eligibility: Individuals, nonprofit organizations, state and local governments.
Objective: To improve foreign language and area studies training in the United States through support of research and studies, experimentation, and development of specialized instructional materials.
Contact: Centers and Research Section, Division of International Education, Department of Education, ROB-3, 7th and D Streets, S.W., Washington, DC 20202, 202-245-2794.

84.018 TEACHER EXCHANGE

Type of Assistance: Grants (dollar amount not available).
Applicant Eligibility: Individuals.
Objective: To increase mutual understanding between the people of the United States and those of other countries by offering qualified American teachers opportunities to teach in elementary and secondary schools, and in some instances in teacher training institutions, technical colleges, polytechnics, or colleges of art, abroad. With the cooperation of American schools, teachers from other countries may teach for an academic year in the United States under the same program. There are also opportunities for American teachers to participate in short-term seminars abroad.
Contact: Teacher Exchange Section, International Exchange Branch, Division of International Education, Department of Education, ROB-3, 7th and D Streets, S.W., Washington, DC 20202, 202-245-9700.

84.019 FULBRIGHT-HAYS TRAINING GRANTS—FACULTY RESEARCH ABROAD

Type of Assistance: Grants ranging from $865 to $18,568.
Applicant Eligibility: Individuals.
Objective: To help universities and colleges strengthen their programs of international studies through selected opportunities for research and study abroad in foreign language and area studies; to enable key faculty members to keep current in their specialties; to facilitate the updating of curricula; and to help improve teaching methods and materials.
Contact: Division of International Education, Department of Education, ROB-3, 7th and D Streets, S.W., Washington, DC 20202, 202-245-2794.

84.020 FULBRIGHT-HAYS TRAINING GRANTS—FOREIGN CURRICULUM CONSULTANTS

Type of Assistance: Grants ranging from $9,420 to $14,298.
Applicant Eligibility: Nonprofit organizations, state and local governments.
Objective: To benefit American education at all levels by helping institutions bring specialists from other countries to the United States to assist in planning and developing local curricula in foreign language and area studies.
Contact: Division of International Education, Department of Education, ROB-3, 7th and D Streets, S.W., Washington, DC 20202, 202-245-2795.

84.021 FULBRIGHT-HAYS TRAINING GRANTS—GROUP PROJECTS ABROAD

Type of Assistance: Grants ranging from $30,000 to $217,628.
Applicant Eligibility: Nonprofit organizations, state and local governments.
Objective: To help educational institutions improve their programs in foreign language and area studies.
Contact: Division of International Education, Department of Education, ROB-3, 7th and D Streets, S.W., Washington, DC 20202, 202-245-2796.

84.022 FULBRIGHT-HAYS TRAINING GRANTS—DOCTORAL DISSERTATION RESEARCH ABROAD

Type of Assistance: Grants ranging from $2,705 to $35,075.
Applicant Eligibility: Individuals.
Objective: To provide opportunities for advanced graduate students to engage in full-time dissertation research abroad in modern foreign language and area studies. The program is designed to develop research knowledge and capability in world areas not widely included in American curricula.
Contact: Division of International Education, Department of Education, ROB-3, 7th and D Streets, S.W., Washington, DC 20202, 202-245-2797.

84.023 RESEARCH IN THE EDUCATION OF THE HANDICAPPED

Type of Assistance: Grants ranging from $4,000 to $500,000.
Applicant Eligibility: Nonprofit organizations, state and local governments.
Objective: To improve the education of handicapped children through research and development projects, and demonstrations of model programs.
Contact: Chief, Research Project Branch, Division of Innovation and Development, Bureau of Education for the Handicapped, Department of Education, 400 Maryland Avenue, S.W., Washington, DC 20202, 202-245-2275.

84.024 HANDICAPPED EARLY CHILDHOOD ASSISTANCE

Type of Assistance: Grants ranging from $50,000 to $150,000.
Applicant Eligibility: Nonprofit organizations, state and local governments.
Objective: To support experimental demonstration, dissemination, and state

implementation of preschool and early childhood projects for handicapped children.

Contact: Program Development Branch, Handicapped Children's Early Education Assistance, Division of Innovation and Development, Department of Education, 400 Maryland Avenue, S.W., Washington, DC 20202, 202-245-9722.

84.025 HANDICAPPED INNOVATIVE PROGRAMS—DEAF-BLIND CENTERS

Type of Assistance: Grants ranging from $600,000 to $1,600,000.

Applicant Eligibility: Nonprofit organizations, state and local governments.

Objective: To establish model single-state and multistate centers to provide all deaf-blind children with comprehensive diagnostic and evaluative services, programs for their education, adjustment, and orientation, and effective consultative services for their parents, teachers, and others involved in their welfare.

Contact: Coordinator, Centers and Services for Deaf-Blind Children, Bureau of Education for the Handicapped, Division of Assistance to States, Department of Education, 400 Maryland Avenue, S.W., Washington, DC 20202, 202-472-4825.

84.026 HANDICAPPED MEDIA SERVICES AND CAPTIONED FILMS

Type of Assistance: Direct payments ranging from $1,350 to $1,650,000.

Applicant Eligibility: Nonprofit organizations, state and local governments.

Objective: To maintain a free loan service of captioned films for the deaf and instructional media for the educational, cultural, and vocational enrichment of the handicapped; provide for acquisition and distribution of media materials and equipment; offer contracts and grants for research into the use of media; and train teachers, parents, and others in media utilization.

Contact: Captioned Films and Telecommunications Branch, Division of Media Services, Bureau of Education for the Handicapped, Department of Education, 400 Maryland Avenue, S.W., Washington, DC 20202, 202-472-4640.

84.027 HANDICAPPED PRESCHOOL AND SCHOOL PROGRAMS

Type of Assistance: Grants ranging from $182,600 to $70,607,419.

Applicant Eligibility: State governments.

Objective: To provide grants to states to assist them in providing a free appropriate public education to all handicapped children.

Contact: Division of Assistance to States, Bureau of Education for the Handicapped, Department of Education, 400 Maryland Avenue, S.W., Washington, DC 20202, 202-472-2263.

84.028 HANDICAPPED REGIONAL RESOURCE CENTERS

Type of Assistance: Grants ranging from $100,000 to $800,000.
Applicant Eligibility: Nonprofit organizations, state and local governments.
Objective: To establish regional resource centers that provide advice and technical services to educators for improving education of handicapped children.
Contact: Division of Media Services, Bureau of Education for the Handicapped, Department of Education, 400 Maryland Avenue, S.W., Washington, DC 20202, 202-472-1494.

84.029 HANDICAPPED PERSONNEL PREPARATION

Type of Assistance: Grants ranging from $8,000 to $360,000.
Applicant Eligibility: Nonprofit organizations, state and local governments.
Objective: To improve the quality and increase the numbers of teachers, supervisors, administrators, researchers, teacher educators, and speech correctionists working with the handicapped, and specialized personnel such as specialists in physical education and recreation, paraprofessionals, and vocational/career education volunteers (including parents and parent coalitions).
Contact: Director, Division of Personnel Preparation, Department of Education, Bureau of Education for the Handicapped, 400 Maryland Avenue, S.W., Washington, DC 20202, 202-245-9886.

84.030 HANDICAPPED TEACHER RECRUITMENT
AND INFORMATION

Type of Assistance: Grants ranging from $10,000 to $400,000.
Applicant Eligibility: Nonprofit organizations, state and local governments.
Objective: To disseminate information that can help parents, consumer organizations, professionals, and others interested in special education in making decisions that affect the education and general well-being of handicapped children.
Contact: Bureau of Education for the Handicapped, Department of Education, 400 Maryland Avenue, S.W., Washington, DC 20202, 202-245-9661.

84.031 HIGHER EDUCATION—STRENGTHENING
DEVELOPING INSTITUTIONS

Type of Assistance: Grants ranging from $37,000 to $2,000,000.
Applicant Eligibility: Nonprofit organizations, state and local governments.
Objective: To strengthen developing colleges qualifying within the definition of the Higher Education Act of 1965 in their academic, administrative, and student services programs.
Contact: Assistant Director, Division of Institutional Development, Bureau of Higher and Continuing Education, Department of Education, 400 Maryland Avenue, S.W., Washington, DC 20202, 202-245-2384.

84.032 HIGHER EDUCATION ACT INSURED LOANS (GUARANTEED STUDENT LOANS)

Type of Assistance: Guaranteed/insured loans up to $5,000 annually per student.

Applicant Eligibility: Individuals.

Objective: To authorize low-interest deferred loans for educational expenses available from eligible lenders such as banks, credit unions, savings and loan associations, pension funds, insurance companies, and schools to vocational, undergraduate, and graduate students enrolled at eligible institutions. The loans are insured by a state or private nonprofit agency or the federal government.

Contact: Guaranteed Student Loan Branch, Division of Policy and Program Development, Bureau of Student Financial Assistance, Department of Education, 400 Maryland Avenue, S.W., Washington, DC 20202, 202-245-2475.

84.033 COLLEGE WORK-STUDY PROGRAM

Type of Assistance: Direct payments ranging from $176 to $8,286,574.

Applicant Eligibility: Nonprofit organizations and local governments.

Objective: To promote the part-time employment of students, particularly those with great financial need, who require assistance to pursue courses of study at institutions of higher education.

Contact: Campus-Based Branch, Division of Policy and Program Development, Bureau of Student Financial Assistance, 400 Maryland Avenue, S.W., Washington, DC 20202, 202-245-9720.

84.034 PUBLIC LIBRARY SERVICES

Type of Assistance: Grants (dollar amount not available).

Applicant Eligibility: State governments.

Objective: To assist in extending public library services to areas without service or with inadequate service; establishing and expanding state institutional library services; offering library service to the physically handicapped; establishing and expanding library services to the disadvantaged in urban and rural areas, and strengthening the metropolitan public libraries which serve as national or regional resource centers; providing programs and projects to serve areas with high concentrations of persons of limited English-speaking ability; and strengthening major urban resource libraries.

Contact: State and Public Library Services Branch, Office of Libraries and Learning Resources, Bureau of Elementary and Secondary Education, Department of Education, 400 Maryland Avenue, S.W., Washington, DC 20202, 202-472-5150.

84.035 INTERLIBRARY COOPERATION

Type of Assistance: Grants (dollar amount not available).

Applicant Eligibility: State governments.

Objective: To provide for the systematic and effective coordination of the

resources of school, public, academic, and special libraries, and special information centers, to improve service to their particular clienteles.
Contact: State and Public Library Services Branch, Office of Libraries and Learning Resources, Bureau of Elementary and Secondary Education, Department of Education, 400 Maryland Avenue, S.W., Washington, DC 20202, 202-472-5150.

84.036 LIBRARY TRAINING
Type of Assistance: Grants ranging from $10,000 to $84,200.
Applicant Eligibility: Nonprofit organizations, state and local governments.
Objective: To assist institutions of higher education and library organizations and agencies in training persons in the principles and practices of librarianship and information science.
Contact: Library Education and Postsecondary Resources Branch, Division of Library Programs, Office of Libraries and Learning Resources, Bureau of Elementary and Secondary Education, Department of Education, 400 Maryland Avenue, S.W., Washington, DC 20202, 202-245-9530.

84.037 NATIONAL DEFENSE/DIRECT STUDENT LOAN CANCELLATIONS
Type of Assistance: Direct payments ranging from $4 to $129,821.
Applicant Eligibility: Nonprofit organizations, state and local governments.
Objective: To reimburse institutions for their share of National Defense Student Loan recipients who cancel their loans by becoming teachers or performing active military service in the U.S. Armed Forces.
Contact: Campus and State Grant Branch, Division of Program Operations, Bureau of Student Financial Assistance, 400 Maryland Avenue, S.W., Washington, DC 20202, 202-245-2991.

84.038 NATIONAL DEFENSE/DIRECT STUDENT LOANS
Type of Assistance: Direct payments ranging from $100 to $4,738,389.
Applicant Eligibility: Nonprofit organizations, state and local governments.
Objective: To establish loan funds at eligible higher education institutions to permit needy undergraduate and graduate students to compete their education.
Contact: Policy Section, Campus-Based Branch, Division of Policy and Program Development, Bureau of Student Financial Assistance, 400 Maryland Avenue, S.W., Washington, DC 20202, 202-245-2991.

84.039 LIBRARY RESEARCH AND DEMONSTRATION
Type of Assistance: Grants ranging from $1,800 to $320,000.
Applicant Eligibility: Nonprofit organizations, state and local governments.
Objective: To award grants and contracts for research and/or demonstration projects in areas of specialized services intended to improve library and information science practices and principles.

Contact: Chief, Research and Demonstration Branch, Division of Library Programs, Office of Libraries and Learning Resources, Bureau of Elementary and Secondary Education, Department of Education, 400 Maryland Avenue, S.W., Washington, DC 20202, 202-245-2994.

84.040   SCHOOL ASSISTANCE IN FEDERALLY AFFECTED AREAS—CONSTRUCTION

Type of Assistance: Grants ranging from $2,000 to $3,000,000.
Applicant Eligibility: Nonprofit organizations, state and local governments.
Objective: To provide assistance for the construction of urgently needed minimum school facilities in school districts that have had substantial increases in school enrollment as a result of new or increased federal activities, or where reconstruction of facilities is necessary because of natural disaster.
Contact: Division of School Assistance in Federally Affected Areas, Bureau of Elementary and Secondary Education, Department of Education, 400 Maryland Avenue, S.W., Washington, DC 20202, 202-245-8427.

84.041   SCHOOL ASSISTANCE IN FEDERALLY AFFECTED AREAS—MAINTENANCE AND OPERATION

Type of Assistance: Grants ranging from $1,000 to over $12,000,000.
Applicant Eligibility: Local governments.
Objective: To provide financial assistance to local educational agencies when enrollments or availability of revenue are adversely affected by federal activities; where the tax base of a district is reduced through the federal acquisition of real property; or where there is a sudden and substantial increase in school attendance as the result of federal activities. Also to assist local agencies in the education of children residing on federal or Indian lands and children whose parents are employed on federal property in the Uniformed Services.
Contact: Director, Division of School Assistance in Federally Affected Areas, Bureau of Elementary and Secondary Education, Department of Education, 400 Maryland Avenue, S.W., Washington, DC 20202, 202-245-8427.

84.042   SPECIAL SERVICES FOR DISADVANTAGED STUDENTS

Type of Assistance: Grants ranging from $35,911 to $307,488.
Applicant Eligibility: Nonprofit organizations, state and local governments.
Objective: To assist students who may be educationally, economically, or culturally deprived, or physically handicapped, or have limited English-speaking ability, who are enrolled or accepted for enrollment by institutions which are recipients of grants, to complete their postsecondary education.
Contact: Director, Division of Student Services and Veterans Programs, Bureau of Higher and Continuing Education, Department of Education, 400 Maryland Avenue, S.W., Washington, DC 20202, 202-245-2511.

84.043 STRENGTHENING STATE EDUCATIONAL AGENCY MANAGEMENT

Type of Assistance: Grants ranging from $400,000 to $4,000,000.

Applicant Eligibility: State governments.

Objective: To strengthen the leadership resources of state educational agencies and to assist in identifying and meeting the critical educational needs of their state.

Contact: Bureau of Elementary and Secondary Education, Division of State Educational Assistance Programs, Department of Education, 400 Maryland Avenue, S.W., Washington, DC 20202, 202-245-2495.

84.044 TALENT SEARCH

Type of Assistance: Grants ranging from $43,779 to $240,000.

Applicant Eligibility: Nonprofit organizations and local governments.

Objective: To identify youths of financial or cultural need with exceptional potential for postsecondary educational training, and assist them through financial aid in obtaining admissions to postsecondary schools; and to decrease the rate of secondary and postsecondary school dropout and increase the number of secondary and postsecondary school dropouts who reenter educational programs.

Contact: Director, Division of Student Services and Veterans Programs, Bureau of Higher and Continuing Education, Department of Education, 400 Maryland Avenue, S.W., Washington, DC 20202, 202-245-2511.

84.045 TEACHER CORPS—OPERATIONS AND TRAINING

Type of Assistance: Grants up to $300,000.

Applicant Eligibility: Nonprofit organizations, state and local governments.

Objective: To strengthen the educational opportunities available to children in areas having concentrations of low-income families; to encourage colleges and universities to broaden their programs of teacher preparation; and to encourage institutions of higher education and local education agencies to improve their programs of training and retraining for in-service teachers, teacher aides, and other educational personnel.

Contact: Operations Branch, Teacher Corps, Department of Education, 400 Maryland Avenue, S.W., Washington, DC 20202, 202-653-8334.

84.046 CONTINUING EDUCATION OUTREACH

Type of Assistance: Grants ranging from $17,214 to $760,470.

Applicant Eligibility: State and local governments.

Objective: To encourage colleges and universities to assist in the solution of community problems by strengthening community service programs; to strengthen existing community service mechanisms or create new ones; to expand continuing education opportunities; and to plan for resource materials sharing that will expand learning opportunities for adults.

Contact: Chief, CSCE Branch, Division of Training and Facilities, Bureau of Higher and Continuing Education, Department of Education, 400 Maryland Avenue, S.W., Washington, DC 20202, 202-245-9868.

84.047 UPWARD BOUND

Type of Assistance: Grants ranging from $49,000 to $400,000.

Applicant Eligibility: Nonprofit organizations, state and local governments.

Objective: To generate the skill and motivation necessary for success in education beyond high school among young people from low-income families who have academic potential, but who may lack adequate secondary school preparation. The goal of the program is to increase the academic performance and motivational levels of eligible enrollees so that such persons may complete secondary school and successfully pursue postsecondary educational programs.

Contact: Director, Division of Student Services and Veterans Programs, Bureau of Higher and Continuing Education, Department of Education, 400 Maryland Avenue, S.W., Washington, DC 20202, 202-245-2511.

84.048 VOCATIONAL EDUCATION— BASIC GRANTS TO STATES

Type of Assistance: Grants ranging from $144,449 to $41,212,931.

Applicant Eligibility: State governments.

Objective: To assist states in improving planning for, and in conducting, vocational programs on the local level for persons of all ages who desire and need education and training for employment.

Contact: Director, Division of State Vocational Program Operations, Bureau of Occupational and Adult Education, Department of Education, 400 Maryland Avenue, S.W., Washington, DC 20202, 202-472-3440.

84.049 VOCATIONAL EDUCATION—CONSUMER AND HOMEMAKING EDUCATION

Type of Assistance: Grants ranging from $13,253 to $3,781,128.

Applicant Eligibility: State governments.

Objective: To assist states in conducting programs in consumer and homemaking education. Emphasis is placed on programs located in economically depressed areas or areas with high rates of unemployment.

Contact: Director, Division of State Vocational Program Operations, Bureau of Occupational and Adult Education, Department of Education, 400 Maryland Avenue, S.W., Washington, DC 20202, 202-472-3440.

84.050 VOCATIONAL EDUCATION—PROGRAM IMPROVEMENT AND SUPPORTIVE SERVICE

Type of Assistance: Grants ranging from $35,782 to $8,991,128.

Applicant Eligibility: State governments.

Objective: To assist the states in improving their programs of vocational education and in providing supportive services for such programs.

Contact: Director, Division of State Vocational Program Operations, Bureau of Occupational and Adult Education, Department of Education, 400 Maryland Avenue, S.W., Washington, DC 20202, 202-472-3440.

84.051 VOCATIONAL EDUCATION—PROGRAM IMPROVEMENT PROJECTS
Type of Assistance: Grants ranging from $100,000 to $5,000,000.
Applicant Eligibility: Individuals, nonprofit organizations, state and local governments.
Objective: To provide support for a National Center for Research in Vocational Education, projects for research, curriculum development, and demonstration in vocational education, and six curriculum coordination centers.
Contact: Director, Division of Research and Demonstration, Bureau of Occupational and Adult Education, Department of Education, 400 Maryland Avenue, S.W., Washington, DC 20202, 202-245-9634.

84.052 VOCATIONAL EDUCATION—SPECIAL PROGRAMS FOR THE DISADVANTAGED
Type of Assistance: Grants ranging from $6,094 to $1,738,570.
Applicant Eligibility: State governments.
Objective: To provide special vocational education programs for persons who have academic or economic handicaps and who require special services and assistance in order to succeed in vocational education programs.
Contact: Director, Division of State Vocational Education Program Operations, Bureau of Occupational and Adult Education, Department of Education, 400 Maryland Avenue, S.W., Washington, DC 20202, 202-245-3488.

84.053 VOCATIONAL EDUCATION— STATE ADVISORY COUNCILS
Type of Assistance: Grants ranging from $91,135 to $172,920.
Applicant Eligibility: State governments.
Objective: To advise state boards for vocational education on the development and administration of state plans; evaluate vocational education programs, services, and activities and publish and distribute the results; and prepare and submit through the state boards an annual evaluation report to the Commissioner and the National Advisory Council.
Contact: Director, Division of State Vocational Program Operations, Bureau of Occupational and Adult Education, Department of Education, 400 Maryland Avenue, S.W., Washington, DC 20202, 202-472-3440.

84.055 HIGHER EDUCATION—COOPERATIVE EDUCATION
Type of Assistance: Grants ranging from $20,000 to $175,000.
Applicant Eligibility: Nonprofit organizations.
Objective: To provide federal support for cooperative education programs in institutions of higher education, for the training of persons in the planning,

establishment, administration, and coordination of programs of cooperative education; for projects demonstrating or exploring the feasibility or value of innovative methods of cooperative education; and for research into methods of improving, developing, or promoting the use of cooperative education programs in institutions of higher education. Cooperative education programs are those in which periods of academic study alternate or parallel periods of public or private employment related to the student's academic program or professional goals.

Contact: Chief, Cooperative Education Branch, Division of Training and Facilities, Bureau of Higher and Continuing Education, Department of Education, 400 Maryland Avenue, S.W., Washington, DC 20202, 202-245-2146.

84.056   EMERGENCY SCHOOL AID ACT—BASIC GRANTS TO LOCAL EDUCATIONAL AGENCIES

Type of Assistance: Grants averaging $391,728.
Applicant Eligibility: Local governments.
Objective: To assist the process of eliminating, reducing, or preventing minority group isolation. Funds are to be made available only to local educational agencies.
Contact: Division of Equal Educational Opportunity Program Operations, Bureau of Elementary and Secondary Education, Department of Education, 400 Maryland Avenue, S.W., Washington DC 20202, 202-245-7965.

84.057   EMERGENCY SCHOOL AID ACT—GRANTS TO NONPROFIT ORGANIZATIONS

Type of Assistance: Grants averaging $100,000.
Applicant Eligibility: Nonprofit organizations.
Objective: To assist the process of eliminating, reducing, or preventing minority group isolation. Funds are to be made available to public or private nonprofit agencies, institutions, or organizations other than local educational agencies.
Contact: Division of Equal Educational Opportunity Program Operations, Bureau of Elementary and Secondary Education, Department of Education, 400 Maryland Avenue, S.W., Washington, DC 20202, 202-472-2286.

84.058   EMERGENCY SCHOOL AID ACT—EDUCATIONAL TELEVISION AND RADIO

Type of Assistance: Grants (dollar amount not available).
Applicant Eligibility: Nonprofit organizations.
Objective: To assist the process of eliminating, reducing, or preventing minority group isolation. Funds are available to public or private nonprofit agencies, institutions, or organizations with expertise in the development of television and radio programming which has positive cognitive and affective value and presents multiethnic children's activities. Programs developed will

be made reasonably available for transmission, free of charge, and will not be transmitted under commercial sponsorship.

Contact: Chief, ESAA Broadcast Branch, Division of Educational Technology, Bureau of Elementary and Secondary Education, Department of Education, 400 Maryland Avenue, S.W., Washington, DC 20202, 202-245-9225.

84.060 DEVELOPMENTAL AWARDS PROGRAM, INDIAN EDUCATION—LOCAL EDUCATIONAL AGENCIES AND TRIBAL SCHOOLS

Type of Assistance: Grants ranging from $526 to $998,293.

Applicant Eligibility: Local governments.

Objective: To provide financial assistance to local educational agencies and tribally controlled schools to develop and implement elementary and secondary school programs designed to meet the special educational and culturally related academic needs of Indian children. More specifically to increase academic performance with special emphasis on basic skills; reduce dropout rates and improve attendance; and increase the relevance of academic offerings by the schools to the cultural heritage of Indian children.

Contact: Office of Indian Education, Department of Education, 400 Maryland Avenue, S.W., Washington, DC 20202, 202-245-9159.

84.061 INDIAN EDUCATION— SPECIAL PROGRAMS AND PROJECTS

Type of Assistance: Grants ranging from $5,580 to $400,000.

Applicant Eligibility: State and local governments.

Objective: To plan, develop, and implement programs and projects for the improvement of educational opportunities for Indian children.

Contact: Office of Indian Education, Department of Education, 400 Maryland Avenue, S.W., Washington DC 20202, 202-245-2673.

84.062 INDIAN EDUCATION—ADULT INDIAN EDUCATION

Type of Assistance: Grants ranging from $20,600 to $195,000.

Applicant Eligibility: State and local governments.

Objective: To plan, develop, and implement programs for Indian adults to decrease the rate of illiteracy, increase the mastery of basic skills, increase the number who earn high school equivalency diplomas, and encourage the development of programs relevant to the culture and heritage of Indian adults.

Contact: Office of Indian Education, Department of Education, 400 Maryland Avenue, S.W., Washington, DC 20202, 202-245-2673.

84.063 PELL GRANT PROGRAM

Type of Assistance: Direct payments ranging from $200 to $1,800.

Applicant Eligibility: Individuals.

Objective: To assist in making available the benefits of postsecondary education to qualified students.

Contact: Division of Policy and Program Development, Basic Grants Branch, Bureau of Student Financial Assistance, Department of Education, 400 Maryland Avenue, S.W., Washington, DC 20202, 800-638-6700; in Maryland call 800-492-6602.

84.064 HIGHER EDUCATION—VETERANS' COST OF INSTRUCTION PROGRAM

Type of Assistance: Direct payments ranging from $879 to $118,000.
Applicant Eligibility: Nonprofit organizations, state and local governments.
Objective: To encourage colleges and universities to serve the special needs of veterans, especially Vietnam-era and disadvantaged veterans.
Contact: Chief, Veterans' Program Branch, Division of Student Services and Veterans' Programs, Bureau of Higher and Continuing Education, Department of Education, 400 Maryland Avenue, S.W., Washington, DC 20202, 202-245-2806.

84.065 EDUCATIONAL TELEVISION AND RADIO PROGRAMMING

Type of Assistance: Grants (dollar amount not available).
Applicant Eligibility: Nonprofit organizations, state and local governments.
Objective: To carry out the development, production, evaluation, dissemination, and utilization of innovative television and/or radio programs designed for broadcast and/or nonbroadcast educational uses.
Contact: Educational Technology Development Branch, Division of Educational Technology, Office of Libraries and Learning Resources, Bureau of Elementary and Secondary Education, Department of Education, 400 Maryland Avenue, S.W., Washington, DC 20202, 202-245-9228.

84.066 EDUCATIONAL OPPORTUNITY CENTERS

Type of Assistance: Grants ranging from $106,000 to $410,000.
Applicant Eligibility: Nonprofit organizations, state and local governments.
Objective: To provide and coordinate services for residents in areas with a concentration of low-income people to facilitate entry into postsecondary educational programs, and to provide tutoring, counseling, and other supportive services for enrolled postsecondary students from the target community.
Contact: Director, Division of Student Services and Veterans' Programs, Bureau of Higher and Continuing Education, Department of Education, 400 Maryland Avenue, S.W., Washington, DC 20202, 202-245-2511.

84.067 USE OF TECHNOLOGY IN BASIC SKILLS INSTRUCTION

Type of Assistance: Grants (dollar amount not available).
Applicant Eligibility: Nonprofit organizations.
Objective: To support development and demonstration activities related to

the improved use of television and other technology to contribute to the instruction of children in reading, mathematics, and written and oral communication. To expand the variety and improve the quality of instructional efforts involving the use of technology.
Contact: Division of Educational Technology, Office of Libraries and Learning Resources, Bureau of Elementary and Secondary Education, Department of Education, 400 Maryland Avenue, S.W., Washington, DC 20202, 202-245-9228.

84.068   INDOCHINESE REFUGEE CHILDREN ASSISTANCE
Type of Assistance: Grants ranging from $7,000 to $2,500,000.
Applicant Eligibility: State governments.
Objective: To provide federal assistance to states in order to assist local educational agencies to provide supplemental educational services to the Indochinese refugee children enrolled in public and nonpublic elementary and secondary schools.
Contact: Director, Indochinese Refugee Children Assistance Staff, Office of Compensatory Educational Programs, Bureau of Elementary and Secondary Education, Department of Education, 400 Maryland Avenue, S.W., Washington, DC 20202, 202-472-7177.

84.069   GRANTS TO STATES FOR STATE STUDENT INCENTIVES
Type of Assistance: Grants ranging from $1,613 to $12,000,000.
Applicant Eligibility: State and local governments.
Objective: To make incentive grants to the states to develop and expand assistance to eligible students in attendance at institutions of postsecondary education.
Contact: Chief, State Student Incentive Grant Program, State Programs Branch, Bureau of Student Financial Assistance, Department of Education, 400 Maryland Avenue, S.W., Washington, DC 20202, 202-472-4265.

84.070   ETHNIC HERITAGE STUDIES PROGRAM
Type of Assistance: Grants ranging from $10,000 to $60,000.
Applicant Eligibility: Nonprofit organizations, state and local governments.
Objective: To recognize the contributions of ethnic groups to American society; to provide students opportunities to learn more about the nature of their own heritage and that of other groups; and to reduce social divisiveness by promoting awareness of ethnic and cultural diversity in the nation.
Contact: Ethnic Heritage Studies Staff (Attn: Application Officer), Bureau of School Improvement, Department of Education, 400 Maryland Avenue, S.W., Washington, DC 20202, 202-245-3471.

84.072 INDIAN EDUCATION—GRANTS TO INDIAN CONTROLLED SCHOOLS

Type of Assistance: Grants ranging from $50,000 to $160,000.
Applicant Eligibility: State and local governments.
Objective: To provide financial assistance to nonlocal educational agencies to develop and implement elementary and secondary school programs designed to meet the special educational needs of Indian children. Nonlocal educational agencies are schools on or near a reservation which are governed by a nonprofit institution or organization of an Indian tribe.
Contact: Office of Indian Education, Department of Education, 400 Maryland Avenue, S.W., Washington, DC 20202, 202-245-2673.

84.073 NATIONAL DIFFUSION PROGRAM

Type of Assistance: Advisory services, dissemination of technical information, and grants ranging from $20,000 to $305,000.
Applicant Eligibility: Nonprofit organizations and local governments.
Objective: To promote and accelerate the systematic rapid dissemination, and adoption by public and nonpublic educational institutions nationwide, of educational practices, products, and programs that were developed through federal, state, and local government funds and whose effectiveness has been substantiated by the Joint Dissemination Review Panel of the Department of Education.
Contact: National Diffusion Network Division, Department of Education, Rm. 802, 1832 N Street, N.W., Washington, DC 20036, 202-653-7000.

84.074 CAREER EDUCATION

Type of Assistance: Grants ranging from $83,750 to $497,000.
Applicant Eligibility: Nonprofit organizations, state and local governments.
Objective: To demonstrate the most effective methods and techniques in career education and to develop exemplary career education models at elementary, secondary, and postsecondary levels of instruction.
Contact: Office of Career Education, Department of Education, ROB-3, Rm. 3100, 7th and D Streets, S.W., Washington, DC 20202, 202-245-2284.

84.077 BILINGUAL VOCATIONAL TRAINING

Type of Assistance: Grants ranging from $105,723 to $366,746.
Applicant Eligibility: Nonprofit organizations, state and local governments.
Objective: To train individuals of limited English-speaking ability for gainful employment as semiskilled or skilled workers, technicians, or subprofessionals in recognized, new, and emerging occupations.
Contact: Demonstration Branch, Division of Research and Demonstration, Bureau of Occupational and Adult Education, Department of Education, 400 Maryland Avenue, S.W., Washington, DC 20202, 202-245-2600.

84.078 REGIONAL EDUCATION PROGRAMS FOR DEAF AND OTHER HANDICAPPED PERSONS
Type of Assistance: Grants ranging from $75,000 to $450,200.
Applicant Eligibility: Nonprofit organizations and local governments.
Objective: To develop and operate specially designed or modified programs of vocational, technical, postsecondary, or adult education for deaf or other handicapped persons.
Contact: Program Development Branch, Regional Education Programs, Division of Innovation and Development, Bureau of Education for the Handicapped, Department of Education, 400 Maryland Avenue, S.W., Washington, DC 20202, 202-245-9722.

84.079 EDUCATION FOR THE USE OF THE METRIC SYSTEM OF MEASUREMENT
Type of Assistance: Grants ranging from $14,824 to $95,972.
Applicant Eligibility: Nonprofit organizations, state and local governments.
Objective: To provide assistance to state and local educational agencies, institutions of higher education, and public and private nonprofit organizations, groups, and institutions in their efforts to teach students, teachers, parents, and other adults to use the revised metric system of measurement.
Contact: Director, Metric Education Program, Bureau of Occupational and Adult Education, Department of Education, 3700 Donohue Building, 400 Maryland Avenue, S.W., Washington, DC 20202, 202-426-7220.

84.080 EDUCATION FOR GIFTED AND TALENTED CHILDREN AND YOUTH
Type of Assistance: Grants ranging from $6,000 to $190,000.
Applicant Eligibility: Nonprofit organizations, state and local governments.
Objective: To support state and local planning, development, operation, and improvement of programs and projects designed to meet the special educational needs of the gifted and talented at preschool, elementary, and secondary levels; development and dissemination of information pertaining to such education; in-service training of educational personnel and their supervisors working with the gifted and talented; professional development and leadership training; and model or exemplary projects.
Contact: Director, Gifted and Talented Staff, Office of the Deputy Commissioner, Bureau of Education for the Handicapped, Department of Education, 400 Maryland Avenue, S.W., Washington, DC 20202, 202-245-2482.

84.081 COMMUNITY EDUCATION
Type of Assistance: Grants ranging from $7,800 to $81,800.
Applicant Eligibility: Nonprofit organizations, state and local governments.
Objective: To provide educational, recreational, cultural, and other related community services in accordance with the needs, interest, and concerns of the community, through the establishment of the community education pro-

gram as a center for such activities in cooperation with other community groups.
Contact: Director, Community Education Program, Bureau of School Improvement, Department of Education, 400 Maryland Avenue, S.W., Washington, DC 20202, 202-245-0691.

84.082 CONSUMERS' EDUCATION
Type of Assistance: Grants ranging from $14,440 to $105,000.
Applicant Eligibility: Nonprofit organizations, state and local governments.
Objective: To provide consumers' education to students and the general public.
Contact: Director, Office of Consumers' Education, Bureau of School Improvement, Department of Education, 400 Maryland Avenue, S.W., Washington, DC 20202, 202-426-9303.

84.083 WOMEN'S EDUCATIONAL EQUITY
Type of Assistance: Grants ranging from $10,000 to $480,000.
Applicant Eligibility: Nonprofit organizations, state and local governments.
Objective: To promote educational equity for women and girls at all levels of education, and to provide financial assistance to local educational institutions to meet the requirements of Title IX of the Education Amendments of 1972.
Contact: Women's Educational Equity Act Program, Department of Education, Rm. 1105, Donohue Building, 400 6th Street, S.W., Washington, DC 20202, 202-245-2181.

84.084 ELEMENTARY AND SECONDARY SCHOOL EDUCATION IN THE ARTS
Type of Assistance: Grants ranging from $25,000 to $100,000.
Applicant Eligibility: State governments.
Objective: To encourage and support programs that recognize and stress the essential role that the arts play in elementary and secondary education, and conduct programs in which the arts are an integral part of elementary and secondary school curricula; to develop performing arts for children and youth; and to identify, develop, and implement model projects or programs in all the arts for handicapped persons.
Contact: Arts and Humanities Staff, Department of Education, 400 Maryland Avenue, S.W., Washington, DC 20202, 202-472-7793.

84.086 INNOVATIVE PROGRAMS FOR SEVERELY HANDICAPPED CHILDREN
Type of Assistance: Grants ranging from $54,680 to $189,900.
Applicant Eligibility: Nonprofit organizations, state and local governments.
Objective: To improve and expand innovative educational and training services for severely handicapped children and youth, and improve the accep-

tance of such people by the general public, professionals, and possible employers.
Contact: Projects for Severely Handicapped Children and Youth, Special Needs Section, Bureau of Education for the Handicapped, Department of Education, 400 Maryland Avenue, S.W., Washington, DC 20202, 202-472-2535.

84.087   INDIAN EDUCATION—
FELLOWSHIPS FOR INDIAN STUDENTS

Type of Assistance: Grants ranging from $2,300 to $13,000.
Applicant Eligibility: Native Americans.
Objective: To provide support that enables American Indians to study for careers in medicine, law, engineering, natural resources, business administration, education, and related fields.
Contact: Office of Indian Education, Department of Education, 400 Maryland Avenue, S.W., Washington, DC 20202, 202-245-2673.

84.088   INSTRUCTIONAL MATERIALS
AND SCHOOL LIBRARY RESOURCES

Type of Assistance: Grants ranging from $53,545 to $16,949,647.
Applicant Eligibility: State governments.
Objective: To carry out a program of making grants to states for the acquisition of school library resources, textbooks, and other printed instructional materials for use by children and teachers in public and private elementary and secondary schools; for the acquisition of instructional equipment (such as laboratory and other special equipment, including audiovisual materials) for use by children and teachers in elementary and secondary schools; and for guidance, counseling, and testing.
Contact: Office of Libraries and Learning Resources, Bureau of Elementary and Secondary Education, Department of Education, 400 Maryland Avenue, S.W., Washington, DC 20202, 202-245-2488.

84.089   IMPROVEMENT IN LOCAL EDUCATIONAL PRACTICE

Type of Assistance: Grants ranging from $865,473 to $18,352,051.
Applicant Eligibility: State governments.
Objective: To provide assistance to state educational agencies so that they, in turn, may provide assistance to local educational agencies to improve their educational practices, including activities to improve achievement of children in basic skills; activities to encourage parental participation; development of programs to diagnose learning problems and assess achievement of children (including those in nonpublic schools); improving school management and professional development programs for teachers, administrators, and other instructional personnel; early childhood and family education programs; and expanding education beyond the school building.
Contact: Division of State Educational Assistance Programs, Bureau of Ele-

mentary and Secondary Education, Department of Education, Rm. 3010, 400 Maryland Avenue, S.W., Washington, DC 20202, 202-245-1990.

84.090 HEALTH EDUCATION ASSISTANCE LOANS

Type of Assistance: Guaranteed/insured loans up to $10,000 per year.
Applicant Eligibility: Individuals.
Objective: To authorize loans for educational expenses available from eligible lenders such as banks, credit unions, savings and loan associations, pension funds, insurance companies, and eligible educational institutions. Loans are made to graduate students enrolled at eligible health professions institutions. The loans are insured by the federal government.
Contact: Health Loan Branch, DHHS, PHS, Health Services Administration, Bureau of Health and Personal Development Services, Division of Student Services, P. O. Box 1837, Rm. 1165, 6525 Bellcrest Road, Hyattsville, MD 20782, 301-436-5986.

84.091 STRENGTHENING RESEARCH LIBRARY RESOURCES

Type of Assistance: Grants ranging from $69,000 to $750,000.
Applicant Eligibility: Individuals, nonprofit organizations, and local governments.
Objective: To promote high quality research and education throughout the United States by providing financial assistance to help major research libraries maintain and strengthen their collections; and to assist major research libraries in making their holdings available to individual researchers and scholars outside their primary clientele and to other libraries whose users have need for research materials.
Contact: Library Education and Postsecondary Resources Branch, Division of Library Programs, Office of Libraries and Learning Resources, Bureau of Elementary and Secondary Education, Department of Education, 400 Maryland Avenue, S.W., Washington, DC 20202, 202-245-9530.

84.093 EMERGENCY ADULT EDUCATION PROGRAM FOR INDOCHINESE REFUGEES

Type of Assistance: Grants (dollar amount not available.)
Applicant Eligibility: State and local governments.
Objective: To provide emergency adult education programs and educational support services for Indochinese refugees.
Contact: Director, Division of Adult Education, Bureau of Occupational and Adult Education, Department of Education, 400 Maryland Avenue, S.W., Washington, DC 20202, 202-245-2278.

84.094 GRADUATE AND PROFESSIONAL STUDY

Type of Assistance: Grants ranging from $4,500 to $32,000.
Applicant Eligibility: Individuals, nonprofit organizations, state and local governments.

Objective: To provide funds to institutions of higher education to strengthen and develop programs which would assist in providing graduate or professional education to persons with varied backgrounds and experiences including, but not limited to, members of minority groups that are underrepresented in colleges and universities and in academic and professional career fields. To provide fellowships to institutions to support full-time graduate and professional training of women and of members of minority groups, especially those who have been underrepresented in academic and other professional careers of importance to the national interest.

Contact: Bureau of Higher and Continuing Education, Division of Training and Facilities, Graduate Training Branch, Department of Education, ROB-3, 7th and D Streets, S.W., Washington, DC 20202, 202-245-2347.

84.095 INTERNATIONAL UNDERSTANDING PROGRAM

Type of Assistance: Grants ranging from $25,000 to $100,000.

Applicant Eligibility: Nonprofit organizations, state and local governments.

Objective: To provide assistance to projects that will increase the availability of information about the cultures, actions, and policies of other nations to students in the United States so that they might make more informed judgments with respect to the international policies and actions of the United States.

Contact: Section 603 Task Force, Division of International Education, Department of Education, 400 Maryland Avenue, S.W., Washington, DC 20202, 202-245-2794.

84.096 INCENTIVE GRANTS FOR STATE STUDENT FINANCIAL ASSISTANCE TRAINING

Type of Assistance: Grants up to $30,000.

Applicant Eligibility: State governments.

Objective: To make incentive grants to states to design, develop, and implement programs to increase the proficiency of state and institutional financial aid administrators in all aspects of student financial assistance. Designated state agencies responsible for student grants administer this program in consultation with statewide financial aid administrator organizations.

Contact: Director, Division of Training and Dissemination, Bureau of Student Financial Assistance, Department of Education, 400 Maryland Avenue, S.W., Washington, DC 20202, 202-472-3278.

84.097 LAW SCHOOL CLINICAL EXPERIENCE PROGRAM

Type of Assistance: Grants ranging from $22,000 to $56,000.

Applicant Eligibility: Nonprofit organizations.

Objective: To establish and expand programs in law schools to provide clinical experience to students in the practice of law, with preference being given to programs providing such experience, to the extent practicable, in the preparation and trial of cases.

Contact: Graduate Training Branch, Bureau of Higher and Continuing Education, Department of Education, 7th and D Streets, S.W., Washington, DC 20202, 202-245-2347.

84.099   BILINGUAL VOCATIONAL INSTRUCTOR TRAINING

Type of Assistance: Grants ranging from $129,234 to $226,377.
Applicant Eligibility: Nonprofit organizations, state and local governments.
Objective: To provide training for instructors of bilingual vocational training programs.
Contact: Demonstration Branch, Division of Research and Demonstration, Bureau of Occupational and Adult Education, Department of Education, 400 Maryland Avenue, S.W., Washington, DC 20202, 202-245-2600.

84.100   BILINGUAL VOCATIONAL INSTRUCTIONAL
MATERIALS, METHODS, AND TECHNIQUES

Type of Assistance: Grants averaging $280,000.
Applicant Eligibility: Nonprofit organizations, state and local governments.
Objective: To develop bilingual instructional materials, and encourage research programs and demonstration projects to meet the shortage of such instructional materials available for bilingual vocational training programs.
Contact: Demonstration Branch, Division of Research and Demonstration, Bureau of Occupational and Adult Education, Department of Education, 400 Maryland Avenue, S.W., Washington, DC 20202, 202-245-9614.

84.101   VOCATIONAL EDUCATION—PROGRAM FOR INDIAN
TRIBES AND INDIAN ORGANIZATIONS

Type of Assistance: Grants ranging from $33,883 to $672,705.
Applicant Eligibility: Native Americans.
Objective: To make grants to Indian tribal organizations to plan, conduct, and administer programs or portions of programs that provide occupational training opportunities.
Contact: Director, Division of Research and Demonstration, Bureau of Occupational and Adult Education, Department of Education, 400 Maryland Avenue, S.W., Washington, DC 20202, 202-245-9634.

84.102   EMERGENCY SCHOOL AID ACT—MAGNET
SCHOOLS, UNIVERSITY/BUSINESS COOPERATION
AND NEUTRAL SITE PLANNING

Type of Assistance: Grants averaging $376,144.
Applicant Eligibility: Local governments.
Objective: To encourage the voluntary elimination, reduction, or prevention of minority group isolation in elementary and secondary schools with substantial proportions of minority group students.
Contact: Division of Equal Educational Opportunity, Program Operations,

Bureau of Elementary and Secondary Education, Department of Education, 400 Maryland Avenue, S.W., Washington, DC 20202, 202-245-7965.

84.103 TRAINING FOR SPECIAL PROGRAMS STAFF AND LEADERSHIP PERSONNEL

Type of Assistance: Grants (dollar amount not available).
Applicant Eligibility: Nonprofit organizations, state and local governments.
Objective: To provide training for staff and leadership personnel associated with projects funded under the Special Programs for Students from Disadvantaged Backgrounds.
Contact: Division of Student Services and Veterans Programs, Bureau of Higher and Continuing Education, Department of Education, 400 Maryland Avenue, S.W., Washington, DC 20202, 202-245-2511.

84.104 CAREER EDUCATION STATE ALLOTMENT PROGRAM

Type of Assistance: Grants ranging from $125,000 to $1,682,000.
Applicant Eligibility: State and local governments.
Objective: To enable state and local education agencies to implement career education in elementary and secondary schools.
Contact: Office of Career Education, Department of Education, Rm. 3100, ROB-3, 7th and D Streets, S.W., Washington, DC 20202, 202-245-2284.

84.105 BASIC SKILLS IMPROVEMENTS

Type of Assistance: Grants (dollar amount not available).
Applicant Eligibility: Nonprofit organizations, state and local governments.
Objective: To provide facilitative services and resources to stimulate educational institutions, governmental agencies, and private organizations to improve and expand their activities relating to reading, written and oral communication skills, and mathematical skills.
Contact: Basic Skills Program Office, Department of Education, 400 Maryland Avenue, S.W., Washington, DC 20202, 202-245-8537.

EDUCATION—II

84.106 EMERGENCY SCHOOL AID ACT—PLANNING GRANTS

Type of Assistance: Grants (dollar amount not available).
Applicant Eligibility: State governments.
Objective: To assist the process of eliminating, reducing, or preventing minority group isolation.
Contact: Division of Equal Educational Opportunity Program Operations, Bureau of Elementary and Secondary Education, Department of Education, 400 Maryland Avenue, S.W., Washington, DC 20202, 202-245-7965.

84.107 EMERGENCY SCHOOL AID ACT—
PREIMPLEMENTATION ASSISTANCE GRANTS

Type of Assistance: Grants averaging $78,766.

Applicant Eligibility: Nonprofit organizations, state and local governments.

Objective: To assist the process of eliminating, reducing, or preventing minority group isolation. Funds are to provide help to a local educational agency that has adopted, but not yet implemented, a required plan to prepare for the reassignment of children or faculty.

Contact: Division of Equal Educational Opportunity Program Operations, Bureau of Elementary and Secondary Education, Department of Education, 400 Maryland Avenue, S.W., Washington, DC 20202, 202-245-7965.

84.108 EMERGENCY SCHOOL AID ACT—
OUT-OF-CYCLE GRANTS

Type of Assistance: Grants averaging $976,000.

Applicant Eligibility: Nonprofit organizations, state and local governments.

Objective: To assist the process of eliminating, reducing, or preventing minority group isolation. Funds are to provide help to a local education agency to meet education needs that arise from the implementation of a plan adopted too late to serve as the basis for a basic grant application in the most recent competition.

Contact: Division of Equal Educational Opportunity Program Operations, Bureau of Elementary and Secondary Education, Department of Education, 400 Maryland Avenue, S.W., Washington, DC 20202, 202-245-7965.

84.109 EMERGENCY SCHOOL AID ACT—SPECIAL
DISCRETIONARY ASSISTANCE GRANTS

Type of Assistance: Grants averaging $256,000.

Applicant Eligibility: Nonprofit organizations, state and local governments.

Objective: To assist the process of eliminating, reducing, or preventing minority group isolation. Funds are to provide help to a local education agency to meet unexpected educational needs that arise from the implementation of a qualifying plan after the deadline for receipt of basic grant applications.

Contact: Division of Equal Educational Opportunity Program Operations, Bureau of Elementary and Secondary Education, Department of Education, 400 Maryland Avenue, S.W., Washington, DC 20202, 202-245-7965.

84.110 EMERGENCY SCHOOL AID ACT—
STATE AGENCY GRANTS

Type of Assistance: Grants averaging $500,000.

Applicant Eligibility: Nonprofit organizations.

Objective: To meet special needs incident to the elimination of segregation and discrimination against minority group students and faculty, and to encourage the voluntary elimination, reduction, and prevention of minority group isolation in public education.

Contact: Division of Equal Educational Opportunity Program Operations, Bureau of Elementary and Secondary Education, Department of Education, 400 Maryland Avenue, S.W., Washington, DC 20202, 202-245-7965.

84.111 EMERGENCY SCHOOL AID ACT— GRANTS FOR THE ARTS

Type of Assistance: Grants averaging $100,000.
Applicant Eligibility: Local governments.
Objective: To assist the process of eliminating, reducing, or preventing minority group isolation. Funds are to provide, through the arts, opportunities for interracial and intercultural communication and understanding, and to meet the special needs incident to the implementation of a qualifying plan.
Contact: Division of Equal Educational Opportunity Program Operations, Bureau of Elementary and Secondary Education, Department of Education, 400 Maryland Avenue, S.W., Washington, DC 20202, 202-245-7965.

84.112 BIOMEDICAL SCIENCES FOR TALENTED DISADVANTAGED SECONDARY STUDENTS

Type of Assistance: Grants ranging from $240,000 to $300,000.
Applicant Eligibility: Nonprofit organizations.
Objective: To educate and motivate talented, but economically disadvantaged, youth to prepare them for admission into postsecondary schools leading to careers in the biomedical sciences.
Contact: Biomedical Sciences, Bureau of School Improvement, Department of Education, 400 Maryland Avenue, S.W., Washington, DC 20202, 202-472-2649.

84.113 ADULT EDUCATION PROGRAM FOR ADULT IMMIGRANTS

Type of Assistance: Grants (dollar amount not available).
Applicant Eligibility: Nonprofit organizations, state and local governments.
Objective: To provide adult education programs and educational support services for adult immigrants.
Contact: Director, Division of Adult Education, Bureau of Occupational and Adult Education, Department of Education, 400 Maryland Avenue, S.W., Washington, DC 20202, 202-245-2278.

OFFICE OF THE SECRETARY FOR EDUCATION

84.114 CAPACITY BUILDING FOR STATISTICAL ACTIVITIES IN STATE AGENCIES

Type of Assistance: Grants ranging from $29,500 to $69,750.
Applicant Eligibility: State governments.
Objective: To provide grants to increase the statistical capabilities of state

agencies by facilitating improvements or automation in their statistical systems.

Contact: National Center for Education Statistics, Rm. 3065, 400 Maryland Avenue, S.W., Washington, DC 20202, 202-245-8744.

84.115 INSTITUTE OF MUSEUM SERVICES

Type of Assistance: Grants ranging from $1,000 to $35,000.

Applicant Eligibility: Nonprofit organizations, state and local governments.

Objective: To help ease the increasing costs borne by museums as a result of their increasing use by the public; to encourage and assist museums in their educational and conservation roles; and to assist museums in modernizing their methods and facilities so that they may be better able to conserve our cultural, historic, and scientific heritage.

Contact: Director, Institute of Museum Services, Department of Education, Rm. 326H, 200 Independence Avenue, S.W., Washington, DC 20201, 202-245-7653.

84.116 FUND FOR THE IMPROVEMENT OF POSTSECONDARY EDUCATION

Type of Assistance: Grants ranging from $4,000 to $300,000.

Applicant Eligibility: Nonprofit organizations, state and local governments.

Objective: To provide assistance for innovative programs which improve the access to and the quality of postsecondary education.

Contact: Fund for the Improvement of Postsecondary Education, Department of Education, 400 Maryland Avenue, S.W., Washington, DC 20202, 202-245-8091.

NATIONAL INSTITUTE OF EDUCATION

84.117 EDUCATIONAL RESEARCH AND DEVELOPMENT

Type of Assistance: Grants ranging from $1,500 to $3,900,000.

Applicant Eligibility: Nonprofit organizations, state and local governments.

Objective: To improve the quality of educational practice, to promote the national policy of providing equal educational opportunities to all persons, and to support scientific inquiry into the educational process and dissemination activities through grant awards to projects that are most likely to contribute to new knowledge and increased understanding of the Institute's priority research areas: to improve student achievement in the basic skills of reading and mathematics; to help schools provide equal educational opportunities for non-English-speaking students, for women, and for disadvantaged students; to help educational institutions solve financial, productivity, and management problems; to help youth and adults enter and progress in careers; and to improve dissemination of the results of and knowledge gained from research and development.

Contact: Public Affairs Office, National Institute of Education, 1200 19th Street, N.W., Washington, DC 20208, 202-254-7150.

84.118 NATIONAL ADULT EDUCATION DEVELOPMENT AND DISSEMINATION PROGRAM AND PLANNING GRANTS

Type of Assistance: Grants (dollar amount not available).
Applicant Eligibility: State governments.
Objective: To provide development, demonstration, and dissemination projects and planning grants.
Contact: Division of Adult Education, Office of Vocational and Adult Education, Department of Education, 400 Maryland Avenue, S.W., Washington, DC 20202, 202-245-2278.

84.119 PRE-COLLEGE TEACHER DEVELOPMENT IN SCIENCE PROGRAM

Type of Assistance: Grants ranging from $11,500 to $50,000.
Applicant Eligibility: Colleges, universities, and nonprofit organizations.
Objective: To promote the offering of quality science, mathematics, and social studies to the nation's elementary school students.
Contact: Pre-College Teacher Development in Science Program, Professional Development and Dissemination, Department of Education, 400 Maryland Avenue, S.W., Washington, DC 20202, 202-282-7795.

84.120 MINORITY INSTITUTIONS SCIENCE IMPROVEMENT PROGRAM

Type of Assistance: Grants ranging from $5,000 to $300,000.
Applicant Eligibility: Colleges, universities, and nonprofit organizations.
Objective: To assist institutions to improve the quality of preparation of their students of minority work or careers in science. To increase the number of minority students graduating with majors in one of the sciences, mathematics, or engineering. To improve access for minorities to careers in science and engineering through community outreach programs at eligible colleges and universities. To improve the capability of minority institutions for self-assessment, management, and evaluation of their science programs and dissemination of their results.
Contact: Minority Institutions Science Improvement Program, Division of Science Education Resources Improvement, National Science Foundation, 1800 G Street, N.W., Washington, DC 20550, 202-282-7760.

84.121 VOCATIONAL EDUCATION— STATE PLANNING AND EVALUATION

Type of Assistance: Grants ranging from $1,324 to $434,757.
Applicant Eligibility: State governments.
Objective: To assist the states in fulfilling federally mandated planning and

evaluation requirements by providing a special allocation to each which does not have to be matched by state and/or local funds.
Contact: Division of State Vocational Program Operations, Office of Vocational and Adult Education, Department of Education, 400 Maryland Avenue, S.W., Washington, DC 20202, 202-472-3440.

84.122 SECRETARY'S DISCRETIONARY PROGRAM

Type of Assistance: Grants ranging from $5,000 to $300,000.
Applicant Eligibility: State and local governments and nonprofit organizations.
Objective: To assist in the development or demonstration of innovative techniques or approaches that contribute to the solution of educational problems.
Contact: Secretary's Discretionary Program, Office of School Improvement, Department of Education, 400 Maryland Avenue, S.W., Washington, DC 20202, 202-472-4594.

84.123 LAW-RELATED EDUCATION

Type of Assistance: Grants ranging from $15,000 to $35,000.
Applicant Eligibility: Nonprofit organizations, and state and local governments.
Objective: To assist in carrying out law-related education; in helping others develop programs; and in promoting research and development.
Contact: Law-Related Education Program, Office of School Improvement, Office of Educational Research and Improvement, Department of Education, 400 Maryland Avenue, S.W., Washington, DC 20202, 202-426-9303.

84.124 TERRITORIAL TEACHER TRAINING ASSISTANCE PROGRAM

Type of Assistance: Grants ranging from $100,000 to $500,000.
Applicant Eligibility: U.S. territories.
Objective: To provide assistance for the training of teachers in schools in Guam, American Samoa, the Commonwealth of the Northern Mariana Islands, the Trust Territory of the Pacific Islands, and the Virgin Islands.
Contact: Territorial Teacher Training Assistance Program, Office of School Improvement, Department of Education, 400 Maryland Avenue, S.W., Washington, DC 20202, 202-426-7220.

84.126 REHABILITATION SERVICES—BASIC SUPPORT

Type of Assistance: Grants ranging from $400,000 to $55,784,000.
Applicant Eligibility: State governments.
Objective: To provide vocational rehabilitation services to persons with mental and/or physical handicaps. Priority service is placed on needs of those persons with the most severe disabilities.

Contact: Director, Division of Resource Management, Rehabilitation Services Administration, Office of Human Development Services, Department of Education, Washington, DC 20201, 202-245-0085.

84.128 REHABILITATION SERVICES—SPECIAL PROJECTS

Type of Assistance: Grants (dollar amount not available).
Applicant Eligibility: Nonprofit organizations, state and local governments.
Objective: To provide funds to state vocational rehabilitation agencies and public nonprofit organizations for projects and demonstrations which hold promise of expanding and otherwise improving services for the mentally and physically handicapped over and above those provided by the basic support programs administered by states.
Contact: Director, Division of Innovation Programs, Rehabilitation Services Administration, Office of Human Development Services, Department of Education, Washington, DC 20201, 202-245-3186.

84.129 REHABILITATION TRAINING

Type of Assistance: Grants ranging from $5,000 to $200,000.
Applicant Eligibility: Nonprofit organizations, state and local governments.
Objective: To support projects to increase the numbers of personnel trained in providing vocational rehabilitation services to handicapped individuals.
Contact: Director, Division of Manpower Development, Rehabilitation Services Administration, Office of Human Development Services, Department of Education, Washington, DC 20201, 202-245-0079.

84.130 REHABILITATION SERVICES— INNOVATION AND EXPANSION

Type of Assistance: Grants ranging from $50,000 to $1,699,000.
Applicant Eligibility: Nonprofit organizations, state and local governments.
Objective: To provide part of the cost of planning, preparing for, and initiating special programs under the state plan in order to expand and improve vocational rehabilitation services for the mentally and physically handicapped.
Contact: Director, Division of Resource Management, Rehabilitation Services Administration, Office of Human Development Services, Department of Education, Washington, DC 20201, 202-245-0546.

84.132 CENTERS FOR INDEPENDENT LIVING

Type of Assistance: Grants (dollar amount not available).
Applicant Eligibility: Nonprofit organizations, state and local governments.
Objective: To provide independent living services to severely handicapped individuals in order for them to function more independently in family and community settings and secure and maintain appropriate employment.
Contact: Special Assistant for Independent Living Projects, Rehabilitation

Services Administration, Office of Human Development Services, Department of Education, 330 C Street, S.W., Washington, DC 20201, 202-245-0890.

84.133 NATIONAL INSTITUTE OF HANDICAPPED RESEARCH

Type of Assistance: Dissemination of technical information and grants ranging from $10,000 to $1,500,000.

Applicant Eligibility: Nonprofit organizations and local governments.

Objective: To support research and its utilization to improve the lives of people of all ages with physical and mental handicaps, especially the severely disabled, through identifying and eliminating causes and consequences of disability; maximizing the healthy physical and emotional status of handicapped persons and preventing or minimizing adverse personal, family, physical, mental, social, educational, vocational, and economic effects of disability; and reducing or eliminating the barriers to service and assistance and to using their abilities in daily life.

Contact: Director, National Institute of Handicapped Research, Office of Human Development Services, Department of Education, 330 C Street, S.W., Washington, DC 20201, 202-245-0565.

84.134 TELECOMMUNICATIONS DEMONSTRATIONS FOR HEALTH, EDUCATION, AND OTHER SOCIAL SERVICES

Type of Assistance: Grants ranging from $50,000 to $200,000.

Applicant Eligibility: Nonprofit organizations, state and local governments.

Objective: To promote the development of nonbroadcast telecommunications facilities and services for the transmission, distribution, and delivery of health, education, and social service information.

Contact: Office of Telecommunications Policy, HHH403E, Department of Education, Washington, DC 20201, 202-245-1891.

84.135 AID TO LAND-GRANT COLLEGES

Type of Assistance: Grants up to $50,000.

Applicant Eligibility: State governments where land-grant colleges are located.

Objective: To provide funds to be used for instructor's salaries or instructional equipment in the approved disciplines.

Contact: Office of Postsecondary Education, Department of Education, 400 Maryland Avenue, S.W., Washington, DC 20202, 202-245-7868.

84.136 LEGAL TRAINING FOR THE DISADVANTAGED

Type of Assistance: Grants up to $1,000.

Applicant Eligibility: Individuals from a low-income or economically disadvantaged background and who will have graduated from college at the beginning of the summer of 1981.

Objective: To provide educationally and economically disadvantaged students, many with marginal or less-than-traditional admissions credentials, an opportunity to attend an ABA-accredited law school, by operating seven six-week institutes.

Contact: Graduate Training Branch, Office of Postsecondary Education, Division of Institutional and State Incentive Programs, Department of Education, Rm. 3060, 7th and D Streets, S.W., Washington, DC 20202, 202-245-2347.

84.138 EDUCATIONAL SERVICES TO CUBAN AND HAITIAN ENTRANT CHILDREN

Type of Assistance: Grants (dollar amount not available).

Applicant Eligibility: Educational institutions and nonprofit organizations.

Objective: To provide federal assistance to the state and local educational agencies to meet the special educational needs of Cuban and Haitian entrant children.

Contact: Director of Refugee Assistance Program, Office of Bilingual Education and Minority Languages Affairs, Department of Education, 400 Maryland Avenue, S.W., Washington, DC 20202, 202-472-7177.

84.139 SCHOOLS IN CITIES

Type of Assistance: Grants ranging from $17,000 to $600,000.

Applicant Eligibility: Educational institutions and nonprofit organizations.

Objective: To increase school attendance and decrease the dropout rate; to improve academic achievement and social development; to help youth develop skills with which to function in society; and to coordinate existing community resources with schools as the focal point.

Contact: Urban Initiatives Staff, Office of School Improvement, Office of Educational Research and Improvement, Department of Education, 400 Maryland Avenue, S.W., Washington, DC 20202, 202-245-7852.

84.140 PUSH FOR EXCELLENCE

Type of Assistance: Grants up to $1,000,000.

Applicant Eligibility: Local education agencies.

Objective: To design and establish school-based programs in inner-city schools that improve the quality of education for inner-city students and assist students in attaining educational excellence; develop a close working relationship between school and community; and instill personal responsibility.

Contact: Urban Initiatives Staff, Office of School Improvement, Office of Educational Research and Improvement, Department of Education, 400 Maryland Avenue, S.W., Washington, DC 20202, 202-245-7852.

84.141 HIGH SCHOOL EQUIVALENCY AND COLLEGE ASSISTANCE MIGRANT PROGRAM

Type of Assistance: Grants ranging from $325,000 to $499,000.
Applicant Eligibility: Postsecondary schools.
Objective: To provide assistance to older migratory and seasonal farmworker children to attend college and/or attain a job or high school diploma.
Contact: Office of Migrant Education, Department of Education, 400 Maryland Avenue, S.W., Washington, DC 20202, 202-245-2222.

84.142 HOUSING FOR EDUCATIONAL INSTITUTIONS

Type of Assistance: Loans ranging from $25,000 to $5,000,000.
Applicant Eligibility: Public and private colleges and universities.
Objective: To alleviate severe student and faculty housing shortages through construction, acquisition, or rehabilitation to provide student and faculty housing and related dining facilities. To reduce fuel consumption or other operating costs of existing eligible housing and related dining facilities.
Contact: Office of Institutional Support, Office of Postsecondary Education, Department of Education, 400 Maryland Avenue, S.W., Washington, DC 20202, 202-245-7868.

84.143 EMERGENCY SCHOOL AID ACT— EVALUATION CONTRACTS

Type of Assistance: Direct payments ranging from $4,880 to $549,123.
Applicant Eligibility: Educational institutions and nonprofit organizations.
Objective: To evaluate specific programs receiving Emergency School Aid Act Assistance.
Contact: Office of Elementary and Secondary Education, Equal Educational Opportunity Programs, Division of Program Operations, Department of Education, 400 Maryland Avenue, S.W., Washington, DC 20202, 202-245-7965.

84.144 MIGRANT EDUCATION— DISCRETIONARY INTERSTATE/INTRASTATE COORDINATION PROGRAM

Type of Assistance: Grants (dollar amount not available).
Applicant Eligibility: State educational agencies.
Objective: To carry out activities, in consultation with the states, to improve the interstate and intrastate coordination among state and local educational agencies servicing migratory children and to operate a system for the transfer of migrant student records.
Contact: Office of Migrant Education, Department of Education, 400 Maryland Avenue, S.W., Washington, DC 20202, 202-245-2222.

HARRY S TRUMAN SCHOLARSHIP FOUNDATION

85.001 HARRY S TRUMAN SCHOLARSHIP PROGRAM
Type of Assistance: Direct payments ranging from $1,000 to $5,000 per year.
Applicant Eligibility: Individuals.
Objective: To honor the former President Harry S Truman through the operation of a perpetual educational scholarship program to develop increased opportunities for young Americans to prepare for and pursue careers in public service.
Contact: Executive Secretary, Harry S Truman Scholarship Program, 712 Jackson Place, N.W., Washington, DC 20006, 202-395-4831.

INDEX